The Underground Railroad Ran Through My House!

By
Ruth Deters

The Underground Railroad Ran Through My House!

By Ruth Deters

Cover design by Alex Buss and Evan Waters

Published by
Eleven Oaks Publishing
Quincy, IL

Library of Congress Cataloging in Data has been applied for.

ISBN 978-0-578-00213-2

Dedication

I dedicate this book to my loving husband Bill who accompanied me on this journey and was my navigator in finding these stations. He took most of the pictures shown in this book.

TABLE OF CONTENTS

Acknowledgments

Many people have contributed to this book in large and small ways over the decades of research this book represents. I want to thank my eleven children who encouraged me to write this book. I especially want to acknowledge the efforts of my daughter Ellen Waters for pushing me to get this information on paper, and who helped me type, sort, research and document my findings over several years. I must acknowledge my sons Rich and Ray who hid from the babysitter in the "hiding place" that started my exploration. Rich also took several of the pictures in the book. My son Greg helped with the internet research as well as researching documents and books. My daughter Gerri Buss researched Mendon area homes and helped put some of the information on paper. My daughters Ann Vogel and Kay Waters helped type. My grandsons, Alex Buss and Evan Waters designed the cover. Alex also provided many hours of editing to the document. My grandson Adam Buss spent countless hours formatting pictures for use in the book.

In addition to my family, many friends provided help and support: Father Landry Genosky, Quincy College history professor who gave me the first information which helped me begin my research, Carl Landrum, local historian who provided support and encouragement, Burks and Grace Oakley who gave me my first copy of Dr. Nelson's book The *Cause and Cure of Infidelity,* my dear friend, Carolyn Altenhein spent many hours helping me with my research in the library, courthouse and attics of old houses, Dorothy Nelson Watson, Dr Nelson's descendent, sent information on the Nelson family, Joe Dickman gave me a copy of the Platt letters, Zona Platt Galle, descendent of Deacon Jireh Platt, gave me the Enoch Platt Journal, Janie and Leo Rothweiler took me to the sugar camp and the remaining buildings of Marion College, Kate Ray Kuhn told me about Missouri history and provided me with old photos, English professor, Judy Harvey provided editing advice. Thanks to all the people who let me explore their houses whether or not they turned out to be authentic underground stations. I wish to acknowledge the abolitionists and their families who risked their lives and wealth and left a legacy to my grandchildren and great grandchildren that all people have the right to be free.

Chapter One

THE UNDERGROUND RAILROAD RAN THROUGH MY HOUSE!

"Rich Hid From The Babysitter Last Night In WHAT Hole?"

One morning, after an evening out with my husband, my daughter Ellen came to me quite concerned and said, "Last night, Rich hid from the babysitter in that hole in the floor upstairs." Alarmed, I asked, "What hole?" She took me upstairs into the boys' bedroom and lifted a section of the floorboards. The hole revealed nothing but darkness. I asked if he just put his feet in the hole. "No," she answered, "He got all the way in and put the lid on top of him." A flashlight inspection revealed a small room as deep as the first floor. The area in the little room was surrounding our living room fireplace. From the floor below, the view of the area around the fireplace only seems to suggest a large, wide chimney.

My husband Bill and I knew when we moved into the house as newlyweds that our home-- east of Quincy, Illinois-- was built by Dr. David Nelson: a noted abolitionist in the 1800s. We also knew he was known to have been involved in the Underground Railroad. We had not expected that Nelson's participation in this important movement of American history would suddenly unveil itself so vividly within our own home.

Obviously curious about what we had just discovered in our home, I called Quincy College History professor, Fr. Landry Genosky and described to him what my son led me to discover. He inquired, "Is it Dr. Nelson's home?" I confirmed that it was. "Oh, I've been looking for that," he replied. Genosky had come to believe that the house was no longer standing, because the missionary school that once stood behind it was now gone. Soon, he was peering into that dark hole as I had done. He gave me a little background on Nelson which further sparked my curiosity. I started researching Dr. Nelson's life and early Quincy history and got "hooked"! I started a journey of research-- learning more about the Abolition movement in the area and the fascinating lives of those abolitionists who gave up so much for a cause in which they believed. Each story developed even more curiosity about those who engaged in this remarkable movement known as the Underground Railroad. I carried my research with me wherever I went. While waiting for my children to finish school activities and orthodontist appointments, I read everything I could about Dr. David Nelson. I stayed in touch with Fr. Landry as we became "history" friends, sharing information that we discovered.

This photo was taken from upstairs looking down through the open trap door. On the back left you can see the brick of the regular chimney on the back wall. It continues upward along the wall of the second floor bedroom. The bricks in the front provide a ledge with which to climb down.

This is a picture of the fireplace in the living room directly below the boys' bedroom. Evidence suggests that a tunnel left the basement below this room.

The upstairs bedroom showing the narrow chimney and the opening to the hiding place below.

The sitting area outside the bedroom has a door that leads to the balcony on the front of the house and a view that includes Payson twelve miles away. From here the lights of Hannibal, Missouri can be seen on a clear night. Amanda Nelson used to sit there and do her needlework.

View looking down the old wooden steps into the semi-circular entry way of the home.

Artist's representation of Nelson hiding place

Amid my research on Dr. Nelson and the Underground Railroad, I was able to satisfy my curiosity about the interesting history behind the trap door in our home. The Nelsons would slide a pot bellied stove over the opening in the floorboards on the second floor, put the flue into the opening in the chimney above it, and light up the fire. If someone wanted to check for a trap door, they would be thwarted by the hot, heavy stove.

Inside the hiding place was bricked so that tapping on it would not sound hollow. The burning fireplace would keep the area warm for the hiding slave(s) inside. This view faces the north side wall with the front wall on the left and the edge of the actual chimney on the very right of the picture. (Photo by Kelsey Deters)

In this photo six of my children are in the space that Dr. Nelson built to camouflage a hiding place for escaping slaves. The smiling faces of Susie, Greg and Kay are visible. The hands in the photo belong to Gerri, Mark, and Mike.

In 1966, Fr. Landry was asked to organize the *People's History of Quincy and Adams County, Illinois* for the sesquicentennial. He asked me to write the section on the Underground Railroad activities in Adams County. When I agreed, I knew I would have to broaden my information beyond Dr. Nelson's activities to the rest of the county. Sure enough, I began to find other houses in Adams County that were also stations in the Underground Railroad. Like our house, they all had secret hiding places remaining within--just waiting to be discovered.

Carl Landrum, Quincy historian with exceptional research abilities soon became another "history friend" as we shared information with each other. My children report fond memories of our 'history' dinners when Carl and his sweet wife Shirley would come to our house with Fr. Landry and discuss local historical events and characters. My children were impressed by Mr. Landrum's wealth of information and his modesty about it. At one such event Carl gave me a note, which I still have, reporting that Rev. John Cross came through Quincy in 1840 to survey the stations on the Underground Railroad from Quincy to Chicago. Cross was having difficulty getting stations within one days travel time of each other. He actually traveled on the line to evaluate its effectiveness. This is significant because Cross, of Princeton, Ill. was announced as the general superintendent of the Illinois line. Many interesting anecdotes are documented about Rev. John Cross who was succeeded as superintendent by Owen Lovejoy.

It was through history research that we met and became friends with Burks and Grace Oakley, a charming couple who shared an interest in the history of the Underground Railroad in Quincy. Burks was a retired city engineer from Ohio and a descendent of a close friend of Dr. Nelson's granddaughter Lucy Nelson. Burks shared excerpts from the Quincy Diary of James A. Burks. It tells of Misses Maude and Kitty Burks having spent their vacation at H. A. Nelson's (David Nelson's son) near Philadelphia, MO in 1890. Burks was also aware that a distant relative, William Oakley attended Marion College in the years when Dr. Nelson was teaching there.

For my family, Sundays often became field trips to sites related to the Underground Railroad. As you'll notice, my children are dressed in their "Sunday best" in some of the photos. My children still remember (I think fondly) that family vacations were to places of historical significance—Civil War battlegrounds, other Underground Railroad stations and places of significance to Dr. Nelson.

The influences of history vacations and continued research always around the house apparently left a mark on my children. Several of my children continue to research Underground Railroad history today. My youngest, Greg, has made it his lifelong hobby to study Dr. Nelson. He has read much of Dr. Nelson's writings and has a passion for learning more about the mind of the brilliant man. He continues to call and tell me remarkable things he learned about Nelson. My children's enthusiasm about this topic continues to keep me energized about compiling the information.

Over the years I met with many descendants of the station owners as well as descendents of neighbors to those station owners. I value my continued correspondence with these gracious offspring of the likes of David Nelson and Jireh Platt. Even though Nelson was an integral part of the activities, I realized the topic was more involved than just Nelson. My research and interviews led me to find many other Underground Railroad stations, which I photographed and am sharing in this book. I took additional photos of places I discovered and soon I was giving presentations at schools and clubs in the area. Some of these photos were taken by friends or family, but most are from my original slideshow presentation. These photos are not of professional quality, as I did not realize that most of these historic buildings would be torn down before the opportunity to preserve them or professionally photograph them.

From those early years and until this day, my research includes gathering biographies, letters from descendents and reading diaries of descendents.

As a result of my research, I realized that the men who were involved in the abolition movement were often of the Congregational, Presbyterian, Campbellite or Quaker religion. They were connected to each other by religious affiliation and political beliefs. I began searching for members of those churches, which tended to have small congregations in the 1830's. I looked on old plat books and other records and found where they lived. When I inspected their houses they usually had a hiding place in them, just as in my home. I noticed that the houses in our region were built before 1850. I believe this was in part because after the Fugitive Slave Act of 1850 was passed the abolitionists could be much more severely punished for helping slaves escape. In addition, most of the people involved in the

Underground Railroad in our region moved here from other parts of the country, mostly out East, for the purpose of promoting abolition views. Land was purchased and homes built with the Underground Railroad in mind. The hiding places were included in the initial construction. After 1850 they continued their Underground Railroad activities but they could not take the chance of building a new home with a hiding place in it. Also, the homes were strategically located on or near creeks, or tributaries to creeks. Most of the stories in this book tell of conductors escorting the fugitives to the next station under cover of darkness. Those traveling the route would follow the creeks against the current. They knew that moss grows on the north side of the trees and by paying attention to that they would know which direction they were heading. An additional reason for following creeks was that if they were being tracked by dogs, the water disturbed the scent. The success of the railroad was in part due to each "station" having at least two alternative routes to move the fugitives forward. If trouble was brewing in one direction, an alternative had to be available. For this reason, a map of the Underground Railroad is not one line to the north, but multiple spokes with lines going several directions that ultimately led to Canada. This was all done with extreme secrecy.

While doing some of the more mundane household chores such as hanging laundry in our rustic basement in the winter, I would look at those hand hewn timber beams and rock walls and wonder about the man whose dedication drove him to build his home to be used for such a noble purpose. I also wondered about and admired the wife of such a man. She had to have been involved in her own mundane chores, but also sacrificed so much in supporting her husband's cause. It should be noted that it was Amanda, Dr Nelson's wife, who first influenced her husband's beliefs opposing slavery.

In more recent years, I continued the research with my dear friend Carolyn Altenhein, who I met as a result of a shared article on an Underground Railroad station. Together, we rummaged attics of old homes finding Civil War and pre-Civil War era letters and documents. We also read old documents in the basement of the Adams County Court House. Each outing led to increasingly intriguing information that tied together the history and stories of the Underground Railroad movement in the area of Adams County, Illinois.

The beams in the basement still hold the bark of the trees from which they were cut.

This is the story of my journey along the Underground Railroad, having spent much of my lifetime researching this fascinating subject and along the way having made warm friendships with wonderful people who shared my curiosity on this provocative subject. I have attempted to report the history as accurately as possible. It is not my intent to take credit for anyone's work. My intent is to share my journey through my research of the history of the Underground Railroad because these stories of moral conviction and bravery should not go unreported.

I caution the reader that I have included many original quotes. I feel that where I have available to me the actual words, for authenticity, I report them as written. Some of the language has different interpretations in today's culture. For example, Dr. Nelson writes of "infidelity" and "infidels" meaning primarily lack of belief in God. Other words that are considered offensive today are left in the original quotes, not to offend, but for the reader to know what the people wrote and said in those days and how they said it. I did not do this to offend the reader but to be authentic.

Chapter Two

BUILDING UP STEAM -- HISTORICAL OVERVIEW

American school children, at least since the 1950s, were taught about the Underground Railroad primarily with the story of Harriet Tubman. Her story was usually presented as a romanticized legend of Tubman leading groups of runaway slaves following secret messages. Children were led to believe that there were a few "bad" Southern white men who were chasing them, and that most of the people at that time, at least those from the North, were against slavery. Many people today believe that once a slave reached a free state, they were automatically free. While the story of Harriet Tubman is true, misconceptions about the Underground Railroad are usually the result of a lack of understanding of the attitudes and beliefs in the United States in the early 1800s.

The Underground Railroad was not a railroad but a network of safe houses, homes, or barns used to hide fugitive slaves while escaping to Canada. The term "Underground Railroad" was coined in 1831, when a slave named Tice Davids escaped from Kentucky and crossed the Ohio River. When the owner searched all through the area and could not find a trace of him, he returned to Kentucky and told his friends that it seemed as if he escaped on an underground road. At this time, the railroad was a new mode of travel. It provided a speed of travel never before experienced by American citizens. The abolitionists began to call their operation the Underground Railroad. They incorporated the terms used in the railroad into their operation. Each stop that had a hiding place was called a "station." The men who operated these stations were called "conductors." The slaves were referred to as "freight." There were also "presidents of the line," who were men who organized the Underground Railroad in certain areas. The route they took was referred to as the "track" and so on.

Slavery existed in the United States since the days of Jamestown. Efforts to help slaves escape existed as well. In fact, the Fugitive Slave Act was first passed in this country in 1793. This legislation sought to punish those that facilitated a slave's escape. The years that lead up to the Civil War saw the efforts to free the slaves intensify and become more organized throughout the entire United States. While those who opposed slavery were passionate about abolishing it, most American citizens accepted slavery as a way of life and an economic necessity. Most citizens did not want a change in the "status quo" and resented the abolitionists' efforts to disrupt the practice. Even in "free" states, those who sought to abolish slavery were met with hostility - sometimes physical - by their fellow citizens. Slaves were not free once they reached a free state, such as Illinois.

According to Illinois law, no free black or mulatto could settle or reside in the state without a certificate of freedom. This certificate must be shown to the Commissioner of the Court of the county in which residence was desired. In addition, a bond of one thousand dollars had to be furnished by the slave owner as security that the black man would obey the laws and not be a county charge. Further, it was illegal for any person to hire a black man who possessed no certificate of freedom. The unfortunate individuals who had no certificates were to be advertised by a justice of the peace, or by a county sheriff, and bound out to service again by the end of the year or month.

Under the law, *any* African-American who entered the State as a free man without a duly certified testimonial of freedom, or who became free within the State by completing his required term of apprenticeship without receiving papers from his master, was legitimate prey of the kidnappers. The kidnappers were usually poor, white, indiscriminate men in search of a quick dollar. More often than not, the master was perfectly willing to sign the certificate of freedom but was not able or willing to furnish the one thousand dollars bond. Rarely was the person in question capable of furnishing the bond.

Once under the control of their kidnappers, the victims would be taken to a spot on the Mississippi or Ohio River. Then they were smuggled on board ships and forwarded to Memphis or New Orleans, where they were sold into slavery. Young, able-bodied men brought good prices. Making less than one hundred dollars a slave was rare. Often it was considerably more, and consequently kidnapping proved to be a profitable business.

In this political climate emerged some brave people willing to risk everything in attempts to influence citizens against slavery.

Among them, the first white martyr to the movement, Elijah Lovejoy had direct ties with many of the people whose lives are told in this book.

Elijah Parish Lovejoy, 1802-1837, was a minister and journalist. Originally from Maine, he moved to St. Louis after studying at the Princeton Theological Seminary. He first worked at the *St. Louis Observer*, writing a series of articles critical of slavery. He received death threats, rocks were thrown into his windows and eventually his office was ransacked and his printing presses destroyed. The second press was thrown into the river at St. Charles, Mo. (I was told the press remains in the river there.) In September, 1836 he was forced to move across the Mississippi. In Alton, Illinois he became the editor of the *Alton Observer*, an abolitionist newspaper. On the 21st of September the third press arrived in Alton and was placed in a warehouse on Second Street, State and Piasa. This press Lovejoy had ordered on his own account, and he was not fully decided whether to continue the *Observer* in Alton or to remove it to Quincy where protection had been offered. He chose to stay in Alton where he became increasingly more vocal against slavery. After the third press was destroyed, on November 7, 1837, a fourth printing press was delivered secretly at 3 am. This printing press was supplied by the Ohio Anti-Slavery Society or possibly the Anti-Slavery Society of Illinois–(records conflict).They moved quickly to carry the press to the third floor of the Gilman warehouse when a mob arrived. When he tried to prevent them from setting the building on fire, Lovejoy was shot five times and died inside the warehouse. The fourth printing press was dismantled and thrown into the river while Lovejoy's body lay on the floor. While in Alton and in Missouri many people quietly approved of the mob's actions, nationally the news of Lovejoy's murder galvanized abolitionists even more in their anti-slavery cause.

In our modern world it is hard to imagine how encompassing the issue of slavery was in the early 1800s. Many of the famous people in history who are not known for their connection to slavery in fact were impacted by it. One example is William Frederick Cody, later known as "Buffalo Bill". From *Horse and Rider* magazine this event is recorded:

> *The unaccustomed taste of adventure was force-fed to little Will at an early age when his father – who had been stabbed in the back by an irate Kansan because of the former's abolitionist leanings – fled to Leavenworth, Kansas. Mary Ann Cody learned that the proslavery advocates knew where her*

husband was hiding and were planning to kill him. She dispatched eight year old Will on a pony to warn his father. Years later, Buffalo Bill recalled the incident with his father's enemies: "As I galloped past," he wrote later, "one of them yelled, 'There's Cody's kid now.....Stop you, and tell us where your old man is!"

A pistol shot, to terrify me into obedience, accompanied the command. I may have been terrified, but it was not into obedience. I got out of there like a shot, and though they rode hard on my trail, my pony was too fast for them. My warning was in time.

Like the other youngsters you will read about in later chapters, Buffalo Bill's first encounter with high adventure and escaping danger came about as the result of his family's belief that no man should be a slave to another.

It is important to distinguish that there were roughly three levels of anti-slavery attitudes: the first was the person who said they were "anti-slavery" but did or professed nothing else that supported this attitude. Most people in the North seemed to fall in this category. They said they were against slavery but did not want any change in the practice and resented the abolitionists and Underground Railroad operators for acting on their beliefs. These people reflect that old saying: "All that is needed for evil to prevail is for good men to do nothing." The next level is that of the proclaimed 'abolitionist'. These abolitionists supported and encouraged the immediate abolition of all slavery but through political and religious means. The citizens who found themselves in the third category, Underground Railroad Conductors –actively involved in forcing a change – were driven by the conviction that God's laws superceded man's laws when it came to the treatment of fellow human beings. The Underground Railroad was an *illegal* operation but the conductors, who were also abolitionists, felt that the *moral* directive from God justified their efforts to help slaves find the freedom and liberty they deserved as human beings. However, it is important to note that the majority of Americans in the early 1800's felt the idea of immediate abolition was too extreme because of the impact on the economy and the effects that would have on the entire nation.

Interestingly, some of the most pro-slavery demonstrations took place in New York City. Lewis Tappan's New York City mansion was ransacked by an angry mob while he was attending an anti-slavery meeting. Lewis and his brother Arthur Tappan were wealthy merchants in New York City who used much of their wealth to finance the abolitionist cause. Lewis helped found the American Anti-Slavery Society, sponsored speakers and meetings, and sent mailings of Anti-slavery pamphlets, (tracts) throughout the country. In 1836 he opened a mailed package and found a slave's ear and a piece of rope warning him he'd be hung. A Southerner offered $50,000 for his head. That did not deter him, in 1839, from pleading with and paying former president John Quincy Adams (for whom Quincy and Adams County was named) to represent the African slaves of the Amistad in the landmark case that has been made into an Oscar nominated movie. Fr. Landry told me that the Tappans helped finance Dr. David Nelson in some of his abolitionist undertakings. This would seem likely as Dr. David Nelson served on the board of American Anti-Slavery Society (AASS) with Arthur Tappan from 1836 to 1840. Nelson served as vice–president representing Illinois on the AASS during this time. Nelson and the Tappans also attended many of the same anti-slavery conventions.

The abolitionists knew that slavery was deeply entrenched in this country. To destroy it through politics would have been a long, slow, complicated task. Nevertheless, they considered the laws concerning slavery unjust. They believed the laws gave the white man absolute power over African-Americans. In spite of their religious beliefs, the citizens conducting the Underground Railroad chose to break the law in order to abide God's work and help the slaves get to freedom. When studying the Underground Railroad, you cannot underestimate the overwhelming motivation of the people who so ably organized and conducted it. It is also important not to underestimate the danger these brave people faced.

The following incident reported in *Quincy and Adams County* demonstrates the real danger these men and their families faced (I have no information to support Mr. Schaller's involvement in any anti-slavery activities):

"In 1859, while conducting business in LaGrange (Missouri), Frederick Schaller was the victim of a brutal outrage, perpetrated by unknown men. Eleven Negro slaves had escaped to Illinois, gaining their freedom by means of the so-called "underground railway." A number of masked men appeared at the home of Frederick Schaller in the night, dragged him out, accused him of having aided the slaves

and in spite of his most earnest denial and protestation, tied him to a tree, lashed and horsewhipped him, until his body was streaming with blood and life almost extinct. He was found by friends, who brought him to Quincy, where relatives nursed him back to health."

The men and their families who ran the Underground Railroad stations put everything they had into the cause. They had to be extremely secretive or they and their families would be subject to great abuse and possibly death. People (including close neighbors) were not always in agreement with their actions and sometimes condemned them publicly. It was especially hard for the children who helped in the hiding and transporting the slaves, as I'll discuss in later chapters.

The following map is provided in order to present a visual guide to the geographic layout in relation to the Mississippi River, creeks, towns and other Underground Railroad stations in west central Illinois mentioned in this book:

Map Key

1	Oakland & M. I. #1	17	Hubbard station
2	Terwische Woods	18	Hoffman station
3	Mission Institute #2	19	Fowler station
4	Amanda's house	20	Pulman station
5	Maple Lane Station	21	Pottle station
6	Sam Turner station	22	Hunter station
7	Jos. Turner station	23	Payson Windmill
8	Van Dorn Sawmill	24	Seymour station
9	Eells house	25	Collins station
10	Everett Station	26	McAnulty farm
11	Kemp house	27	Mission Institute 4
12	Hackberry farm	28	Josiah Read farm
13	E. Barr station	29	Terrill farm
14	Ballard station	30	Fielding Station
15	Platt station	31	Marion College
16	Tallcott station	32	Charles Brown station

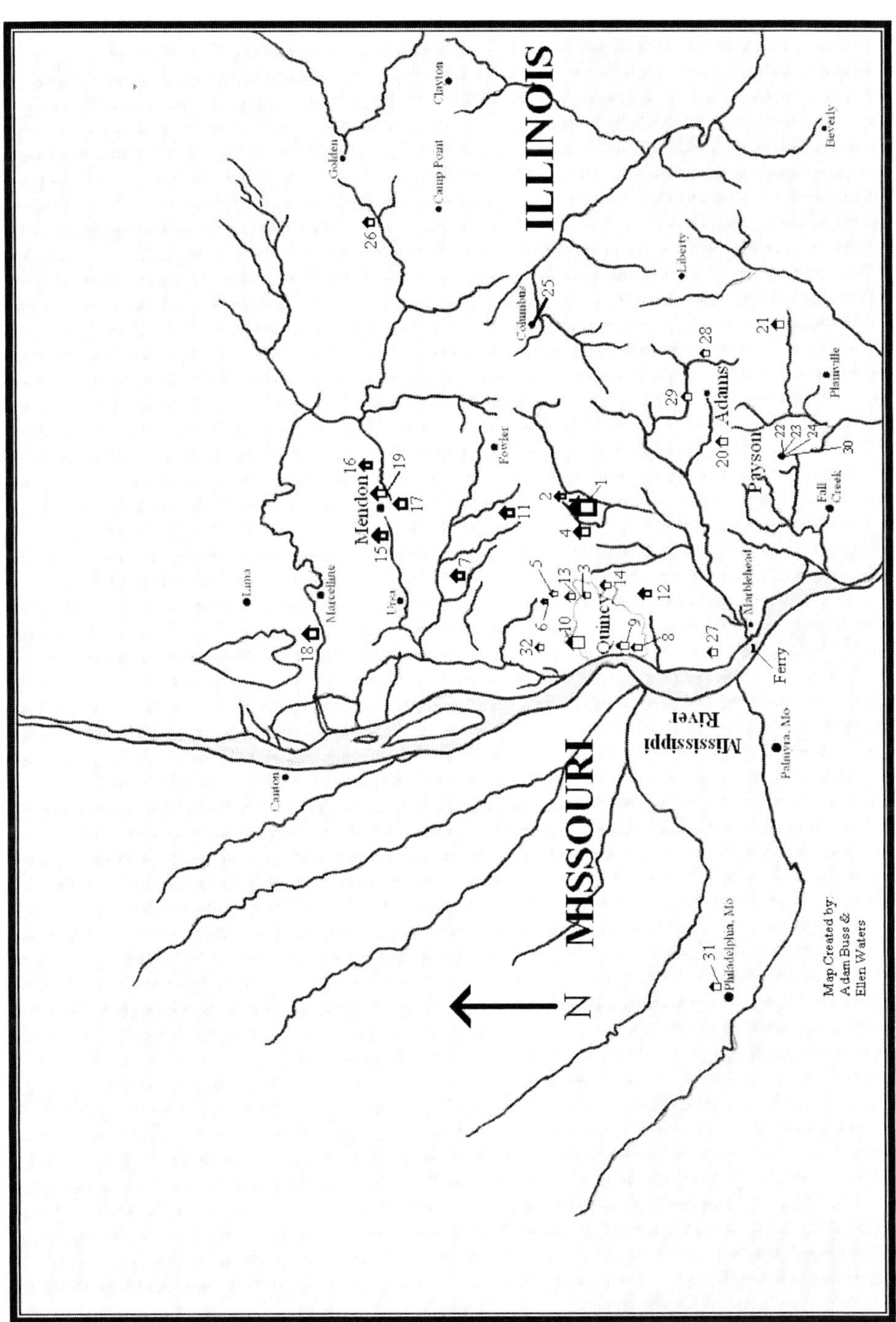
ILLINOIS
Clayton
Golden
Camp Point
Beverly
Liberty
Columbus
Mendon
Fowler
Adams
Payson
Plainville
Fall Creek
Lima
Marcelline
Ursa
Quincy
Marblehead
Ferry
Mississippi River
Palmyra, Mo
Canton
MISSOURI
N
Philadelphia, Mo
Map Created by:
Adam Buss &
Ellen Waters

Chapter Three

THE INTRIGUING LIFE OF DR. DAVID NELSON

Dr. David Nelson

So who was this Dr. David Nelson who built his home with an Underground Railroad hiding place in it? It became my mission to answer this question. The internet was unheard of at the time I began researching. In the 1960s you had to physically go to the libraries, court houses and churches to read the documents on paper. My grandchildren can't imagine that! Fr. Landry told us that Nelson was born in Tennessee. We wanted to know what influenced this Southern gentleman to develop such opposition to the institution of slavery. Bill and I went on a road trip to look for answers, or at least some clues. First we traveled to Jonesborough, Tennessee, a quaint little old town, and found the library-- a little old brick building downtown. The charming southern librarians were happy to help us research the history of David Nelson and his wife Amanda Deaderick. They showed us the old building where Amanda's father's business once thrived. The ladies were really nice and told us how to get to Washington College where both of David Nelson's parents Henry and Anna (Kelsey) Nelson taught. We crossed the Nolachucky River. Nelson was born two miles from there and used to skip rocks over the river. We stopped to take in the river and Bill couldn't resist the urge to skip a few rocks over the Nolachucky. At Washington College (now a prep school) a friendly gentleman at the reception desk told us more about the college and showed us the original buildings that remained from Nelson's time. He, too, shared historical information about Nelson who attended Washington College, near his home, from which he graduated at age sixteen. We learned that it was here that Nelson's anti-slavery views began to take shape.

Washington College was previously called Doak College which produced many of the first abolitionists. Samuel Doak had a strong influence on David Nelson and was associated with the early names of the antislavery movement. From the book *The United States of Appalachia: How Southern Mountaineers Brought Independence, Culture, and Enlightenment to America,* Jeff Biggers tells:

> *Many of Doak's students took his sentiments to heart. The school turned out some notable iconoclasts, like David Nelson, a mercurial preacher, college founder, and medical doctor who had a penchant for poetry and who wrote some memorable church hymns and The Cause and Cure of Infidelity, a popular religious text for his times. Nelson, though, and several other Washington College students became important for their contributions to the most diverse trigger issue in the early nineteenth century: pioneering the antislavery movement a generation before William Lloyd Garrison and Frederick Douglass, the rise of Abraham Lincoln, and the irreconcilable currents that led to the Civil War.*

Later in Biggers' book he goes on:

In effect, the Midwest, East Coast and the western territories inherited more than one generation of progressive thinkers and activists. Southern Appalachia provided these regions with some of the most outspoken leaders of the antislavery movement. The expatriated roles of Benjamin Lundy, Charles Osborn, David Nelson, John Rankin and Levi Coffin remind us of the Southern Appalachian influence on the abolitionist movement in the country.

It is apparent that Samuel Doak had a strong influence on Nelson and his independent style of critical thinking. Doak College produced many of the first Abolitionist leaders. It is especially interesting that many of the people we now attribute to the beginning of abolitionism such as William Lloyd Garrison were actually influenced by the Eastern Tennessee (Jonesborough area) abolitionists. In Garrison's case it was Nelson's college cohort, Benjamin Lundy.

It was incredulous to us that we were living in Nelson's home with his connection to the very beginnings of the profound movement that changed America – and we had no idea!

Our trip to the Jonesborough area continued to help fill in the details about Nelson. We knew that David Nelson was born on September 24, 1793 – perhaps ironically this was the same year that the United States passed the original Fugitive Slave Act. His very pious parents encouraged the study of catechism and the daily reading of the bible. His father was a ruling elder of the Presbyterian Church, and his mother was reported to be of exceptional intellect. He would later influence and be influenced by the significant historical, political and religious events of our country.

We went to the Presbyterian Church to learn more of Nelson's religious influences. The very kind minister got out all the old archives for us. We learned that David Nelson's brother Samuel preached there at the church they attended as children. The papers indicated Samuel died suddenly and they asked David to take over for him. But that is getting ahead of the story. David's desire was to be a doctor and all of the adult references to him refer to him as a surgeon – a very important distinction as abdominal surgery had never been performed on a living person when David was aspiring to study medicine.

We wanted to know how a man with such medical credentials wound up running an Underground Railroad station in Quincy, Illinois. Our road trip took us to Danville, Kentucky. There we learned even more about his remarkable life.

Remarkable Teen Years

In September, 1809, Nelson moved with his brother to Danville, Kentucky, where his brother, Sam, had become the pastor of the Danville church. It was in Danville that Nelson studied medicine under the famed Dr. Ephraim McDowell, son-in law of Kentucky Governor Isaac Shelby. David's brother, Sam, was married to another of the Governor's daughters. Medical school in those years only lasted 12 to 16 weeks. Surgery training consisted of an additional 12 - 16 weeks. (Back then, surgery pretty much meant amputation of limbs as no other surgery had yet been performed). McDowell would train about a half dozen students at a time.

Within three months of Nelson beginning his medical school training a landmark event in the history of modern medicine took place. Dr. Ephraim McDowell became the first surgeon ever to successfully remove an ovarian tumor. In fact, it was the first successful surgery ever performed within the abdominal cavity! It was under this impressive man and in this unique environment that the intelligent young Nelson learned to become a surgeon.

In December of 1809, (Nelson was just finishing the first session of medical school) a courageous Kentucky woman of 46 named Mrs. Jane Todd Crawford rode 60 miles by horseback to reach Danville. She rested a huge ovarian tumor on the horn of the saddle. Dr. McDowell described her as a woman of small stature whose abdomen had become so pendulous with the tumor as to reach almost to her knees.

The surgery was carried out in Dr. McDowell's house on Christmas Day. A mob gathered outside the McDowell home prepared to kill the doctor if Mrs. Crawford did not survive. He was assisted in the operation by one of his nephews, Dr. James McDowell, who had recently graduated in Philadelphia, Pennsylvania. This nephew, from the time of Mrs. Crawford's arrival in Danville, made frequent attempts to dissuade his uncle from operating on her as no surgery of this type had ever been done and the tumor was so large. Several other attendants were present to observe the surgery and to help restrain Mrs. Crawford who was operated on without anesthesia.

In the times prior to the use of anesthesia, an alcoholic or narcotic potion was commonly administered before an operation, yet the patient was not numb to the pain. Mrs. Crawford is said to have repeated psalms to distract her attention from the pain.

Not in recorded history had any doctor performed open abdominal surgery, but Dr. McDowell readied to remove a large tumor from a Kentucky woman's ovary. The surgery lasted about thirty minutes, during which time her intestines rushed out of the abdomen and remained exposed until the solid portion of the tumor was removed. In all, the tumor weighed 22 ½ pounds. Mrs. Crawford did not develop peritonitis or wound infection. She was making her bed within five days and returned home in 25. She lived another 33 years until her death in 1842. Dr. McDowell became known as the "Father of Abdominal Surgery." All this was witnessed by a young David Nelson who continued to study medicine for three more years at the Medical College in Philadelphia, Pennsylvania. Saving lives had become a passion for him.

Wanting to know more about Nelson's training under Dr. McDowell, we took a vacation to Danville, Kentucky where we toured the Ephraim McDowell house. Bill took this photo inside the house.

The Military Years

As David Nelson was entering the practice of medicine at age nineteen, he signed on as a surgeon in the Kentucky Regiment. In 1812, he left Danville for Canada to fight in the war with Great Britain, with his cousin, a prominent Danville lawyer. From *The Cause and Cure of Infidelity* his experience in the military is described in the following passage:

> *In the military, he suffered every privation. In one march, in the severe cold and deep snows of a wild Indian territory, exhausted by hunger and fatigue, he suffered himself to be left unobserved, and resolved there to lie down and die. But his friend and cousin, the brave Col. Allen who afterwards fell at Tippecanoe, missed him, went back, roused him from his deathlike slumber, took him on his powerful horse, and thus saved him for the work God had appointed him to do. Returning from his northern campaign, he entered on his practice of medicine in Jonesborough but at the call of Generals Jackson and Coffee, he enlisted again as surgeon of a regiment for the South, and in the wilds of Alabama flooded with rain was seized by fever, reduced to the utmost extremity, and at Mobile, Alabama on the eve of an expected battle, received the news of peace.*

These military experiences left an impression on Nelson that continued to shape his attitudes for his actions in the future. He learned how to survive in the wilderness under extreme conditions and he no longer seemed to fear death.

David and Amanda

After the end of the war, Nelson returned to Jonesborough and resumed his medical profession. Beginning while a student in Danville, he imbibed in "infidelity," (Nelson's choice of word) in connection with gambling and other army habits, which continued on his return. But being talented, genial, social, and handsome, he was a popular young physician. Soon he had a practice worth $3000 per year. The journal of his grandson Harry Nelson records this description:

> "*He was big, fun-loving, and attractive: he drank and played cards to an extent distressing to his family...*"

Eventually, Nelson fell in love with Amanda Frances Deaderick. She was the daughter of a highly respectable merchant. She was said to be an athletic girl who was full of pranks and liked climbing trees – not exactly typical of a Southern Belle! Idolized by her father, he sent her to boarding school in Salem, North Carolina, but she resented the strict rules and persuaded him to bring her home. It is reported that she excelled in botany, at that time the only science taught to women. Later in life her knowledge of botany would help her family survive very difficult times. While studying music and art in Washington City, Tennessee her dramatic vivacity made her popular. Originally called Frances, while in Washington City, she was re-christened with the name Amanda. It is said that this scandalized her older relatives. Throughout her life Amanda continued to make independent decisions that would scandalize the traditions of older Southern relatives but not in any immoral way.

When David first saw Amanda she was playfully wearing a wreath of flowers in her hair on the lawn of her home. She looked whimsical at barely five feet tall. Nelson was immediately smitten. The beautiful Amanda was slower to warm to Nelson as she had many suitors. Amanda's pious parents did not approve of the card playing Nelson. When the two decided to elope, Amanda's father had planned to take her on a trip that included jewelry shopping. Her father had planned to purchase diamonds and pearls for his favorite child. The night before the scheduled elopement, Amanda had second thoughts. She went to her mother who was reading her bible and told her she wanted to talk to her. Amanda's mother responded that she was reading the bible and Amanda should go and leave her alone. Amanda did leave – by way of the window.

On May 15, 1816, Amanda Frances Deaderick married Dr. David Nelson, the brilliant young surgeon of Jonesborough, TN. Upon hearing of her marriage it is said that her father fainted and refused to allow her to come home. They did not speak for three years, until, at the time of her son's birth, Amanda was having a difficult time and it was feared she might not survive. They reconciled and remained close from then on. Amanda who was sincerely religious is credited for influencing David to return to his religious upbringing.

Tennessee Years

Nelson continued to practice medicine and officiated as a ruling elder in the Jonesborough Presbyterian Church as his father did before him. Little seems to be written of the next years but we know that Nelson read much and at some point became interested in the writings of John Newton of England. Newton ran a slave ship to and from Africa and England before being converted into an abolitionist. Nelson attended Colonization Society meetings in the Jonesborough area at this time. (Colonization may have been a prelude to abolitionism and was a concept about giving the slaves freedom in an established colony.) Nelson subsequently studied theology privately under the instruction of the Rev. Robert Glenn. Nelson and another Presbyterian ministry student, Frederick A. Ross were licensed to preach the gospel, by the Abingdon Presbytery at Glade Spring Church in Virginia. They were ordained six months later on October 3, 1825 at Rogersville, Tennessee. Dr. Nelson preached for two years in East Tennessee.

In those days it was not uncommon for preachers to travel giving sermons in a variety of towns. Religious revivals were becoming popular as religion was experiencing what is called in history the Second Great Awakening. Both Nelson and Ross traveled through Ohio, Tennessee and Kentucky as guest preachers in churches and revivals.

From the *Western Sketch-Book*, Rev. James Gallaher writes an anecdote from one of Dr. Nelson's travels out east that gives us a glimpse into Nelson's unique personality and his interesting logic when making a point:

> *Nelson worked very hard at preaching in the rugged west. It grieved him to see a series of articles in print that criticized the practice of holding revivals which was the custom of preachers in Missouri. The professor who wrote these articles, although a worthy man, had always been in the seclusion of a seminary.*
>
> *Nelson's heart was filled with sorrow that such disastrous influences should emanate from such a quarter. But what can a plain, western man do, when a cold, blighting stream of 'east wind" comes sweeping over the garden of the Lord, chilling and nipping the tender plants, and freezing all before it? Alas*

for the churches in the west, when "the star in the east" is overspread with mist and darkness!

Such was the attitude of things when Nelson made a visit to the east. He was walking along a street in one of the principal cities, when he discovered an extensive bookstore. At one side of the door, on a broad sheet, was an advertisement in large letters, "Dr. ___ on Revivals, for sale here." At the other side of the door hung a similar advertisement, "Dr. ___ on Revivals, for sale here." Nelson paused, surveyed the broad sheets for a moment, then stepped into the store, and, addressing the bookseller, said, "Have you got here the Treatise of the Emperor Nicholas of Russia on the proper method of cultivating cotton and Sugar-Cane?"

"Why n-no," said the bookseller, drawling out the answer; "we have not got it, and I should think that Nicholas, out in the far north, among the snows of Russia, would be likely to know very little on the subject, as, most certainly, he has never seen a plant of either cotton or sugar-cane."

"Well," continued Nelson, "have you got the Dissertation of President Boyer of Hayti on the Proper Method of building Ice-Houses?" "No," replied the bookseller; "and there again, I should think that Boyer, in the West Indies, having never seen ice, would be a most unsuitable person to attempt to write a dissertation on the subject."

"Ah!" said Nelson, turning towards the door, "I see that you have "Dr___ on Revivals," and I did not know but that you might have those other works. Good morning, sir."

To reach more faithful, Ross and Nelson collaborated with a third preacher Rev. James Gallaher on a religious magazine. (Gallaher was later involved in the Underground Railroad in Ohio.)

From 1827-1829, *The Calvinistic Magazine* included sermons by Dr. Nelson. One in particular discouraged preaching by "shouting," and encouraged influencing by speaking softly and rationally. This reflected his own style of preaching and influenced those around him.

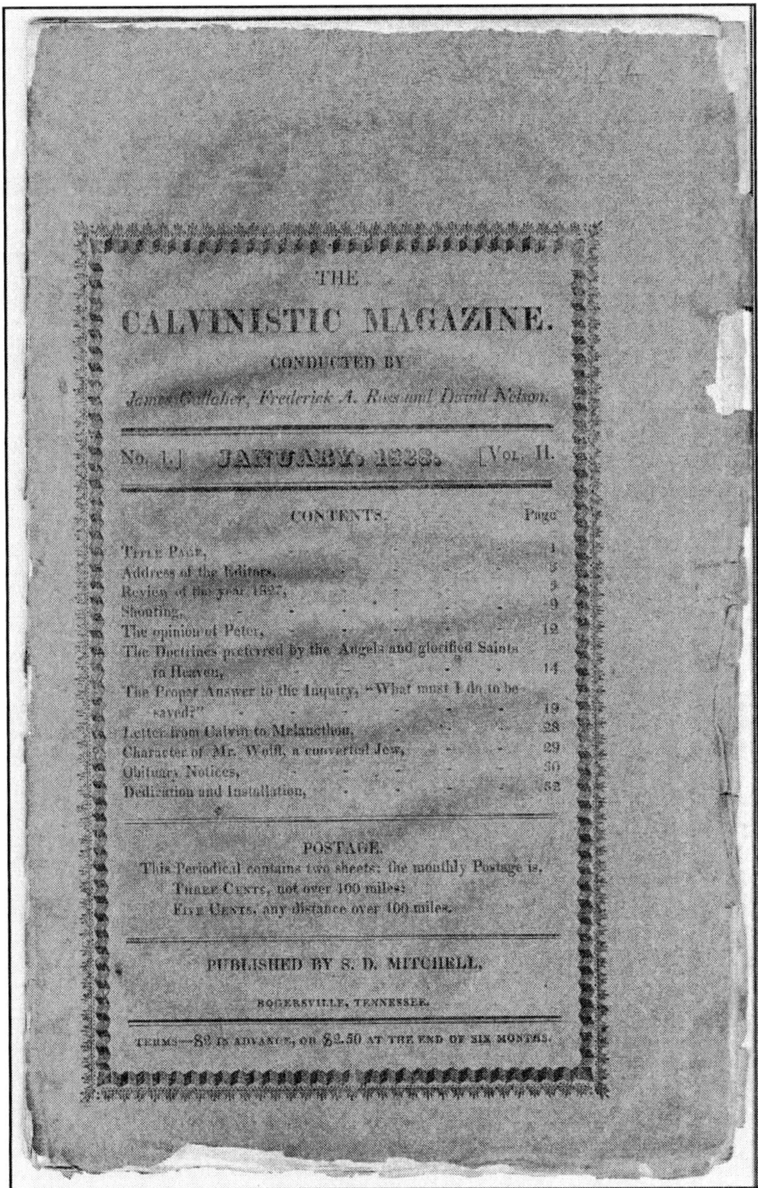

THE

CALVINISTIC MAGAZINE.

CONDUCTED BY

James Gallaher, Frederick A. Ross and David Nelson.

No. 1.] JANUARY, 1828. [Vol. II.

CONTENTS. Page

POSTAGE.

This Periodical contains two sheets: the monthly Postage is,
Three Cents, not over 100 miles:
Five Cents, any distance over 100 miles.

PUBLISHED BY S. D. MITCHELL,

ROGERSVILLE, TENNESSEE.

TERMS—$2 IN ADVANCE, OR $2.50 AT THE END OF SIX MONTHS.

The cover of the first *The Calvinistic Magazine*. I have 32 original *Calvinistic Magazines* which I acquired several years ago. They provide me with a glimpse of Nelson's preaching style and philosophy.

In the years between 1827 and 1829 Dr. Nelson was in the Danville, Kentucky area serving in several capacities. He was on board of Centre College, he was minister of the Presbyterian Church and by some accounts he was teaching medicine at Centre College in Danville and/or Transylvania University in Lexington. Interestingly, it was just 2 years earlier that Jefferson Davis was a student at Transylvania University. What a small world that two men who would go on to have such great influence on the history of slavery in the United States, for completely opposite reasons, would be at the same small college at nearly the same point in history. Nelson also crossed paths with another man of considerable fame at this time. The biography of Samuel B Cunningham, builder and president of the East Tennessee & Virginia Railroad, states that Cunningham was a physician and surgeon who "studied medicine under the instruction of Dr. David Nelson" at Centre College.

It was during this time that Dr. Nelson met and inspired two Centre College students, Charles Spilman and Benjamin Shaw. Spilman and Shaw were classmates as well as roommates at the college. They were also members of Dr. Nelson's Presbyterian Church. I believe Benjamin Shaw was the same man who later presented a very famous speech in Boston which outlined the illegality of slavery. It was presented in very legal terms and I find it interesting that one of the few degrees someone could obtain at Centre College in the 1820's was a law degree.

Nelson, recognizing the need for a book which would provide a better and more comprehensive collection of hymns for the church, approached Spilman and Shaw to compile such a book. It is likely that Nelson was looking for a book of hymns which would align more closely with the needs of the revival oriented movement taking place at both churches and camp meetings. The songs needed to be inspirational but also easy to remember – the nature of camp meetings meant it was unlikely most attendees would have access to a hymn book so it was better if the songs could be memorized and sung by heart.

These two students knew Dr. Nelson well and in fact considered him a mentor and they accepted Dr. Nelson's challenge. They worked for some time on this book and in 1829 published their book titled *Columbian Harmony*. These are extremely rare and hard to find. I found one at the American Antiquarian Society. Interestingly one of the songs Spilman and Shaw put in the book is titled "Nelson" in honor of their mentor, Dr. Nelson:

Nelson Hymn from Colombian Harmony

Clearly, Dr. David Nelson must have had a powerful effect on the students he taught to have honored him in this way. I believe the words to the song discuss Nelson's own struggle with religious infidelity. More on the significance of this book is covered in the later chapter, "Rhythm of the Tracks."

In 1828, Dr. David Nelson accepted a job to succeed his deceased brother, Samuel K. Nelson, as the pastor of the church in Danville. Both Nelsons were successful and influential as pastors of this church. In *Asa Turner and His Times, First President of Iowa College* this story is told:

Nelson having been approached when he was leaving the pulpit of an Old School Presbyterian church in Kentucky, by an infidel who said "You have been preaching lies." Dr Nelson looked the man up and down and said, "You are dressed like a gentleman. If you will behave like one and come and hear me preach six evenings, I will show you that I have forgotten more infidelity than you ever knew. I can wind you around my little finger as easily as I could a tow-thread." In a few evenings the man and fifty of his friends were in seats listening to the vibrant preacher.

These stories hopefully will give a sense for the kind of man Dr. Nelson had evolved into while preaching and ministering these years.

Missionary work was an important part of Presbyterian ministry. As a result, Nelson traveled throughout unsettled regions on behalf of the American Education Society. In his travels he was drawn to a new unsettled region ripe for settling and preaching —Missouri! Dr. Nelson decided to move his family to an area of the state north of St. Louis and just west of the Mississippi River. Later, in 1829, Nelson, referred to as "a Presbyterian minister of distinction" in the *History of Marion County, Missouri*, moved to Missouri.

In order to understand the effect of that move, I quote from the diary of his brother-in-law, David Anderson Deaderick. In 1829 he wrote:

> *There was a great disposition in many of our citizens to remove to the fertile countries west and north of us. The rage now seems for Indiana, Illinois and Missouri, some to the Western District of this state. I was again, the fourth time, in the Western District on business connected with our mercantile establishment. Doctor Nelson has bought land in Missouri, 130 miles north of St. Louis and intends to remove to it in the fall of 1830.*
>
> *...Early in May of this year (1830), I made a journey to Missouri, in company with my brother-in-law and cousin, Gen'l A. Anderson, Col. W. B. A. Ramsey, and John H. Grozier, the two last of Knoxville.*
>
> *The General's object and mine was to see the country with a view of moving to it. We went by way of Lexington and Georgetown, Ky., to Cincinnati, Ohio, thence by Madison and Salem, Indiana, to Vincennes on the crossing at St. Charles the Missouri river, to Palmyra about 130 miles N. of St. Louis. In this neighborhood Wabash, thence direct to St. Louis, Missouri, and thence, Doctor Nelson, my brother-in-law, had bought land, and since our return from Missouri, has removed to it. We visited the spot where he intended residing: one cabin for a smoke house was then up and no other preparation for his reception.*
>
> *He was expected in two or three months. There was, at the time of our visit in June, but one cabin, if even that, west of him. We were on a large prairie twelve or fourteen miles west of the Doctor's location, on which we were told by Doctor Clarke, a domestic animal had never grazed, and on which a single location had not been made. This I mention to show how far in (to) the Far West the Doctor's fancy had led him. I endeavored to dissuade him from removing to his land for a year or two until more settlers*

come in, but he would not listen to me. If he will become a sportsman an ample supply of game is at his door, consisting of prairie fowl (a sort of grouse), turkeys, deer, prairie wolves, and even elk are not twenty miles west of him.

Chapter Four

THE MISSOURI JUNCTION

Given the Missouri we know today, David Deaderick's account of what Missouri was like before the Nelsons arrived is hard to imagine. They came to an unsettled land. Deaderick's account helps us appreciate the remarkable achievements made by those early settlers: David and Amanda Nelson and their children settled and established a community and a distinguished college there within the next six years.

Dr. David Nelson and his family settled in Union township, about thirteen miles northwest of Palmyra and purchased 600 acres of land. Palmyra was on the border of frontier settlements. It was not even known if any civilized men lived beyond this point. Nelson became active in church work immediately upon his arrival on the Missouri frontier.

Here is a picture of what remains of a sugar pit on the grounds. The mound of earth is built up and a fire pit is in the center. Here they would put huge pots of maple sap over the pit to process it into sugar. This picture was provided to me by Leo "Bud" Rothweiler of Palmyra, MO. He was helping me locate it after I discovered the mention of it in the Nelson's wills. One man he asked said "It's across the road from my house."

On this pictured property was a 40 acre plot that was known as the Sugar Camp. It was necessary in those days to be self sufficient. Even sugar was manufactured locally by the means of the time – drawing sap from Maple trees and turning it to sugar.

Church records reported in *History of Marion County Missouri* show that Dr. David Nelson, the "well known Presbyterian divine" preached on the old camp ground on section 24 (n.w.qr.) in 1829. Area church records indicate that Nelson was very busy at this time spreading the word of God.

The First Presbyterian Church of Palmyra was organized March 27, 1831. The first congregation included two "colored" women, "Sarah" and "Ann". Dr. David Nelson served as the first pastor. To illustrate how things were about to change for Dr. Nelson, it was only a few years later, a member of that same church, the Palmyra sheriff, said that Dr. Nelson did not deserve to live because of his anti-slavery preaching.

The earliest Presbyterian services in Hannibal were said to be held in a small frame warehouse adjacent to the river. On August 19th 1832, they were organized in the home of Lyman Nash by Dr. David Nelson. Interestingly, Samuel Clemens' mother converted to Presbyterianism in the year 1841 in Hannibal about the same time her husband, John Clemens, was serving on the jury of the famous Underground Railroad case of Thompson, Work & Burr as told in a later chapter. A young Samuel Clemens—Mark Twain--would later attend Sunday school in the church organized by Dr. Nelson.

In Round Grove Township, north of Union and west of the Fabius townships, the New Providence Church was organized in August 3, 1834. Records show that the first child baptized in the church, was Rebecca Jane McAfee, by the Rev. David Nelson.

Nelson had the idea of creating a college for the education of young men in the ministry. Because money was scarce, he liked the idea of creating a manual labor college. The students would pay for their college by working a required number of hours. The institution would be self sufficient. In 1832, having taught for a few months, he chartered and presided over Marion College. His goal was to educate ministers and missionaries. During this time, he made tours to the eastern cities to secure adequate means for his educational enterprise. There he left the "impression that he was a man of extraordinary faith and power."

This picture was given to me by Kate Ray Kuhn, author of *A History Of Marion County Missouri*. It was the home of the President of Marion College, Dr. David Nelson, in Philadelphia, Missouri. It is not in her book.

My children, Mike, Susie and Kay show off this original door and door knocker, taken from the original home of the president of Marion College, in Philadelphia, Missouri. Dr. Nelson was the first president of the college. When we went back the door knocker was not there. I hope it is being preserved by someone somewhere.

Last remaining building of Marion College – an outhouse!

At the time these pictures were taken, this was the only building left of the original Marion College in Philadelphia, Missouri. It is a three-holer outhouse, possibly the oldest outhouse in Missouri. It was built around 1830, and was still in use when I visited!

The Regulations For The Theology Department Of Marion College lists details of how the college was run, including the names of trustees, professors and students. The trustees applied for the charter to the legislature of Missouri during the winter of 1830-31. Initially, a log school house was erected on eleven acres. Nelson became both the presiding officer required by the charter as well as teacher of the school. The college was located on Section 16, Township 58 North, Range 7 West. Having financial difficulties, the school had to borrow money. As a corporate body, the Trustees held property at zero value, and consequently, a private estate must be pledged to receive a loan. In April, 1833, three of the Trustees – David Nelson, Dr. David Clark, and Col. William Muldrow – went to New York City where they borrowed $20,000 for ten years, at 7% interest. (They reportedly borrowed from the Tappan brothers, who are known to have financed much of the Underground Railroad.) As a condition of the loan, no less than 4000 acres of land could be purchased in one body. With this money, 470 acres were purchased in the vicinity of the college. For the large body of land required by the agreement, it was necessary to go a distance of 14 miles. In the midst of a beautiful and well watered prairie, 4019 acres were purchased at the reduced government price. The college needed to be self sufficient, with ability to secure timber and coal for fuel. It was subsequently necessary to purchase 480 additional acres at a higher price.

Nelson, Clark, and Muldrow borrowed this money in their own names and felt duty bound to their families to retain the ownership of the property until the loan was repaid. They organized themselves into an association by the title of the "Education Company of the West." This arrangement left two bodies in management of the institution. The Board of Trustees had the legal right to control the institution, while the property and means of support belonged to the Education Company. When the loan was paid off, they-- by deed-- conveyed the title of the whole property to the Trustees of the College, in trust, for Education purposes. They maintained control of their planned college.

A large farm was connected with the institution. Each student was assigned a certain number of acres, and he was required to cultivate saleable grain, vegetables, or other marketable produce. They were also required to work a certain number of hours each day in addition to hours of study and recitation.

The students of Marion College taught the slave children at Sunday school to read the Bible. William Nelson, son of David Nelson, reports seeing the "slave holder's flunkeys go into the Sunday school with sleeves rolled up and chase the student teachers out of the house, and they did not dare to teach the Negro children again."

On February 9, 1832, the First Presbyterian Church in St. Louis held an important revival. Among the converts was Elijah Lovejoy. An account in the anti-slavery publication called the *Emancipation* states that Lovejoy was converted in St Louis by Dr. David Nelson. Theodore Weld, a nationally prominent abolitionist, was also in St. Louis working against slavery. Perhaps Nelson, Lovejoy and Weld met at the First Presbyterian Church in St. Louis. Weld was already more interested in abolition than religion. Neither Nelson nor Lovejoy was known publicly to be an abolitionist at this time, but their pattern of thinking was receptive.

Around this time, seven young graduates of the Divinity School of Yale University signed a compact to go to Quincy, Illinois and establish a seminary of learning to educate the surrounding country. Members of the 'Yale Band' settled in the area in 1829-30. Both education and religion profited highly by their efforts. Although these men were not abolitionists before they came to Illinois, they were instrumental in arousing the anti-slavery crusade in this area. In November of 1830, Rev. Asa Turner, a member of the Yale Band, arrived in Quincy with his bride, Martha Bull. A month later he helped organize the Presbyterian Church, which within three years reorganized as Congregational. In November 1834, at Rev. Turner's home in Quincy, an Association of Congregational Churches was formed. The group was solidly anti-slavery and used every means to support the abolition movement. Based on Turner's own accounts it would seem that Asa Turner and Nelson might have already been acquainted.

As Nelson became increasingly open about his long-held opposition to slavery so did the aggressiveness of the response to his abolitionist leanings. N. A. Hunt's letter, re-printed in a later chapter, explains that Nelson freed his slaves in Kentucky except for a few he brought to Missouri to help with the college. Nelson's son, William D. Nelson, M.D., then tells in his unpublished autobiography that his father made it known that he intended to free his slaves. This inflamed the Missouri community against him. As with everything Dr. Nelson did, even freeing a slave provides an interesting story. William Nelson relates this story:

Father had a slave named Cyrus (Si). He fell in love with a young colored woman named Lucy. Knowing he would get his free papers in a few days he started with her to Canada, but Joseph Rodgers her owner, came to Father to get him to go with him to hunt them and bring them back. Father told him that he did not own Cyrus which made the slave-holders hate him still more. Rodgers went after them and found them at LaGrange, Missouri on the river above Quincy, Illinois. They were a short distance from town. Rodgers and his men sent four Indians to bring him to town.

Si got hold of a club and beat them with it. They returned without him. Rodgers went with a few men and Si surrendered without a fight. When he came home, I asked him why he surrendered to the whites, and would not to the Indians. He gave me a scornful look and said: "Do you suppose dat I would let an Injen take me?" I could not help laughing until it was hard to quit. Si thought it a great disgrace to be taken prisoner by an Indian, but not by a white man. Father reproved Si for his act and to punish him made him make him several hundred rails to fence a few acres of land. When the job was finished he got his free papers and a wad of money.

The following journal entry by William Nelson demonstrates the increasing danger that Nelson faced by more openly opposing slavery:

Not long after Dr. Nelson freed Cyrus, the slave holders raised a mob of 75 men in Palmyra, the county seat, and came to the college to lynch Father.

Oliver Allen, a lawyer and a relative of father's rode with the mob from town to the college and arrived in advance, told father that they were coming to lynch him, and to get ready to fight. Father told him that it would not be Christ-like and he would not fight.

Oliver Allen was a man that did not know what fear was. He had killed two men in a duel before he was 21 years old.

As he rode from Palmyra to the college with his pockets full of pistols with the butts sticking out, he told them that before they killed father they would have to kill him first, and said; "I know you could do that, but before you do a dozen of you will bite the dust."

When the mob came they asked father if he had his abolition papers in the house, he told them that he had but they could not have them if they intended to destroy them. When they started to go through the gate into the front yard father stepped into the middle of the gate and drew a knife from his pocket and declared he would cut the carotid artery of any man who would dare to go through the gate.

Oliver Allen walked back and forth in front of the mob and reminded them of what he had told them on the road from Palmyra to the college; the mob backed out. They had no legal papers which was the reason father lost his peace principals and became angry.

The Boone Farm

In order to give my audiences a sense of how strongly the slave culture was engrained in Missouri at this time, I would begin my speeches and slide presentations with this picture of a typical

Missouri plantation home near Philadelphia, Missouri. This is an example of the life the slaves were trying to leave. My friend and Missouri historian Kate Ray Kuhn took us here. It was called The Boone Farm. She told that it was built by a descendant of Daniel Boone. Daniel Boone was known to have lived west of St. Charles, Missouri, approximately 90 miles south of this location. He also owned property in other locations throughout Missouri. The location of this home, near Philadelphia, Missouri, is in proximity of the anti-slavery activities that triggered many subsequent events with far reaching consequences. These controversial events provided the fascinating stories that drew me further into the continued research of the men, women and children working on the Underground Railroad.

In this home the slave quarters were still evident. This basement of the Boone home was believed to be the slave quarters. She told that some slaves slept on the wooden plank in the picture. Other rooms in the basement were plastered which suggests that they were also used as living quarters.

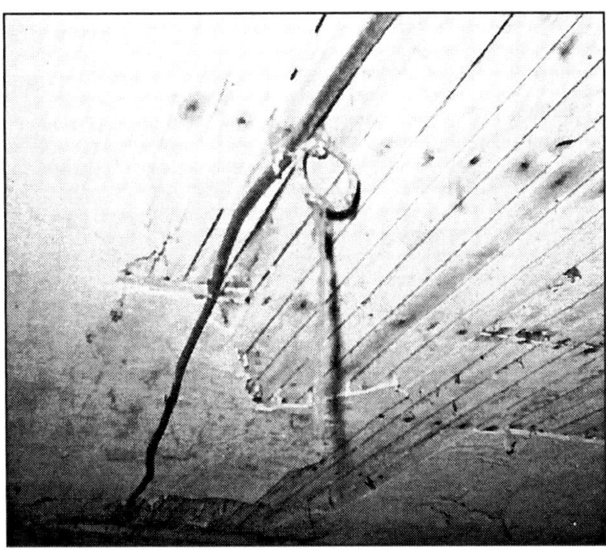

This second picture shows a large ring secured to the ceiling of the room used to tie a slave to if necessary.

Dr. Nelson's progress toward becoming an outwardly open abolitionist took another step when he heard Theodore Weld speak at the Presbyterian General Assembly in Pittsburgh in 1835. Additional evidence that Nelson was now becoming more transparent regarding his abolitionist leanings came on June 16 of that year, the Agency Committee of the American Anti-Slavery Society voted to recommend that Rev. David Nelson of Missouri be appointed an agent for one more year.

By the spring of 1836, abolition was a hot topic in the vicinity of Marion College in Philadelphia, Missouri (a village that was laid out in 1835 by William Muldrow.) An incident that aroused additional unrest in the area resulted when two men arrived in Marion County to promote abolition. Anti-abolition wrath was directed at two individuals only named as Garratt and Williams, recent arrivals from the "Eastern run", (how mid-westerners referred to people from the East). They had brought with them a box filled with abolition tracts (pamphlets). An armed mob, that organized at Philadelphia seized Garratt and Williams, and ordered them to leave the state. The mob went next to Palmyra where the tracts were burned publicly. As Garratt and Williams left the state, a mob waylaid them. Garratt's first hand account follows from the:

Fourth Annual Report of the American Anti-Slavery Society, January 1, 1837

Mr. A.C. Garratt, one of the exiles, gives the following account of his treatment by the mob:

"My case was then held up for investigation. Lawyer Wright was appointed spokesman. On his calling for the manner of punishment, some proposed tar and feathers, others 100 lashes, others to take me to Palmyra, and keep me there until night, then daub me with tar, and burn me with the books. Mr. W. finally made a proposition, to which they agreed, which was, that I must either receive 150 lashes, or leave the state. But when they found that I preferred the lashes to being driven from the state, they would not let that stand, but made another, which was, that I must have 150 lashes well laid on, and if I lived through it, I must lose my life if found within the bounds of the state after the following Saturday. Seeing that it was impossible for me to accomplish anything under these circumstances within the state, I concluded to leave it. Upon these grounds they released me, taking the books with them, which I wished them to read, and added, I hoped they would do them good. But before we separated, Mr. Wright was appointed to reprimand me. After he was done, I wished to defend myself by a reply. But they all cried out, 'We won't hear him.'"

The man who was thus stripped of his rights as an American citizen was of most estimable and upright character. His trustworthiness may be judged from his being superintendent of the Marion College farm. After the banishment of Mr. Garratt and his companion Mr. Williams, also connected with the college, "a public meeting of the citizens of Palmyra and of Marion County, assembled, pursuant to notice, on Saturday, May 21, 1836," at which the following, among other resolutions, was passed:

> *"Be it therefore Resolved, that we approve of the recent conduct of a portion of our citizens towards Messrs. Garratt and Williams (two avowed advocates and missionaries of abolition) who came among us to instruct our slaves to rebellion by the use of incendiary pamphlets, by pictorial representations of imagined cruelty, and by other artful appeals to their passions, eminently calculated to weaken the obligations of their obedience, as characterized by that decision, mildness and dignity, which become a people acting on the principle of self defense."*

Garratt and Williams went to Illinois and later became students of Dr. Nelson in Quincy.

The following is a copy of an Anti-slavery tract similar to one that Garratt and Williams were likely to have been distributing. When you read it, it is easy to see why pro-slavery advocates did not want this information passed out in their communities.

No. 4.

MORAL CONDITION
OF
SLAVES.

[Compiled, chiefly, from recent publications.]

The physical debasement and misery of the slaves in the United States, have often been dwelt upon until the heart has bled, and tears of sympathy have fallen from the eyes of the philanthropist. Such degradation and suffering are enough to awaken deep emotion, and excite to strong effort to relieve the oppressed from the grasp of tyranny. But how much more occasion have we to deplore the degradation and enslavement of the human soul! It is proposed in this little tract to give facts respecting the moral condition of slaves.

The testimony now presented is chiefly from the land of slavery; it is the evidence of disinterested persons who were born, and have long lived, in the midst of it; men who are intimately acquainted with slaveholders, and with slaves; men who have been conversant also with freemen, and with the condition of things in the free states. Their testimony is impartial. "Whoso hath ears to hear let him hear."

American Anti-Slavery Society, No. 143 Nassau street, New York.

THE LICENTIOUSNESS OF SLAVERY.

At the first anniversary of the American Anti-Slavery Society, May, 1834, JAMES A. THOME, of Kentucky, made a disclosure of the licentiousness which grows out of the slave system in his own state. He closed it with the following emphatic words:

"I would not fail to have you understand that this is a *general* evil. Sir, what I now say, I say from deliberate conviction of its truth; let it be felt in the North, and rolled back upon the South, that the slave states are Sodoms, and almost every village family is a brothel. (In this, I refer to the inmates of the kitchen, and not to the whites.) . . . . Let me be understood here: this pollution is the offspring of slavery; it springs not from the *character* of the *negro*, but from the *condition* of the *slave*."

On the very next day in which the above was uttered, and while the statement was denied at a colonization meeting, Mr. Thome's charge was fully sustained by the WESTERN LUMINARY, printed at Lexington, Kentucky. A most remarkable and providential coincidence. The editor in the same slave state of which Mr. Thome had spoken, sent forth, without concert, an independent and almost simultaneous testimony to the very same effect, as follows:

"There is one topic to which I will allude, which will serve to establish the heathenism of this population; for I wish this truth to be known to our *eastern brethren*, that if we ourselves will do nothing, *they* may make our negroes an object of missionary attention. I allude to the UNIVERSAL LICENTIOUSNESS which prevails. It may be said emphatically, that *chastity is no virtue among them*—that its violation neither injures female character in their own estimation, or that of their master or mistress—no instruction is ever given, *no censure pronounced.* I speak not of the world. I SPEAK OF CHRISTIAN FAMILIES GENERALLY. How much longer shall this state of things be unregarded?"

Rev. E. M. P. WELLS, an Episcopal clergyman of Boston, said, soon after the speech of Mr. Thome, he had just conversed with a clergyman who left the South in consequence of slavery, and who told him that what the gentleman from Kentucky said was true, and he *had not told half of what was true.** And he thought these statements came with peculiar propriety and power from a *young man.* The evil was terrible among young men. He believed there was scarcely a young man in the South but was more or less contaminated with it. JAMES G. BIRNEY told the writer of this tract he believed there was

* Slavery in Kentucky, be it remembered, is a different thing from what it is in many of the slave states at the South. If, then, such things are done in Kentucky, what must be the moral condition of slaves and slaveholders at the South?

4 MORAL CONDITION OF SLAVES. [76

scarcely a young man of eighteen years of age, living in a slave state, who was not addicted to this sin.

In the Report of the Synod of Georgia, December, 1833, it is stated as follows: "*Chastity*, in either sex, is an exceedingly rare virtue. Such is the universality and greatness of the vice of lewdness, that to those who are acquainted with slave countries, not a word need be said. On a subject like this, we suffer not ourselves to speak. *All* the consequences of this vice are to be seen, not excepting *infanticide* itself!"

In the circular of the "Kentucky Union for the moral and religious improvement of the colored race" (a society formed of some of the most distinguished gentlemen, both of the clergy and laity, at Lexington, Ken.), to the ministers of the gospel in the state, they say:

"To the female character among the black population, we cannot allude but with feelings of the bitterest shame. A similar condition of moral pollution, and utter disregard of a pure and virtuous reputation, is to be found only *without the pale of Christendom.* That such a state of society should exist in a Christian nation, claiming to be the most enlightened upon earth, without calling forth any particular attention to its existence, though ever before our eyes and in our families, is a moral phenomenon at once unaccountable and disgraceful."

The breaking point between Nelson and the pro-slavery community of Missouri finally took place on May 22, 1836. Dr. Nelson was preaching at Greenfield camp five miles from Marion College. During his sermon, he read a paper given to him by William Muldrow asking for donations to colonize free Negroes. Dr. David Nelson's son, William D. Nelson, M.D. writes the following account.

At the time of the disturbance he was about eleven or twelve years old.

> *After Father read the paper, a Dr. Bosley walked to the pulpit with his cane raised to strike Nelson. Muldrow then rushed up to Dr. Bosley and yelled, "I am the man that had that paper read and if you like, strike me." Dr. Bosley drew from his cane a spear nearly two feet long and tried to run it into Muldrow. Fortunately, Muldrow broke the spear, as soon as it was out of his cane. Dr. Bosley then drew a pistol from his pocket and snapped it twice at Muldrow, but it did not fire. Muldrow drew a knife with a long blade and ran it into Dr. Bosley under the left shoulder and into the left lung. Dr. Bosley then went to a shade tree and sat down and swore that he would die, while the blood ran in a stream out of his mouth.*
>
> *I was an eye witness to all this, except I did not see Muldrow stab the Doctor although I was within ten feet of them when it was done. The reason I did not see the Dr. stabbed was that there were nearly twenty of Bosley's and Muldrow's friends all fighting in a bunch. They fought in the church building, and back and forth in the church-yard, knocking each other right and left using only their fists. They fought until both sides were willing to quit. Several men rode at top speed to raise a mob to kill Father. Mother was frantic until she got Father started to Quincy, Illinois, and it was well she did for if Father had gone home as he wanted to do, he surely would have been killed. It was only by the aid of friends that he got to Quincy alive. He fled to the ford of the Fabius River, on the road to Quincy, and hid on a hillside overlooking the ford. He saw squads of men with rifles hunting him. He did not dare to cross the river until late at night. A short time after he reached Quincy, he had to go back after his family and wrote Mother to go to a friend with the children. Mother went as directed. About midnight or later father came, when all were asleep. His friend, terribly frightened, cried aloud, "Oh Doctor, the mob will come and burn the*

house over our heads." Father said, "No brother, I have been all around your house and there is not a soul within a mile of here." We all started as soon as we could dress and by the aid of Father's friends got to Quincy safe and sound.

When Dr. Nelson and two friends left the campground they made a plan. Nelson headed north toward the shore opposite Quincy while the other two headed south to Hannibal where they were able to cross the Mississippi probably on a ferry – there was one at Marblehead, Illinois. Once on the Illinois side they had to travel back north 20 miles to reach friends in Quincy. Former seafaring captain, John Burns, and a friend crossed the Mississippi by boat to the assigned location and brought Dr. Nelson to the relative safety of Illinois.

Capt. John Burns and either George W. Westgate or Peter McWorthy both of Quincy rescued Nelson from the Missouri shore and brought him to Quincy.

But the extraction of Nelson to Illinois did not necessarily mean he was safe from those in Missouri who would have liked to silence him – perhaps permanently. William Nelson continues:

The slaveholders of Missouri sent men to Quincy and the surrounding country and raised a mob of more than 300 men to lynch Father because he had been making abolition speeches in Quincy and vicinity. They rolled a barrel of tar into the square, intending to tar and feather father and sent two men to the hotel to bring him out. They found him at the top of the stairs of the hotel (Rufus Brown's hotel), reading a newspaper. The men laid their hands on father's shoulders, and told him he was their prisoner. He looked up at them and asked them if they had legal papers to arrest him. They said, "No," but they would take him without them. They had barely spoken before Father was on his feet with his chair drawn back. He ordered them to walk downstairs quickly and they did. Father was not nearly so scared as they expected to find him, even if they did have 300 backers in sight. Father was six feet barefoot, and weighed over 250 lbs.

While the mob was collecting, drinking and swearing, John Wood, afterwards Governor of Illinois, armed thirty abolitionists and went to the hotel, where Father was standing between the hotel and the mob. Wood and his supporters told the Missourians if they took Doctor Nelson, they would do it over the abolitionists' dead bodies. Discovering it was a more hazardous undertaking than they expected, they drank whiskey and swore until night and went home.

Dr. Bosley suffered a terribly long time and came near dying, but recovered and then the mobites liberated William Muldrow. Dr. Bosley and Muldrow had some time previously had a quarrel about a saw mill, which was the real cause of the fight at Father's meeting.

The above account by Dr. William Nelson was given to me by Dorothy Nelson Watson, descendent of Dr. David Nelson.

This brawl is misrepresented in several history books as a response by the crowd to Rev. Nelson's sermon. It is evident by his son's eye witness account that Col. Muldrow's business dealings were the actual cause that ultimately led to Dr. Nelson's move to Quincy, Illinois. Dr. Nelson does not appear to have much to do with Muldrow, who continued to live a controversial life. I do not know how Dr. Nelson met Col. Muldrow, but by April, 1833 they were in New York City together securing funding (reportedly from the Tappan brothers) for Marion College.

Col. Muldrow was a very colorful character in Missouri history. Born at "Muldrow's Hill", Kentucky, on April 12, 1797, he came to Missouri in 1821. Col. Muldrow's fight with Dr. Bosley during Dr. Nelson's speech is told in several places including William Nelson's diary. It is his connection to Dr. David Nelson and their combined efforts in the establishment of Marion College that drew us to visit his tombstone in Little Union Cemetery in Union Township between Palmyra and Philadelphia, Missouri.

A vision of Muldrow was to develop a perfect city-- Marion City. He designed it and went out east and sold lots for large sums of money. Soon people began to move there. The population by 1837 was about 300 people. Haines & Darrow opened a large mercantile, a large packing house was built on the wharf, a warehouse furnished employment and the town prospered. Although it was never completed, the first railroad spike west of the Mississippi was driven to run railroad to Hannibal eight miles south. Unfortunately, a flood wiped out the city along with Muldrow's dream. It was in the area where the formerly named American Cyanamid (now BASF) plant stands. Near Marion City, from the steamboat landing known as

Green's Landing, the ferry ran across the river from Marion City, Missouri to Marblehead, Illinois. An escaping slave could hang on to the rear and use the draft of the ferry and float along to the Illinois shore. Then, walking against the current of the water in the streams and creeks, they were headed north. A tributary of Mill Creek eventually leads to Oakland, Dr. Nelson's Underground Railroad station.

William Nelson, son of David Nelson, describes Muldrow this way.

> *William Muldrow was a very remarkable man. He owned several large farms and was quite wealthy. He had a hundred acres of corn in one field which was very uncommon those days. I saw a breaking plow that turned four feet of prairie sod each round that he had made under his eyes and dictation. He had also 60 acres of mustard. William Muldrow had a few faults but he was such a true friend to Father that I cannot feel my duty to expose them.*
>
> *Muldrow was a powerfully built man with limbs and muscles like an elephant. Father's weight was over 250 pounds and Muldrow's near the same, although father was three to four inches taller than Muldrow.*

Muldrow was such a colorful character that he was immortalized by two of the best writers of all time. Mark Twain, also a resident of Marion County, knew Col. Muldrow very well and he said he drew the character of "Col. Mulberry Sellers" from his recollection of Muldrow. The expression, "There's millions in it," is attributed to Muldrow.

Charles Dickens visited the United States in 1842 and came as far west as St. Louis, where he met with a group of anti-slavery advocates, some from Missouri. Later, when he wrote the book, *Martin Chuzzlewit*, his description of "Eden" was modeled after Muldrow's plan for Marion City.

In 1849 Col Muldrow went to California, where he engaged in business with Capt. John Sutter, the discoverer of gold in California. The two had a falling out, resulting in a lawsuit, and Captain Sutter had to sell his homestead to satisfy the judgment. Col Muldrow returned to Missouri in 1869 and died there in 1872.

Col. William Muldrow is buried in the Union cemetery near Palmyra, Missouri.

Harriet Boekenhoff, a great, great granddaughter of Col. Muldrow, was a classmate of mine in Quincy. Her parents, Mr. & Mrs. Rome Boekenhoff, Jr., operated Boekenhoff's Bakery on Maine Street in Quincy. She became a professional cellist and was living in Texas the last I heard.

Marion College changed to Masonic College in 1845 probably in part to divorce itself from its anti-slavery background. A student of Marion College, Frederick T. Kemper, became a teacher at the college. Eventually the college was moved to Boonville, Missouri and became Kemper Military School. Students of Kemper Military School include humorist Will Rogers and, more recently, Green Bay Packer Torrance Marshall, the MVP of the 2001 Orange Bowl and Jamal Williams, Pro Bowl defensive tackle for the San Diego Chargers. It closed its doors in 2002.

Dr. Nelson Preaches

Dr. Nelson was run out of Missouri for doing the very thing he loved best-- preaching. Soon after he was safely in Quincy he wrote the following letter to the *St. Louis Observer*. I have included it in its entirety because it is such an excellent example of the words of one of the greatest preachers ever in America. Although this was written as a letter, the words read as if he could have intended them to be spoken.

As you read the letter imagine that you are in a campground. The brush has been cleared leaving only the tall trees. Benches are made of planks laid on logs or stumps. Around these pews are tents owned by the families and societies who have come to listen. A preacher's stand has been constructed. It is about 12' x 16' with a roof overhead. (The area beneath the stand is used for a jail for those who get disruptive!) A large crowd has gathered, as this is really the closest thing to entertainment these people experience for many miles around. Familiar hymns are sung. A number of speakers present thoughts and prayers. Then a large man walks forward. He is dressed as if he paid little attention to his appearance. He wears a cravat around his neck. He chooses not to climb the pulpit, but rather stands in front of the crowd as if he wants to be close to the people. He does not shout but speaks clearly and powerfully, challenging those present to think about their moral convictions.

From the *St. Louis Observer*.

DR. NELSON'S LETTER.

To the Presbyterians of Missouri, who hold Slaves: Dear Brethren, I have some acquaintance with a majority of you. I believe we mutually love each other. Through the columns of the "Observer," we may converse, although we meet not face to face. I wish to present you with a thought, which if unimportant you need not notice. I feel that affection moves me to the effort—but should the doctrine be unsound, regard it not—should the argument be unfair or delusive, it will not be hard for you to turn away—but should I advocate the truth, then, in God's name, hear and act. I do hope to sing many a song with the most of you on the other side of the river! Then whilst we are together here, let us help each other on, when we have the smallest opportunity. Connected with the thought which I desire to suggest for your consideration, are two original principles, about which we concur in sentiment with feeling celerity. Nevertheless, I will here write them down, plain as they are, that they may be mentally applied whenever needed, without direct quotation.

FIRST PRINCIPLE.-- The participator in crime is a criminal. The accessory, in the view of heaven, is a principal. Standing near where crime is acted, I participate, if I remove obstacles, if I hold the slightest additional temptation before the eye of the guilty, if I furnish facilities, nay, IF I PREVENT NOT where my ability reaches.

SECOND PRINCIPLE.-- This can be longer remembered by noting the case where a man was urged to cease from habitual adultery. After stating, that should he suddenly neglect his paramour, she, through revenge, would make statements to her husband which would cause him to take his (the adulterer's) life—the law would then execute the husband, and the homeless, unsupported woman, would soon reach death through the avenues of abandonment, leaving her children to certain wretchedness, &c. He received the following answer from his adviser, which contains the principle about which we heartily agree: "The consequences seem awfully threatening, but I am not aware of any permit from the Holy One which authorizes the gradual cessation from that which his soul hateth; or a partial retreat from abominable pollution, the violation of the seventh commandment."

Or the following case may impress upon our memories this all-important principle:

His Bible, his friend, and his conscience, warned M. to repent of murder. He had been in the habit, semi-monthly, of going to a certain road, killing a traveler, and, and with his purse furnishing a dissolute family with the means of revelry. The answer of M. was: "my conscience is awake—my habit must cease, but not suddenly. I must first teach my children industry, they know not how to work; I must restrain their passion for indulgence; should food and raiment, the necessaries of' life, suddenly fail them, with their present lawless habits, my daughters would become prostitutes, my sons robbers; and the increase of murders would be twenty-fold. I should not only destroy my family, but the public would bleed for it at every pore." The reply he received, contains, again, that starting principle, concerning which, I am happy to believe, we have no dispute. The consequences indeed threaten woefully. But results are not to frighten us from ceasing to violate the sixth command—thou shalt not kill. Quitting murder gradually does not comport with the views of all the wicked. Ceasing to dip our hands in blood as soon as circumstances are altogether favorable, is not the doctrine, dear brethren, which you love.

Furthermore: if we may not cease slowly from the crimes of murder and adultery, then it would be hard to show a reason why we may leave off by degrees, the infraction of any one of the remaining eight commandments. God has not intimated to us that an inferior or superior degree of holiness belongs to any one of the ten. But if we may not violate moderately, for a time, one of heaven's awful injunctions; what shall we say of the custom, which in a Christian, amounts to the certain breaking of each one of the commandments, from the first to the tenth, inclusive, as fast as time beats seconds, while passing by us? That is, eighty-eight thousand four hundred times in twenty-four hours, the moments pass our souls to give in their account above. And that account, correctly, is that each man or woman claiming a fellow-creature, has been guilty of each crime pointed at by the decalogue, as often as every second. Do not smile, my dear friend. It requires no effort to prove more than this. Oh! The picture is not the outline of facts. I have lived with slavery for forty years. You are not very likely to deny such facts as I write. Have you courage to turn round and look at yourself in the glass of truth for half an hour? Come, then, and let us be steady and deliberate; for shortly all our characters will be uncovered, even should we be unwilling. Inasmuch, then, as the sixth and seventh commandments have been already noticed, we may begin with one of them.

You own a slave, dear brother or sister. (Permit me to say, dear brother; I have wept with you in the same room and circle, at the mention of Calvary; the recollection of those melting. moments yet continues, and will, I hope, until we meet on high.) Your example then, encourages slavery!! And let me here throw in that which I expect to prove erelong--it upholds it more than the example of one hundred ungodly men. But you agree that example is encouragement, and the strongest of encouragement, in any cause. As long then, as you continue the practice, you help to keep on the chain; and of course, (forget it or not,) participate in the results, Now look at that young colored female; she knows that if she is known as a fornicatress, or an adulteress, her standing in society is not lessened. Nothing else was expected. Her diminution of respectability is imperceptible, at best. She had no standing to lose. Will you say, that keeping any one in a station where no shame, no disgrace, no forfeiture of home is to be dreaded, will not add to the temptation toward adultery? Or will you say, that those who increase temptation do not participate in the crime? (Hold out the temptation of one half cent, or the promise of secrecy, or the smallest additional facility to any one who kills, and human law calls you a murderer. God's rules are as strict.) Or will you say that example does not aid in the perpetuation of slavery? I really do think you will not readily take either of these positions. And yet one of them you must take, or it follows that you are accessory to sins, which, if each polluting act did cover just the space occupied by an individual star, would stain the heavens above us to perfect blackness every hour!

Do you toss your head, with something like anger, my dear relative in the church? Then you have stepped to a hiding place. They are not hard to find when fancied interest prompts—poor indeed is that invention which cannot shape something plausible to shun the plainest inference, where inclination urges. But I will light another lamp, which may shine into the corner you at present occupy. How is it to place males and females, to sleep before the same fire, or in the same narrow room, their beds almost touching? Do not talk to me about bolts or locks. Such statements might pass with some eastern brethren; but I know the truth. Separation, even where it is claimed, exists only in name. And it never will be better, for the profits of slavery will not justify a house with many separate rooms. Will you say that, in their education, they are so trained to chastity and elevation of thought, they are beyond temptation? I presume this is not your plea. Is it that every possible exposure does not amount to temptation? No; this you do not believe. Do you say peace to yourself, because you have but one, or none grown, of different sexes? Ah! Then I must again remind you, that you help to encourage all the slavery in the United States; and this wire of influence links you to every common result. I could mention a variety of ways, by which you do your s h a r e in promoting all the adulteries and fornications connected with slavery; but I have no paper. I shall only pause to say, that your share will be larger than you suppose, and wider than an angel can see across.

Look at an hundred men together, where one murder is committed. One hand alone is extended in the bloody deed; but all encourage—some by smiles, some by words of cheer, others by promises of protection. Do you say that one hundred cases of murder were necessary, in order to constitute each one of these a murderer? No: one crime is not divided, but multiplied into one hundred separate acts. Do not stupefy yourself by hoping that the sins of slaves are divided out to the different families where they happen. If you encourage all the slavery that exists, you encourage all the naturally attendant sins; and the sins we help on in any way, belong to us! When I push away all thoughts and feelings of extravagance; if I yet dare to be faithful and just, I cannot see how anyone can swim across the sea of pollution which surrounds every slaveholder, in half an eternity. Could masters afford to build kitchens with eating rooms, sitting room, and separate bed-rooms; still those females are thrown, by the nature of their employments, into the same field, or under the same shade with the men; or sent on errands through an exposure, (perhaps with profligate white young men,) to which no prudent mother ever subjects her daughter. Dear sister, why do you leave that young slave where you would not leave your own child? Shall I answer for you? It is through a comparative amount of indifference whether her chastity is preserved or not. You would rather she should stand pure; but she is a slave, and you have other employment; you cannot watch her always. Why does not the church shudder? Why is not every member seized with the agony of distraction, remembering that not a communicant sits at the board, who is not influentially united with the sins of ______ deformity; any one of which would stain that white cloth black, oftener and faster than the speaker pronounces words about the blood of Christ? O, sister, long habit may accustom us to almost any spectacle: but we begin to live in a different age. Light is dawning. It is time you should think. You must think; and if you do, it will not be long before you act, unless you are satisfied with the atmosphere of sin, and love the sound of hot rivers that flow into hell. But blessed be the Saviour of the world, and the God of our salvation, we can act. We are not tied to that horrible monster. And of which we heartily repent. I begin to find that I shall not have space to take up each one of the Ten Commandments. I may glance at one or two more, and this will show us what is the awful truth concerning the whole ____ law.

"Remember the Sabbath day to keep it holy."

That slavery which you say you disapprove, (but still continue to practice,) either afraid out of the power of the black to keep holy those blessed hours, or renders it next impossible. This million on the right hand are worked through the week in such a manner, that the Sabbath can only be to them a day of slumber and stupefaction. The others might possibly keep it holy, but never will. Linked with the shape of our soul, is a propensity, not in itself criminal. It cannot be parted with, or annihilated. It is a wish to see our fellow-creatures, and to associate with our kind. The slave can only leave the circle of his toils (uncheered by the thought of wages) on Sunday. He longs to see his equals. If he does ever allow himself to be in company, this is his day, and it is spent in gossip, rambling, and sin!

"Honor thy father and thy mother."

Do you, dear fellow-traveler, (I hope to glory,) suppose it a matter of indifference with the Lord of Hosts, whether this commandment is obeyed or broken? I believe His voice pronounced the words out of Sinai's blaze, as audibly and emphatically as it did the sixth, or tenth. You help to put it out of the power of half a million of children to obey God here. That child is not reared by her parents. This one sees them whipped—hears them called strumpet, harlot, thief, scoundrel, and every name that denotes infamy. These parents cannot learn the art of training children—a most difficult and momentous branch of education. If they did possess the skill of government, they cannot exercise it. They have not time. They possess o n l y a divided authority, &c. Children can never honor parents, who do not act the part of father and mother towards them with diligence and affection.

Thus it is with all the ten commands. Slavery necessarily involves the continued, incessant, and total violation and disregard of everyone, by every victim, every hour. It is not now expedient to explore this dismal forest further. We have already seen more than we can remember. Let us turn a different course. It may be that you have been all this time hoping that you are not answerable for the crimes of South Carolina bondmen; or of slaves anywhere at a distance. Is this your hiding place? Your door can be unlocked, and you can be pushed out where the arrows of conscience will reach you again. I remember well, when I first heard it asserted that the evil done the earth by the daily drunkard, was not to be compared with that of the steady and respectable man who only tasted occasionally. My first thought was, "it is extravagance." My mind then traversed the assertion again, when I was compelled to take it in undiminished. My third reflection was, "How stupid have I been all my life, never to have seen that before!"

A man need not have his eyes entirely open, before he can safely depose that the red-eyed, idiot staggerer, in rags, has nothing alluring about him. His look and smell will rather serve to drive the incautious away from the hot track towards putrefaction. Nay, even those half-gone, smoking, spitting, noisy fools, who vapour around the bar-keeper, disgust the naturally delicate and refined. If you wish to make sure that such shall run the drunkard's race, conduct them into that parlor; and let the man who never was debased, whose conversation is instructive; and whose manners are dignified, hand the glass with a social smile.

Ah! My brother, you decide here at once. I have heard you. You know whose example entices towards the pit of intemperance —the gentleman's or the brute's. You say there is no comparison. And you say correctly. You say that the example of the respectable man will reach an hundred times as far in upholding any vice, as that of the worthless and the hateful. But when you say all this, you seem to forget its import in the case of slavery. I never hear you mention the principle when you talk of slavery. Do you purposely forget it, or what is the cause of your strange avoidance? I fear you will be afraid to answer the question I am about to ask you. It will give you pain to answer it. I, therefore, would not urge the question; but God will shortly, I fear, make some demands of us, to which we cannot reply. As a preventive, then, I must ask the question; whether you, my Presbyterian brethren, have or have not courage to answer honestly. The question is this: whose example is the most stable and efficient, in upholding that slavery with which you agree we are cursed? Is it that of the bloody, little-souled coward, who starves his dependents, and sinks his lash in human flesh daily, loving the sight of gore, and charmed with groans into a feeling of loftiness? No. If none but these owned slaves, it would not be tolerated half a year. The mob in New Orleans, (yes, New Orleans!) pulled down the house of such a character. These tyrants do the cause of emancipation as much service, as the bloated do the cause of' temperance. Is it the example of the professional negro driver, which encourages men to claim souls as property? No: you hate these men yourself. I hear you often say so. (Although I confess I am, and always was, too dull to see much difference between the man who carries a slave from one state to another, and the man who sells him, or owns and chains him to a particular spot.) But you say that all detest the negro driver. Of course, his example is rather against, than in favor of the custom. Whose example is it, then, which quiets the conscience most, and stills perturbation, and makes it seem honest to say, "work without wages;" and thickens every link in that accursed chain? It is the example of the steady professor of religion. It is the example of him whose conduct, in other respects, most adorns the gospel; who pleads against alcohol, who observes the Sabbath, who feeds his slaves and clothes them well, and tasks them lightly. You are generally of that class. You do more to confirm and continue naked slavery, than any other class of men in existence. There is that belonging to the influence which sober walking professors have over the earth that the wicked do not understand. Many Christians forget, and others do not know it. Let us build a platform on which to exhibit that fact.

The time was, when, if I heard an infidel say that religion and the bible had his entire contempt, I believed him. When he told me that he had not the slightest regard of any kind for the name of Jesus, he seemed to think so, and I thought with him. But after this I saw him, whilst Christians were weeping over a praying sinner, gnashing his teeth at the spectacle! Whilst the minister was preaching, I saw him leave the house of God in anger. I remembered that if the minister had been speaking of

Constantine or Tamerlane, it would have been a matter of perfect indifference with that hearer, whether he censured bitterly or warmly eulogized. I spoke with, perhaps, an hundred lofty scoffers, on points of history, science, or law, where we differed in our views. They maintained a rational and smiling debate. I addressed them kindly on their prospects for eternity. Some grew instantly angry; others asked for another subject; others turned pale—all were restless. In short, I found that the name of Jesus Christ has more torturing influence over atheists, deists, and universalists, who profess total indifference, than any other name ever pronounced, "under heaven amongst men." Let us now look at the same principle exhibited in another case. Why were the humble followers of Wesley, in England, more tarred, feathered, stoned, cursed, and hated, than were the horse thieves and gamblers? They had not stolen the property, or assaulted the persons of their countrymen. Yet robbers and murderers did not receive half the hearty hatred, (if we may judge from the malignant invective, and bitter cursings,) as they did these inoffensive men. The Saviour has given us the reason—"If ye are of the world, the world would love its own; but because ye are not of the world, therefore the world hateth you." These men had a powerful influence in England. Their holiness was reproving the multitude so severely, that it almost drove them to madness.

The loudest compliment I ever heard paid a Methodist church, either in England or America, has been the hatred bestowed on them by the carnal professor, and the wicked. The boldest praise I could bestow upon the Presbyterian Church, and the most flattering belief I entertain of them, I here write down; because it is necessary to my ultimate design in this address. I believe they are more hated and reviled in bar-rooms, and groceries, than any other people in the Mississippi valley. If I am correct in this supposition, then it follows that their influence is great indeed. If not correct, it is still true that their influence may be known and measured by the amount of calumnies, sneers, and belchings of animosity, of which they are the subject; and which may be seen in infidel prints, and heard elsewhere. If the character, and testimony, and conduct of Christians, torture not the conscience of the world, there will be no throes of impatience visible. If the doctrine and walk of professors resemble that of the Saviour, they will be hated as certainly as he was; and men will be loud in their abuse of them, as certainly as they were of Him. Now we are prepared to understand that all holy and active professors of every denomination have an influence over the ungodly, which the wicked deny; over the worldly church member, which he does not acknowledge; and over all, far beyond their own apprehension.

Before Christians began to wash their hands, it was in vain to speak in favor of temperance. If Christians did not own slaves, (I mean those, who, in other respects, seem to deserve the name of Christian,) the consciences of thousands who now walk in quiet, would be tortured most unbearably: and yet you are waiting, are you? For what? For the world to set you the good example? No, you dare not say that. Is it that the slaves may be prepared for freedom? If you say this, I have one objection to it; that is, it is not true. For you are not preparing them. I have long heard this; but I know it is sham pretext, for no more is now doing to educate them, than was years ago. You have not now, in this state, as many in Sabbath schools, or in training of any kind, as the natural increase of one year. You cannot, and in many cases you dare not, assemble them in schools. And will you, follower of the Lamb, mock the Lord, by telling him you are waiting to have them trained? Are you waiting for something to be done by the laws? Oh, deceptious statement from the bottomless pit! This song, the Christians of my native state, Tennessee, have been singing for half a lifetime. And at least they obtained their convention. And how did the long-hoped-for convention relieve them? By making it unconstitutional for the legislature to touch the subject.

Do you, the light of the world, (here I address all the slave-holding Christians,) contend for the privilege of holding them for a year or two? Can it then be strange that others should design to hold them forever. But do you reply, "What can I do? The law is against liberation, my servants are unprepared, I am unable to act in the case." Hold there, brother, sister; you can act. You can act tomorrow. No human power can compel you to make, or to continue to make, a slave of your fellow creature. Do not say you cannot emancipate. I know better.

Some have tried it. All the difficulty lies in being willing. Do not say a word about consequences. They cannot be worse than must attend on many additional Southampton cases, in years to come. But no matter what are the consequences, you are not justified in continuing to participate in ten thousand times ten thousand thefts, murders, adulteries, and every imaginable crime. You can say to your slave, tomorrow morning, "you are no longer mine, but I am willing to hire you." Do right, and leave the consequences with God. If you do not do something shortly, my dear friend, I tremble for you.

You have not the excuse you had three years since. Light is beaming. Discussion increases. A few years since, when your preacher came down from the pulpit, your elder handed him a glass of spirits for the sake of his health; (disgusting lies.) What would you think of either of them, were they to act so now? You would pitch them from the church battlement. If you did not, you would not deserve to lay your filthy fingers upon a bible. What is the reason of this? Guilt increases as light strengthens. Just so, in a few years, you will wonder at those who could claim an immortal being as property, and sleep. Did I say just so? The expression is inadequate. You will stand in perplexing doubt, whether he who could claim a brother man long enough to cook one dinner, could possibly have had, at the time, any respect for any part of the law of God. Oh, dear brethren, let us hear that you are doing right, that the maxims of perdition no longer govern you. Do you say, "my wife is unable to work, because of ill health." Then work for her yourself. Do you reply, "I am needed in the field?" Then beg—or do anything lawful, rather than be a thousand times criminal every hour. O, get out of that ocean of sin any way. You will feel happy--exceedingly happy—I know it. To do right brings a blessing with it, worth worlds. Try it, and try it speedily. This is a hurrying age.

I hope in a few weeks, to be able to write an address to the abolitionists, in company with several other classes of men, on a very important subject. Do let me have some good news to tell them. If you would free all your slaves, it would urge the government to do something sooner than any thing else. Do you fear your slaves would become vagabonds? I have known those who feared this, but tried it, and were very agreeably disappointed. Do be a little timorous on other points. Dread, lest growing up in bondage, their souls should be lost. I would give what little I possess of worldly treasure, could I thereby prevail on you to make the following innocent experiment, for the next month, uninterruptedly. As your servant passes near you, just look into that dark face seven times in each day, and say, "there is a deathless being whose natural rights I do not intend to restore until the government does something." And then go to prayer. This, I have little expectation you will or can do. May I then, in conclusion, ask you to comply with a very fair and reasonable demand? Will you go on your knees once in each day, and tell Him, whose eye is every where, that you are faithfully and earnestly educating or preparing your slaves for freedom, and that as soon as they are ready you will free them? No, you dare not tell him such a falsehood. Let me, then, in saying farewell, repeat that which you already believe. The space between you and the gate—either the right or left hand gate—is narrow indeed. The beings who live where the Prince of compassionate mercy is, who are now in his company look very beautiful. The everlasting hills are bright. Heaven is long as well as glorious. They sing there, oh! how sweetly. If you are there some eight or nine hundred millions of years on the other side of the judgment, you will not regret any inconvenience you sustained here by waiting on yourself. You will not sigh when you recollect having diminished your property, (PROPERTY!!!) by doing right. N.

It is difficult to imagine that anyone listening to these words would still condone the horrific conditions of slavery, yet they did. Although Dr. Nelson had a powerful effect on many around him, there were those who were threatened by his words. As you read the extraordinary events in this book you will notice that most of the persons involved in these Underground Railroad activities had heard Dr. Nelson preach and were motivated by him to act against slavery.

Chapter Five

OAKLAND AND MISSION INSTITUTE

Nelson's house and Underground Rail Road station as it appears today.

When Dr. Nelson first came to Quincy, he lived at the home of Capt. John Burns, located on the east side of Fourth Street, south of the Public Library, and north of the "Lord's Barn" (The first church built in Quincy). Burns was one of the men who rescued Dr. Nelson from his Missourian pursuers. He was associated first with Eells' Institute at 3rd and Spring. Until 1838, Capt. Burns was working on the construction of a large grain windmill twelve miles southeast of Quincy in Payson, Illinois. There is more on the mill in a later chapter on Payson.

Nelson's son William remembers a time following Nelson's flight to Quincy after all the excitement had settled. Another brother, Henry Aurelius, who was sixteen years old at the time, had stayed behind with someone in New London, Missouri (ten miles south of Palmyra). He became ill with typhoid fever and nearly died. Dr. Nelson and

Amanda went there to tend to him. While there, a crowd of about fifty men came to lynch Dr. Nelson. When they came to the door, the brave Amanda severely tongue lashed them. Like a mother bear protecting her cubs, she used that spirit to take on a dangerous mob. William quotes her as saying, "You are a brave band of armed soldiers to come against one man, and that man attending to a sick child at death's door. You are a wonderful crowd of heroes." He said his mother gave them much more verbal bashing. At one point, it got so hot for the mob that they rushed into a patch of tall woods to escape her tongue!

And then another interesting thing happened. Dr. Nelson went outside to meet the mob and made a Masonic sign that all Masons understand. The leaders of the mob then persuaded the rest of the mob to return to town. Free Masonry is a fraternal organization that began in the late 16th to early 17th century. Members share moral and ideal beliefs and use signs that are gestures and words to identify members at meetings etc. Apparently, Nelson and the leaders of the lynch mob belonged to the Free Masons.

An event occurred during the latter part of 1837 which created an intense excitement in Adams County. It was what is often mistakenly spoken of as the Nelson riots, being erroneously associated in date with the flight of Dr. Nelson from Missouri and the attempts to kidnap him, though these events occurred during the preceding year.

Anti-slavery and abolition societies were organized in many of the northern cities. Their formation was almost invariably attended with excitement and often violence. Such a society had been organized in Quincy. Several meetings had been held and a good deal of feeling aroused upon the subject.

Dr. William Nelson gives this account of an incident at the "Lord's Barn":

> *Father made an appointment to make an Abolition speech in Quincy. The Mobites declared that he should be mobbed if he tried it. But Gov. Wood and the abolitionists declared that he should. As I was passing through Quincy a few days before his appointment, Gov. Wood came to me and told me to tell father to let nothing prevent him from filling his appointment. Nothing but severe sickness or death would have prevented him. He spoke in the Congregational Church and the mob came and shattered four large windows on the north, but Gov. Wood had*

a pile of brickbats at the door and beat them back, fracturing one man's lower jaw. This was father's last mob.

On September 27, 1837 a call for an Antislavery Convention was signed by Elijah P. Lovejoy and "undersigned" by 245 persons from seventeen communities of the state of Illinois. Dr. Nelson and his adult son David D. Nelson of Jacksonville were among those signers. This list provides a list of persons whose beliefs were strong enough to risk signing their names to the document. Many times I was able to check the list for someone who built a house suspected of being an Underground Railroad station and confirm their anti-slavery sentiments by their signature on this petition. The convention took place in Alton October 26, 27 & 28th of 1837. Only a few days later Elijah Lovejoy was murdered inciting intense emotions on the issues of slavery and free speech.

On April 19, 1838, Dr. Nelson purchased 185 acres from Edward B. Kimball, located in Melrose Township approximately five miles east of Quincy. On the south 105 acres, he built his home, "Oakland", where he lived and died. On the north 80 acres, a chapel and twenty small log cabins for students were built. Dr. Nelson – repeating a plan similar to Marion College – built another college for missionaries. There was also a horse drawn mill built along the creek. This land was conveyed in trust to Rev. Asa Turner, for the purpose of establishing a manual labor missionary college. The land conveyed to Asa Turner was called Adelphia Theological Seminary, or Mission Institute No 1.

In his first summer of residence at his east Quincy home, under the shade of four large oaks, Dr. Nelson wrote *Cause and Cure of Infidelity*. He drew mainly from his own thoughts and memory. In *Asa Turner and His Times, First President of Iowa College,* Asa Turner recalls:

> His well-known book is but a Synopsis of sermons. He could think as well sawing logs or shaving shingles as in the best study in the world, and it was just as easy to arrange it on a log as in a rocking chair. He would ponder over a chapter perhaps a day, or a week or two, and when he got ready sit down and write it off no matter where he was.

Nelson also wrote another treatise entitled *Wealth and Honor*, which he carried to the East for publication. Unfortunately it was lost and never published.

Dr Nelson's home "Oakland" was built with a hiding place around the fireplace in the living room on the first floor. The Grubb family, who sold the house to Bill's family, told us that Sunday services were held in the living room before the chapel was built. The hiding place, later discovered by my sons Ray and Rich Deters as curious young boys, could be entered through a trap door in the room above. It is clear that Dr. Nelson was fully committed to the Underground Railroad as he now lived in a "station".

A close inspection of the left side of this photo taken of the east side of our home shows the foundation is settling where it is believed a tunnel went out of the basement. Several years ago, Richard Elmore of Quincy told us that he was a relative of the Grubb family who lived in the house in the early 1900s and he played in the tunnel as a child. When we were putting in a gas line and digging on that side of the house several rusty metal hand tools were discovered on this site.

Arrow indicates area in basement where original wall was covered with cement many years ago.

Looking southeast from Nelson home toward the ravine where the basement tunnel ran.

Tracing back to the Mississippi from this station would begin here. A ravine on the east side of the house accesses a creek that meanders into Little Mill Creek. Little Mill Creek empties into Mill Creek, which eventually ends up at the Mississippi River in Marblehead, Illinois. From Marion City, Missouri, a ferry ran across the river to Marblehead, Illinois. If a runaway slave were to hang on to the ferry or follow its course to Marblehead, he or she would then walk up Mill Creek by walking against the current and eventually end up at the temporary security of "Oakland" – Dr. Nelson's home.

We wanted to learn more about tunnels as escape mechanisms in the Underground Railroad so we took a family vacation to Nebraska City, Nebraska to tour the Underground Railroad station known as John Brown's Cave-Cabin Museum.

John Brown was known as the abolitionist martyr whose execution for the raid at Harper's Ferry, Virginia is said to have aroused such sentiments that it ultimately caused the Civil War.

Entrance to John Brown's Museum

The trap door under the desk leads down into a secret room.

Tunnel with room to right

Behind a moveable storage cabinet was an opening into the tunnel that led out to a wooded area. The tunnel wasn't tall but was just the right height for Greg and Mark Deters to plan an escape from the Deters family vacation!

Even though the Nelson's were now decisively settled in Quincy, the religious anti-slavery citizens of Missouri still hungered for his dynamic oratory. Dr. Nelson's son, William, tells of a planned return trip to preach in Missouri:

> *After Dr. Nelson had resided sometime in Illinois, in Adams County, a few miles from Quincy, some of the members of one of his old churches in Marion County invited him to preach for them on a sacramental occasion. He agreed to do so, but with the expressed understanding that he would preach the gospel only, without any references to abolitionism, which sentiment he did not deny that he held as his own private opinion. Some of the citizens, however, resolved that he would not preach at all, and went to the meeting well armed and determined to prevent him from opening his mouth on the occasion. Some of these were themselves Presbyterians. Other members of the church armed themselves, and attended the meeting determined that Dr. Nelson should speak if he wanted to! Had the doctor been present, blood would have been mingled with the sacramental wine...*
>
> *But Dr. Nelson did not come. Hearing of the character of the opposition to his presence, he was prudent and wise*

enough to remain away, it must be confessed, to the disappointment of some of his friends who wanted an opportunity of showing their courageous devotion to their former pastor. Old Theodore Jones said that he went to the meeting that day with his pistols in his pockets intending to go armed to the communion table, with the full conviction that he was doing right.

Another account of the same event by a slave-holder identified as "S" is reported in *A Missionary Perseveres In Missouri* (Dr. C. is probably Dr. Clark who worked with Dr. Nelson on Marion College.)

Dr. Nelson had an almost endless control over this community, but he was driven away for his benevolence. Dr. C. had related to Mr. S the following fact. Soon after Dr. N. went to Quincy, he sent over an appointment to preach at the college, but the excitement was very great. A multitude had agreed to mob him, if he came, and all his friends felt that he was in great danger. Dr C. immediately started off for Quincy, in hopes to get there before Dr. N. should start, but on his arrival Dr. N. had gone. Dr. C. started to overtake him, which he did some seven miles from the place in which he was to preach. He was riding in a gig, with a friend. Dr. C. wished to have a few words private conversation with him, and wished him to get out. He did so. Dr. C. stated to him his fears, told him of the excitement, of his own danger, etc.

Dr N. heard him through without interruption, and stood for a while in silence. Dr. C. supposed his object was affected, that Dr. N. was considering his course, and would turn back; but his surprise was great when Dr. N. accosted him. "Dr. C.," said he, "I left a bag of clover seed at your house, when I was there last. Is it safe? I was afraid the rats had eaten it; but I want it, and will call after the meeting is over and get it." Perfectly astonished, Dr. C. knew not what to make of it, when Dr. N. said to him: "You will go with us and hear the sermon, won't you?" and started to go on.

Dr. C then rode up to him and said: "I will go, Doctor. I will stand by you as long as life is left, and so will others. There are many who will be there, and blood will be shed," mentioning the names of several of Dr. N's friends, who were determined to stand by him. Dr. N. stopped. He had no fear for himself; but the thought of his friends' defending him at the expense of their lives was too much. He stopped, a tear started on his courageous cheek. "Let's go back," he said, and turning he did so.

Meanwhile, Mission Institute on the property next to Oakland was being developed as a school for men and women being trained as missionaries in foreign countries.

Whitley Thompson, a student at Mission Institute, wrote a diary, a copy of which was provided to me by a descendent, Aileen Ostendorf, of St. Louis, Missouri. In January, 1837, he tells of crossing the "River" on the ice to get to Missouri on business for Dr. Nelson. He tells of then leaving Marion College, staying overnight at Marion City, before crossing the river again to return to Mission Institute. His days are filled with early rising, prayers and work. On February 4, 1837, he writes:

This day has been spent in helping to raise Mr. Hoods House. I have been too light minded to think of my God as I should. O That I may be prepared to spend the Sabbath holy.

Later, on June 19, 1837, Whitley Thompson writes:

This day has commenced another period of Study. I have attended one recitation today. I have also sold my House to Aten for $46-. I have concluded to take this name of all the Students who are and who may come and those who have left

Arrived			
1 AG Field	*from*	*Boston,*	*June4*
2 J K George	" "	"	" 4
3 A C Garratt	" "	*N York*	
4 John Benson " "	*N Y...*		
5 C W Shane	" "	*Cincinnati Oh.*	
6 IM Hunter	" "	*N York*	*Aug10*
7 W Thompson	" "	*Tenn*	" " *10*
8 O J Kendal	" "	*Utica NY*	*Sep" "*
9John Rendal	" "	" "	" "
10M Kibby	" "	*Conn*	" "
11R S Hood	" "		
12Jacob G Conrad	" "	*Mo*	

13 E M Lenard	*" "*	*Oberlin*
14 William Herrit	*" "*	*N. York*
15 W. P. Doe	*" "*	*" "*
16 Elis E Kirkland	*" "*	*Onidio*
17 Hunt		
18 John Aten		
19 James B Thompson		*Tenn*
20 George Thompson		*Oberlin*
21 Evan Williams		*Walsi*
22 James Wells		*MS*
23 William Fithian		*Philadelphia*

Another student, N. A. Hunt, wrote this letter late in his life describing his life working the Underground Railroad and describing his life there:

Riverside, Cal.
Feb. 12th '96

W.H. Siebert, Dear Sir;
James Rosebrough, of Reno, Bond Co., Ill., died about twenty years ago. His youngest son, Wm. married my daughter, and is now living at the old homestead. On taking your letter directed to his father out of the office, and reading it, he sent it to me, thinking that perhaps I could answer some of the inquiries. I was intimately acquainted with James Rosebrough, for 12 years, in Reno. He was a native of Georgia, went to S. E. Missouri, when a young man, and moved to Bond Co., Ill. about the year '40. He was regarded for years, as an outspoken anti-slavery man, and later earned the appellation of a foremost abolitionist-ready, at all times, to harbor a colored man, slave tho' he might be, and help him on, to where he would be a free man. The early settlers of Reno, (then called Bethel) were largely from Tenn., some from N.C., and a few from Geo. and Mo. It was distinctively an anti-slavery settlement. Being 150 m. from the Ohio river, and 90 from the Mississippi, there was no particular need men of an Underground R.R. In ante-bellum times, fugitive slaves were

not unknown about Reno, but they were not very numerous. When one came along, he was likely to be directed to Rosebrough's, McLain's or Wafer's, and he was safe. There were no particular stations in the settlement.

I was born in N.H., and lived there till I was grown. 'Twas in N.H. that I first heard an address on the subject of slavery, delivered by an ag't of the A.C.(colonization) So.(society). A collection was taken up, and I contributed some trifling amount. In the spring of '34, I went to Oberlin Institute, Ohio. (not a college then) and there, of course, I soon became antislavery in sentiment. In June, of '37 I went to Mission Institute, near Quincy, ILL. Dr. David Nelson, the author of "Cause and Cure of Infidelity," was the founder of M. Institute. He was a Virginian, graduated from college very young, studied medicine, and was a surgeon in the army, in the War of 1812. After he was converted, which was late in the twenties, instead of giving infidel lectures against Christianity, he became a very successful minister of the Gospel of Christ. He began his Christian life in Kentucky. And about the first thing he did, was to set his slaves free. From Kentucky he went to northern Mo., thinking that in that section, with but a few slaves, he could build up an institution of learning to educate ministers, especially for foreign missionary work. He founded Marion College, with that object in view; but his strong antislavery utterances, in the pulpit, and elsewhere, brought many another war upon him; and he had to flee for his life, to the free state of Ill. There, near, Quincy, he founded his Mission Institute. Dr. Nelson still owned landed property in the vicinity of Marion College, after he was driven from Mo., and necessarily had to have communication, back and forth, tho' seldom going in person, for his life was in danger. The Dr. came to me one day, in the spring of '39 or '40, and asked me if I would go with another student, whom he mentioned, over to the western bank of the river, opposite Quincy, and walk up and down the river. We were to signal our presence there at intervals by rapping rocks together in our hands. We were not to speak a word, but if our signals were answered, we were to help such as needed help, to a station 16 m. east of Quincy. At that station there was a barn, painted red, so that no mistake need be made.

Apparently barns painted red were not the norm in the 1830s and 40s as they are today. It may have been an issue of being able to afford that much paint. In all my years of Underground Railroad research I did not know the location of that barn. As I was nearing the completion of this book I believe I came across that barn. I was so excited by the discovery after all these years that I couldn't sleep all night! That story is in a later chapter. Hunt continues:

Sunday night was the time to cross the river, as it would be easier for persons on the other side to be there on that night, than any other day of the week. Four of us were thus spoken to --Two to go each alternate week. To specify particulars in this work would be to write volumes. Two or three will suffice. I should say here that Quincy, in the thirties, and early forties, was noted as an antislavery town, and for that reason, more of this line of business was done there, than at any other town on the Illinois side, between there and St. Louis. I know not how many other lines were operated there, beside the one I was connected with, but I know there was a good deal of work done. A very fine young man came to us from St. Louis. He was to be sold South, and that they all dreaded, some worse than death, and took their own lives. This young man was intelligent and reached Canada safely.

A sister of Wm Bird, the fellow student who always accompanied me over the river, had a sister that married a slaveholder; and one of the female slaves, she thought ought to be free, and she fitted her out, as well as she could, and started her to the Queen's Dominions. She made the journey safely. But who can say as to the right, or the wrong of the mistress? I can't. Two young ladies of my acquaintance, told their father that they would go to the mill with a grist, as the milling must be done, and the father was needed at home with the workmen, who were building a barn. The mill stood upon the bank of the river below Quincy. {Marblehead, IL, south of Quincy, was known as Millville because of the mill there. It also had a Mississippi River ferry landing.} *While at the mill, they saw a black man, at a distance, and went to him. He needed help. They got him into their Dearborn wagon, and secreted him among the bags. When near home, lest he should be seen by the workmen, they had him crall (sic); and at the house they carried him in, as they did the other sacks of meal. He was stored away, in the garret till an opportune time and taken on to the station.*

I will mention but one more incident. At a night meeting, near Quincy, a colored man took me aside, and asked my advice about leaving his master. I laid before him, as well as I could, what were the liabilities, on the way of escape from bondage, and told him, if he had a good master, as he said he had and was not liable to be sold South, it would perhaps be well for him to "bide his time, for the day-star of hope for the slave was rising. And yet I told him if he was determined to make the effort, I was ready to help him. I never persuaded, or even suggested to a slave to leave his master, but if he came to me panting for freedom, I helped him at the perel (sic) of my life. Those scenes are almost forgotten, for I am nearing my 85th mile stone.

N. A. Hunt

It is apparent from this letter that the abolitionists believed that slavery would be abolished soon in the 1840s.

The purpose of Mission Institute was to prepare students for the rigors of becoming missionaries in foreign lands. The Underground Railroad was something they participated in for moral and religious reasons while there. I was fortunate to receive this letter describing incidents at Mission Institute from a student's descendent in 1969:

Oakham, Mass
March 29, 1969

Mrs. Ruth Deters
Oakland
Quincy, Illinois

Dear Mrs. Deters,

In a round-about way I have received an item from the Herald-Whig Quincy, Ill Oct 15, 1968 telling of your interest in Mission Institute. I had wondered about this Institute as I have papers telling that my grandfather, William Mellen attended there in 1838. He later attended Yale Divinity School and then went as a missionary to Africa. I believe he got his inspiration to go to Africa while at Mission Institute. As a child my mother used to tell me stories which her father had told her of his experiences in helping slaves to get away, I wonder if you would be interested in these stories. I know about 3 of them.

Two of his daughters went to Africa as missionaries and one of his granddaughters went to India so you see, this early influence was far reaching.

My sister visited Quincy last summer & inquired about Mission Institute & no one had heard of it—so I was glad to find out about it.

My grandfather lived in Mass. but when 20 years old his uncle sent him on a business trip to Quincy. He traveled with a team & the journey took him 6 weeks.

Sincerely yours,
(Miss) Emily Rood

The follow up letter portrays such innocence in the midst of danger that would astonish young people today:

Oakham, Mass
April 13, 1969

Dear Mrs. Deters,

I have written out for you the two stories which I remember. I never knew my grandfather as he died before my mother was married but she used to tell the stories her father had told her. There may have been more but these are all I remember. It is years since I have heard them, but they made a great impression on me as a child.

The one person I have heard mentioned as also being at the school when he was there was Rev. George T. Thompson {well-known from the infamous Thompson, Work and Burr case as told in a later chapter} who also went to Africa as a missionary. My grandfather went to Africa in 1850 & remained there for 35 years without a vacation & then for the next 10 years he spoke of Africa in churches & Sunday Schools all over this country. I hope this information may be of some little interest or help in your studies.

I have been glad to learn something of this school & if more is printed I would be would be glad to know of it.

Sincerely yours,
Emily Rood

<u>My grandfather told this story.</u>

He used to help every so often to get slaves to the next station. A wagon would be fixed up to look as if he was taking produce to the next town but in straw in the bottom somehow slaves would be hidden. He had a slight acquaintance with a young lady in Quincy & she wanted to help in this service. So on his next trip she was invited to go along & a trunk put on in back & they set out (apparently a young man & his sweetheart going away). They got to the next station but it was late & they were to spend the night. They were taken to their quarters which turned out to be one large room with 2 big double beds. My grandfather tried to sit facing the window with his head in his hands, hoping that the lady would prepare for bed. As she didn't he finally went out into the cold night & walked around till he saw the lights go out in that room. Then he went back in & prepared for bed—Then the problem. It was very dark and he did not know which bed she had chosen but he tried the first one & luckily it was the empty one & he crawled in & had a good sleep. I don't remember what happened in the morning, but I expect he had to get up & leave at an early hour.
They got home safely the next day.

One night he was out with slaves trying to get them to their next stop. A bad thunderstorm was coming up and there were signs that they were being followed & danger that the slaves would be found—so they let the slaves out next to a large cornfield—The corn was up high & the slaves could get in the middle of the field somewhere & it would be impossible to find them. They would come back the next day & pick them up and take them on.

The next day they went back to find them & wondered how they could. There was a farm house nearby & stopped there to make discrete inquiries. The man there said, "Yes, they are hidden in my barn & you can get them & take them on. They were quite safe here, as I am known to be much against aiding run away slaves, so no one would expect me to be helping them & did not come here to hunt for them. They came to the door last night after that bad storm & they were soaking wet & so forlorn looking that I did not have the heart to turn them away. I let them sleep in the barn & have given them breakfast."

They picked them up and carried them on safely.

About twelve miles north of Quincy in Mendon, Illinois was a fearless conductor by the name of Deacon Jireh Platt. His four sons were active in the Underground Railroad and later wrote letters and journals about it. I shared the letters with Zona Platt Galle, Jireh Platt's descendent and in return she shared Enoch Platt's journal with me. The first hand accounts of conducting on the Underground Railroad are incredible to read.

Although the Mission Institute students had much to do with the required manual labor, prayers and studying, several of them were also conductors on the Underground Railroad. This story, from the handwritten journal of Enoch Platt, demonstrates a sense of humor about the serious mission.

One of the students of Mission Institute name G. was thought by some of the faculty to be too thoroughly possessed with a spirit of mischief to ever be of any real use in the world. He keenly enjoyed Running off niggers", and was never better pleased than when exercising his ingenuity in getting out of a "Bad scrape" with them. He was so daring that at first some of the abolitionists feared to trust him, but as he was always ready to go, and always successful, he became for a time the main conductor on that part of the route and figured as a prominent actor in more than one of the incidents recorded in these sketches. {Enoch Platt journal} He was one night to bring three men to Father's. Knowing that the Institute grounds would be watched that night, just at dusk he had them lie down on the bottom of a common farm wagon, his only disguise being to throw an old blanket over them. For a short distance he had to go west toward Quincy to get onto the Mendon road. Just before he got to the corner, he saw four hunters riding rapidly toward him. One moment more and right in their sight he would have taken the Mendon road, which would have insured pursuit and capture. But that one moment was enough for G. Whipping up his horses he drove straight on toward Quincy boisterously singing:

"A life on the ocean wave,
A home on the rolling deep,
My wife she won't behave,
And my child won't go to sleep."

As he met the hunters two rode each side of his wagon, they never dreaming that that rowdy singing along the road had passed their three slaves right under their noses without their even smelling them.

As soon as he was out of their sight he turned toward Mendon, and made his horses travel. Telling Father {Platt} that the hunters were in close pursuit, he hurried home, put the horses in the stable, and went to bed, without his absence being known by either his landlady or his fellow students. He had succeeded in getting them safely away and it made little difference to him if the farmer's horses which he had driven were not fit for work for a week after. In the morning he volunteered to help hunt, but the masters learned that he was a student and declined his services.

The following humorous story in Enoch Platt's journal reflects the confusion people had on what the Underground Railroad was even at the height of the activity:

So many slaves escaped from the border states that it began to seriously affect their market value. So very few that once escaped were ever recovered, that the question "How do they get them away?" was a puzzling one, that was a frequent theme of conversation among the masters. A young man at Mission Institute (in Quincy), who had a much higher opinion of himself than his acquaintances had of him, had heard about the U.G.R.R and large rewards offered for the return of fugitives, conceived the idea that if he could only discover the secret, he could make some money out of it, and distinguish himself at the same time. So he set himself to the task. G. overheard him making some inquiries about it, and confidentially told him "I know all about it" There is a railroad track underground all the way from Quincy to Chicago. I have been over it a number of times and know all about it. If you will promise not to tell anyone I will tell you."

Of course the promise was given, when the student gravely told him that the trains always ran at night, but did not have any regular hour of starting. "You know," said he, "that old unused rail road grade between here and town. Go to the culvert a mile west of here and watch there. Sometime during the night you will hear a rumbling sound. That is the train coming. As it passes a trap door will open into the culvert. Be ready when it opens and drop yourself into it, and you will be on board the train, and can go over the road yourself and find out all about it."

The night was chilly and unpleasant, but just at dark the student saw his friend start out for his night of watching. At daylight the next morning he saw him with chattering teeth coming back and asked, "What luck?"

"I watched there all night, and the train didn't come."

"Is that so? Well, sometimes one night does pass without any train going out, but never two nights in succession. If you go there and watch again tonight you will be sure of it."

But the joke was too good to keep, and he told other students of it. They teased the poor fellow so unmercifully about his trip on the Underground Railroad that he was compelled to leave the place.

The notion that the Underground Railroad was an actual railroad traveling underground is a misconception that many people had at the time and some continue to believe even today. Teachers often begin their instruction of the subject by explaining that it was not an actual railroad. As time passes, less time is spent on the subject of the Underground Railroad in schools and those misconceptions may resurface. In 1941 Henrietta Buckmaster wrote the following in reference to the mystical nature of the Underground Railroad:

Who laid the Underground Railroad? Perhaps a Paul Bunyan equipped with a frontier magic scooped up the earth with his fist and shot out his arm in tunnels north and south in the land. Perhaps a kind of voodooism made a display of black magic and transported a fugitive along rails that vaporized after him...

It may not have been Paul Bunyan or voodoo, but it was enormous and spiritually strong— as it accomplished the liberation of more than 100,000 lives.

Dr. Nelson continued to travel throughout the country, giving speeches and raising money for Mission Institute. In February of 1839 he traveled to New England and gave such a stirring speech that it was printed by the American Anti-Slavery Society as Tract No. 12 shown here. Do not let the antique appearance keep you from reading these powerful words that speak to the beliefs of those opposed to slavery.

No. 12.

DR. NELSON'S LECTURE

ON SLAVERY.

Dr. Nelson was born and educated in Tennessee. For many years he was a surgeon; but having become very deeply impressed with religion, he changed that profession for the ministry; and at length became pastor of a Presbyterian Church, in Danville, Kentucky. His labors there were much blessed; and all classes of people in that region speak of him as having been singularly beloved and respected, until he thought duty called him to become the president of Marion College, in Missouri. Here his able letters on the subject of slavery aroused jealous fears as to the College; and the arrival of two free colored youths, from New-York, one to be employed as a domestic in Dr. Nelson's family, and the other with the intention of fitting himself for a missionary to Africa, served as a breeze to the already kindling flame. Two hundred men, including lawyers, doctors, and various public characters, armed with pistols, dirks, clubs, &c. proceeded to the Mission Farms, with the avowed intention of

American Anti-Slavery Society No. 143 Nassau street, N. Y.

white young men, in whose company the colored youths had arrived; searched their trunks for what they called "incendiary papers;" threatened tar and feathers, or 150 lashes, well laid on: but finally released them, without personal violence, on condition that they left the state forthwith, and never entered it again, under penalty of death. The innocent clored youths, in the mean time, had been secretly conveyed away, and thus escaped the danger.

This outbreak was followed by fresh disturbances of a similar character; in which Dr. Nelson was threatened and distressed, but otherwise received no injury. A public meeting was called at Palmyra, in which resolutions were passed, approving of these violent proceedings, and declaring "a solemn and abiding determination" to follow them up, till fanaticism was crushed. This meeting, in May, 1836, was followed by events which greatly harrassed Dr. Nelson, and many of his friends considered his life in danger. On one occasion, he was obliged to escape from his home at night to avoid the fury of Lynch law. The spirit of slavery, finally drove him from Missouri. He is now zealously engaged in building up a Mission Institute in the neighborhood of Quincy, Illinois. During a visit to New England in February, 1839, to solicit funds for this institution, Dr.

Nelson, being requested publicly to express his sentiments concerning slavery, delivered the following Lecture at Northampton, Mass.

THE LECTURE.*

Dr. Nelson commenced his remarks by stating, that the black and white races were mixing very fast in the slave States. He had been accustomed to hear young men boast so generally of profligate connexions with slaves, that when he was first told such attachments would be disgraceful in the free States, he could not believe it. The gradual lightening of complexions among the slaves was strikingly observable, even within his own recollection. He knew people, married and settled in the free States, who had once been slaves; but they were so perfectly white, that none suspected their origin. He said when he was surgeon in the army, during the last war, an officer, who messed with him, one day stepped up to the ranks, and laying his hand on a soldier, said, 'You are my slave!' The man dropped his knapsack and musket in a moment, and cooked for them during the remainder of the campaign. He was lighter than his master, who happened to have

* The sketch of this lecture was first published in the Boston Liberator, March 1, 1839. It, has been revised, and some slight addition made, by Mrs. Child.

a dark complexion. His astonished comrades would exclaim,' Why, Julius, is it possible you are a slave? You used to be a very respectable and thriving man in Ohio!' To which the 'chattel' replied, 'And I mean to be respectable and thriving again, before I die. Honesty and industry will help a man up in the world.' When his master urged that he ought to serve him several years, in consideration of his kindness, and the money he had paid for him, Julius answered, ' Perhaps I may for a little while, master ; but I can't stay long ; freedom is too sweet.' Dr. N. mentioned having talked with a slave, who said he had run away in obedience to his master's orders. ' My master was always very kind to me,' said he ; ' and when my mistress was first married, she was very kind ; but as her children grew up, the neighbors observed they looked just like me. Then she began to dislike me, and had me punished often. But the older the children grew, the more we looked alike. At last, she said I must be sold to New Orleans. Then my master told me to tie up my clothes and run away.'

The inferences deduced from these facts were, that slavery tended to promote a rapid amalgamation, while freedom checked it ; and that if the admixture of the two races went on in as rapid a ratio as it had done for the last thirty years, it would soon be impossible for us to judge whether our citizens were slaves or not, by their complexion.

The speaker next alluded to the strong local attachments of the colored race. He had frequently met emancipated or runaway slaves, who said, 'How I do long to go back where I lived when I was a child! The climate suits me better; and more than that, all my friends and relations are there. Oh, if slavery was only abolished, so that we could all be free there, I'd be back quicker than I came.'

This was intended to show that there was no danger of colored people all flocking to the North, in case of emancipation, and leaving the South without laborers.

Dr. N. expressed surprise that he had been asked to lecture in New England, because he knew so much about slavery. "Why, my dear friends," said he, "there are things which the smallest boy in this room knows just as well, perhaps better than I can tell him. A dear sister in Christ lately asked me, if I did not think the slaves would cut their masters' throats, if they were freed at once. Said I, Dear sister, you shall answer that question yourself, if you please. Suppose you were compelled to work without wages, year after year—told when you might go to bed, and when you must get up—what you might eat, and what you might wear—should you think it just and right? Suppose your master at last became troubled in conscience, and said, 'I restore your freedom. Forgive the wrong I have done you. Go, or stay, as you please. Your earnings are henceforth your own. If you are in trouble, come to me, and I will be your friend.' Do you think you should feel like cutting that man's throat? She eagerly replied, 'Oh, no, indeed I should not.'

"Although labor is a blessing to man, yet we all feel that a great degree of it is hard. When I plough the fields in a hot day, I feel that there is some things *hard* about it. What is it enables me to go through it with a light heart? It is the hope of receiving wages, for the comfort and improvement of myself and family. But what if I and my family are all compelled to work without wages? This would make the labor seem ten times as hard. My dear fellow travellers to eternity, these things must be just as plain to you, as they are to me.

"I lived many years without having a suspicion that there was any thing wrong in holding slaves. Even after I had an interest in Christ, there seemed to be nothing amiss in it; just as pious people went on making and selling rum, without troubling their consciences about it. Oh, that I then could have had faithful christian brethren, to rouse me with the voice of exhortation and rebuke! I should not then have approached the table of our Lord with fingers all dripping with the blood of souls! I will tell you what first called my attention to this subject. My wife came to me one day, and said that Sylvia (one of our servants) had told her we had no right to hold our fellow-beings in bondage; she had worked for us six years, and she thought she had fully paid for herself. I gave some rough answer, and turned away. A few days after, my wife again remarked that Sylvia said the holding of slaves could not be justified by the Bible. 'Don't mind her nonsense,' said I. By and bye, my wife said, 'Sylvia brings arguments from the Scriptures, which I find it hard to answer.' Well, my friends, the end of it was, that Sylvia made an abolitionist of my wife, and my wife made an abolitionist of me.

"When my feelings were thus roused on the subject, I was anxious to discover some way by which we could benefit the colored race, and best atone for the wrong we had done them. I thought I discovered this in the Colonization plan: and for seven or eight years I labored in that cause with as much zeal as I ever felt on any subject. If you ask why I did not, during this time, boldly remonstrate with others against the sin of slavery, I must answer, that, in addition to the natural depravity of my own heart, I was prevented by the conviction that I was doing enough of my duty by working for Colonization. After a time my views began to change. I will tell you briefly how it happened. If you differ from me in the inferences I draw, I have no controversy with you, my brother. Work in your own way, I only tell you what effected a change in my own mind. I had from the very beginning been occasionally pained by remarks I heard. When I recommended the scheme to slaveholders, they entered into it warmly, and said they should be right glad to get rid of the free colored people; they were convinced such a movement would render their slave property more valuable and secure. These things pained me a little. Still I thought I might do good by laboring for Colonization; and I did labor zealously, until the discussion at the North forced upon me the knowledge that the Society has been working *sixteen years* to carry off *one fortnight's increase of slaves*! Then I was "discouraged; and my hands dropped by my side." A visit to the Cherokees gave me some thoughts concerning Colonization as a Missionary enterprise. Many of the Indians had become converts to Christ; they had improved in the arts of civilized life; and there was a light in the eye, always kindled when men begin to think about the soul and its existence in a future life. But the difficulty was, the same country which sent them messengers of the blessed Gospel, likewise sent among them cart-loads of rum. I remembered how missionaries in Pagan lands dreaded the arrival of a ship from their own country; because where there was one sailor that would speak to the natives of God and the Bible, there were six who would lead them into drunkenness and debauchery. Why, my dear hearers, I should be afraid to take any congregation, in the most moral town—even this audience, if you please,—and set you all down in the midst of a heathen land, as missionaries there. I should be afraid you would not all be fit for your work."

The lecturer neglected to point the moral; but he obviously meant to ask, What then can be expected from ship-loads of ignorant and degraded slaves, landed on a Pagan shore?

"After I emancipated all my other slaves," continued he, "I still held one man in bondage several years. He seemed to be incapable of taking care of himself. My friend said it would be wrong to emancipate him; he was so stupid, he would suffer if he had no master to provide for him, and would soon come upon the county. He certainly did seem very stupid; so I continued to hold him as a slave. But oh, how I bless God that a voice of warning and rebuke reached me from the Free States! Oh! I expect to sing about it through all eternity! It led me to ask myself, are you not deceived in thinking you keep this man from motives of benevolence? Is it not the fact that you like well enough to have him to black your boots, and catch your horse? I called him to me, and said 'I give you your freedom. Whatever you earn is your own. If you get sick, or poor, come to me. My house shall always be a home to you.' About a year after, I met him riding on a pony. 'Well,' said I, 'how do you like freedom?' 'Oh, massa, the sweetest thing in all the world! I've got a hundred silver dollars stowed away in a box!' The last time I talked with him, he had laid by six hundred dollars. If you let a man have the management of his own concerns, though he is stupid, he will brighten up a little.

"When I was three or four years old, I could say off all the alphabet, and spell some small words; but it was soon discovered that I had learnt all this by rote, and did not know one of the letters by sight. I was taken from school, and one of my father's young slaves became my principal teacher. He would lead me out under a shady tree, and try to impress the letters on my mind, by saying, 'That's great O, like the horse-collar; that's H, like the garden gate, that's little g, like your father's spectacles.' He was much brighter than I was; but I was sent to college, and he was sent into the cornfield. He became dull; and I dare say if I could now find him, somewhere in Alabama, I should find him stupid and ignorant. Yet if he had gone to school and college along side of me, he would have been as much superior to me, as I am now superior to him.

"I have been asked concerning the religious instruction of slaves; and I feel safe in answering, that in general it amounts to little or nothing. Hundreds and thousands never heard of a Savior; and of those who are familiar with his name, few have any comprehension of its meaning. I remember one gray headed negro, with whom I tried to talk concerning his immortal soul. I pointed to the hills, and told him God made them. He said he did not believe any body made the hills. I asked another slave about Jesus Christ. I found he had heard his name, but thought he was son of the Governor of Kentucky."

(Dr. Nelson was understood to say this slave was held by a Minister of the Gospel.)

"One of my pious Presbyterian brothers charged me with being too severe upon him: He said he certainly did instruct his people: he did not suffer them to grow up in heathen ignorance. While we were talking, one of his slaves entered the room; and, having asked leave to propose some questions to him, I said, 'Can you tell me how many Gods there are?' 'Oh, yes, massa; there are two Gods.'"

Being asked concerning the treatment of slaves, Dr. N. said, "I have not attempted to harrow your feelings with stories of cruelty. I will, however, mention one or two among the many incidents that came under my observation as family physician. I was one day dressing a blister, and the mistress of the house sent a little black girl into the kitchen to bring me some warm water. She probably mistook her message; for she returned with a bowl full of boiling water; which her mistress no sooner perceived, than she thrust her hand into it, and held it there till it was half cooked.

"I remember a young lady who played well on the piano, and was ready to weep over any fictitious tale of suffering. I was present when one of her slaves lay on the floor in a high fever, and we feared she might not recover. I saw that young lady stamp upon her with her feet; and the only remark her mother made, was, 'I am afraid Evelina is *too much* prejudiced against poor Mary.'

"My hearers, you must not form too harsh a judgment concerning individuals who give way to such bursts of passion. None of you can calculate what would be the effects on your own temper, if you were long accustomed to arbitrary power, and hourly vexed with slovenly, lazy, and disobedient slaves. If sent on an errand, they would be sure to let the cattle into the cornfield; if they gave the horse his oats, they would be sure to leave the peck measure where it would be kicked to pieces. Such is the irritating nature of slave service.

"I am asked whether Anti-Slavery does not tend to put back emancipation. Perhaps there is less said about it in Kentucky, than there was a few years ago; but the quietus seems to be this: in answer to my arguments, slaveholders reply. 'Why, Christian ministers and members of churches, at the north, say *they* do not think slavery is so entirely wrong. Now, they certainly have a better chance to form an impartial judgment than we have.' This operates like a dose of laudanum to the conscience; but the effects are daily growing weaker. I do not know how it is, but there seems to be a class at the North, much more ready to apologize for slavery, than the majority of the slaveholders themselves.

"Much is said about the excitement produced.—For the sake of the little boys here, I will illustrate this by an example. The Greeks were a cultivated and refined people; but it was a part of their worship of Diana to whip boys at her altar, until their sides were worn so thin, they could see their bowels;

and their parents were not permitted to weep, while they witnessed this cruel operation.—When the apostle Paul came among them, he lifted up his voice against their Pagan rites, and told them their Gods were made by the hands of men. Then they all began to scream, 'Great is Diana of the Ephesians!' Some good people hearing the uproar, might have said, 'See how Paul puts back the cause of Christianity! None of the other apostles will dare to come here to preach. Paul himself had to run!' Yet what was the result? The images of Diana were finallly overthrown, and Christ was worshipped in her stead. Just so it will be with the slaveholders. They scream, because they feel the sharp points of truth prick their consciences; but thy can't stand there and scream forever. The postmasters may try to shut out information; but it is like piling up a bar of sand across a rushing river. Let the broad stream roll on, and it will soon carry the sand before it.

"I am glad of organized abolition, because I believe that over all the din, some portion of truth even now reaches the slaveholder's conscience. Already, many have learned that every thing is safe and prosperous in the British West Indies, and that property is fast rising in value there; more will learn it soon. I hear of one acquaintance after another, who begins to feel uneasy about holding human beings in bondage. Members of my former church in Kentucky beg me to print more letters about slavery; and when I tell them the postmaster will destroy them, they answer, 'Then seal them up in the form of letters; we are willing to pay the postage.' Already it is observable that professors of religion are afraid to *sell* their slaves. This shows that the wedge has entered. It will enter deeper yet.

"Am I asked what is the remedy for slavery?—I can only answer, that I have known very many emancipated slaves; and I have never known or heard of one instance where freedom did not make them more intelligent, industrious, and faithful to their employers. Their grateful affection for old master and mistress almost amounts to worship. They seem ready to kiss the very ground they tread on. The plan I propose is, that each and every slaveholder try this blessed experiment. But some inquire, ought they not to be compensated for their property? Sylvia said she had paid all she cost me, when she had worked for us six years; and she said truly. Now a large proportion of slaves have been held three and four times as long; and of course have paid for themselves three or four times over.

"What is the duty of christians at the

North? Dear fellow travellers to eternity, need I remind you that Jesus has said, inasmuch as we neglect the least of his brethren, we neglect him? Jesus is the Brother, as well as the Redeemer, of the human race. If you neglect the poor slave, when he lies in prison, sick, hungry, and naked, how will you answer for it at the judgment seat? Surely it is a solemn duty for christians at the North to rebuke and persuade christians at the South, with all affection, but still with all faithfulness and perseverance.

"I have stated only what I myself have seen and known, in Kentucky, Missouri, Virginia, and Tennessee. To illustrate each point, I have selected one or two instances where I might relate a thousand. If any man doubts my evidence, I think I could convince him of its truth if he would travel with me in the states where I have resided."

This is a hasty abstract of Dr. Nelson's lecture; but I believe it is correct. The audience apparently listened with a great degree of interest. These anecdotes of things personally known to the lecturer are excellent illustrations of principles and are highly attractive. I have often wished that James G. Birney and Angelina E. Grimke made more free use of them.

Published by the American Anti-Slavery Society; Office, 143 Nassau-street, New-York.

While Nelson was publicly speaking against slavery, he was also privately acting on behalf of slaves. An event that occurred in 1840 related to Dr. Nelson's anti-slavery activities was reported in an obituary in the *Mendon Dispatch* in March, 1917:

> *There died in Mendon, Friday at midnight, at the age of 74 years, Mrs. Alice Jones, a daughter of slave parents, and in many respects a remarkable woman. ...*
>
> *Mrs. Jones' father and mother, Jeff and Aunt Annie Christian, were members of a colony of twenty-seven liberated slaves sent to Mendon about 1840 by Rev. David Nelson, M.D. whose name is closely linked with Quincy's early history as an educator, religious worker and abolitionist. Dr. Nelson was a personal friend of Dr. David Ross, a planter and large slave owner in Tennessee, and through the former's efforts they became convinced that slavery was wrong and liberated his slaves in bunches and provided them with means to leave the state where they could live in freedom. He sent three families, twenty-seven persons in two wagons to Quincy, to Dr. Nelson, with instructions to find homes for them. Jeff Christian, the most intelligent man of the lot, was sent ahead on a horse and into his care was given the freedom papers and money for the journey, and Jeff led the procession safely to the "promised land." Dr. Nelson thought that Mendon would be a good place for them. They came here and all lived for a few days in a log cabin where the Mendon M.E. church now stands. ...*
>
> *Under the Illinois black laws, Erastus Benton and others of the prominent Mendon settlers were guardians under $100 bond for the good behavior of the Negroes and insisted that Jeff and Annie be married with the rites of the church and this was done. Alice, Fred and Henry were born after the marriage, several other children before.*
>
> *Dr. Nelson was the man who made Quincy famous as the author of "Shining Shore" (hymn No.1277 in songs for the sanctuary) which was sung all over the world, and of "The Cause and Cure of Infidelity," read in 100,000 homes...*

It is clear that Dr. Nelson acted against slavery in his private life as well as his public life. His influence on his children is evident by the mention of his adult son, David D. Nelson's anti-slavery activity. Remember that an Anti-Slavery convention was held in Alton in

October 1837 a few days before Elijah Lovejoy was murdered. David D. Nelson signed a petition to have that convention. Three years later the Quincy Whig reported on July 25, 1840:

> *The Abolitionists of Illinois, have lately held a State Convention at Princeton, Bureau county. The question was debated in the Convention, whether an abolition electoral ticket—(for Birney and Earle, the abolition candidates for President and Vice President of the United States) – should be formed, and supported by the abolitionists of this State, at the November election. The Convention consisted of 100 members—85 of whom were opposed to forming an electoral ticket—in fact the Convention separated with the understanding that no ticket should be formed. But, fifteen of the members were strenuous for a ticket, and one was subsequently adopted by this small minority of the delegates contrary to the wishes of the Convention. The following is the ticket:*
>
> *Wm Holyoke, of Knox county.*
> *Erastus Benton, of Adams county.*
> *Riply E. W. Adams, of Will county.*
> *Eli Wison, of Peoria county.*
> *William Lewis, of Putnam county.*
>
> *Wm. Holyoke of Galesburg, was President of the Convention, and David D. Nelson, of Quincy, Secretary.*

It may have been this division within the antislavery groups that kept them from working in unison and ending slavery sooner.

Amanda and David's oldest son was now actively involved in anti-slavery activities. Although proud of him, his parents must have been concerned for his safety.

On June 20, 1840 the twelfth child of Dr. David and Amanda Nelson was born. He was named Eugene La Fon Nelson. The name La Fon was after a famous doctor that impressed the Nelson's.

Perhaps an even a more notable event occurred in 1840: a scheduled debate between Dr. David Nelson and Joseph Smith of the Mormon Church of Nauvoo, IL, fifty miles north of Quincy. *The Quincy Whig* on July 11, 1840 included an announcement that read:

> *Dr. Nelson will deliver one or more lectures on Mormonism, on Wednesday, July the 15th at 10 o'clock, forenoon, in the grove, in the east part of Quincy. Any person wishing to reply will have an opportunity to do so if they see fit. — Should the weather be unpleasant the lecture will be given in some meeting house in the city.*

From his memoirs prophet Elder Ells writes that he was chosen by Joseph Smith to conduct a 'discussion' in Quincy with Dr. Nelson (president of the Presbyterian Theological Seminary at Quincy). Elder Ells was honored for the opportunity to represent Joseph Smith in a debate with the famous orator, the esteemed Dr. David Nelson. It is clear that Joseph Smith was not eager to be compared with the speaking skill of the eminent Presbyterian preacher. The debate was to take place at Terwische Woods, now known as Hickory Grove subdivision east of Quincy. Joseph Smith owned property on what is now 48th and Broadway streets east of Quincy. He was present, but did not intend to engage in the debate because he had asked Elder Ells to represent him. Dr. Nelson, an epileptic, suffered a seizure and Joseph Smith did not have the debate continue. The Mormons considered the seizure a sign from God. Elder Ells wrote:

> *The challenge being accepted, to my surprise I was designated to respond. Some forty or fifty persons went down. As the idea had gone abroad that Dr. Nelson had challenged the Prophet, there were many present-clergymen of all denominations, and Governor of the State (Carlin). I do not remember the words of the propositions we agreed upon...The Doctor became confused, and his friends advised him to desist. He remarked that his opponent had treated him courteously, and stepped down. The Seer (Joseph Smith) got upon the stand and challenged any of the clergymen present to continue the discussion, but none responded. The Spirit of God through the weak had silenced the worldly wise.*

The action of Dr. Nelson and his followers can be reported as events, but the events are not as important as understanding the true goals of those people behind the events. My son Greg, whose passion is the study of Dr. Nelson's writings, summarized some of Nelson's views. Old journals and diaries have been quoted in this book, but this time I share Greg's e-mail:

I tend to think that Nelson was primarily influenced in his views regarding the need to abolish slavery by several factors. 1. religion via the Second Great Awakening and 2. by his experiences as a physician having viewed firsthand the physical brutality and insensitivity of slavery. 3. I think he was also concerned (similar to the sentiments you read in *Prison Life and Reflections*) that those who were exposed to the slavery society, and not just the slave owners became increasingly desensitized to the immoral treatment and conditions of slaves. I think he believed this desensitization of morality would eventually drag all of society under.

It seems that Thompson, Nelson and probably many others involved in the Quincy area UGRR were baffled by the contradiction of seemingly religious people in Missouri who would otherwise be upstanding citizens and Christians but were so cruel and immoral in certain areas of their life. I think the belief was that the common thread which was corrupting the morality of those living in the slave states was the slavery culture in general. In many respects I think Nelson and those at the Mission Institute were as motivated by the interest in saving society within the slave states as they were in actually freeing the slaves. In other words, I think the strange paradox of abolitionists is that they may not have been as interested in saving the slave by helping him to freedom as they were in saving the slaves' master and hence society in general.

Success of Mission Institute Students

Mission Institute was a college for instructing missionaries but it was also an institute of the highest quality of advanced learning. The following letter from the *Cincinnati Morning Herald*, Saturday, May 3, 1845 page 2 column 4 the writer gives examples of the courses of study there:

Dr. Nelson's "Mission Institute"

I have just attended the anniversary exercises of this truly _aui-generis institution. Dr. David Nelson, who founded it some nine years ago, was a surgeon in Gen.

Jackson's army—an infidel—afterwards a Christian, then general agent of Marion College, Mo—then hunted into Illinois for his anti-slavery sentiments, lying hid some days, with his family in the brushwood—escaped at last with his life, and, landing at Quincy, found protection, and started Mission Institute, a self-supporting Institution, where students built their own houses, earned their own support, while the teachers found theirs. Four small establishments upon this plan were started, two of which remain, but are soon, it would seem, to be united in one.

The examinations have been sustained beyond any expectations I had or could have formed. Young men who had earned their expenses by hard labor, as they went along, and young women also read such parts of Homer and Sophocles as are contained in the 2nd volume of the Greek Majora with a fluency and ease, certainly unsurpassed, if equaled even by the average of our college classes. The recitations in some branches of the Mathematics, and in Astronomy, were also highly creditable to the industry and efficiency of both teachers and taught. The teachers at the location near Quincy, Rev. William Beardsley, and Mr. Griswold, who was a lawyer by profession, have devoted themselves to their calling with a zeal and single-mindedness worthy of the times when in Greece the best instruction was given by those who "expected and received little or nothing for their labor—with this difference in favor of the moderns, that they look for, and, if faithful will receive their reward hereafter. Farewell,

As ever yours,
J.B.
Jonathon

Indeed, advanced subjects were taught there, as it is known that Isaac Farewell Holton taught Greek and natural history at Mission Institute from 1840 to 1844.

Some may think that Mission Institute was a pioneer school with the resulting education less than the avant guarde schools of the East, but the education was apparently quite successful as many students went on to make considerable contributions to the world. Several students who attended Mission Institutes 1 or 2 have gone on to significant achievements. For example, Mr. Stone's interesting and noteworthy life is reported in his obituary in the *Quincy Daily Journal*, Thursday, May 5, 1910:

DEATH OF A PIONEER
REV. ABRAHAM T. STONE, FATHER OF MRS. JOHN PUTMAN OF NORTH FIFTH STREET,
Died Last Night—Was One of the First Settlers in Adams County and was a Friend of Lincoln.

Rev. Abraham T. Stone, one of the early pioneers of this county, died last night about 7 o'clock at the home of his daughter, Mrs. John Putman, 902 North Fifth street, with whom he had made his home for many years. He was aged 92 years and died of old age. He had been feeble for several years, but was bedfast only about ten days.

Mr. Stone had lived a long, useful and eventful life and such men as Gov. John Wood and Abraham Lincoln had been his friends. In the early days he was a prominent citizen of these parts, and was intimately connected with the early development and growth of Adams County.

He was widely known and highly esteemed and in his death one of the sturdy pioneers of this vicinity has passed to a reward well earned and richly deserved.

When Mr. Stone located in Illinois Pike county embraced all the territory lying south of Wisconsin, east of the Mississippi and west of the Illinois rivers. He brought the first sheep into the county, lived in the first house built, witnessed the organization of the first church, was a member of the first school, traded a big fat hog for the only axe in Quincy, gave a full load of good wheat for 500 feet of rough pine boards, spent three years in the territory before the county was organized, remembered the first marriage license issued, knew the first sheriff of the county, and his memory took him back more than three-quarters of a century.

Deceased was born in Licking county, Ohio, six miles west of the city of Newark, on the fifth day of March, 1818, and was one of a family of four children. In the spring of 1822 the Stone family moved to Adams county and located on a tract of land that afterward became a part of what was known as Stone's Prairie and is now a part of Payson township.

The trip here was made in a wagon drawn by two horses and the family brought a lamb with them, thinking to kill if for food, but the animal became such a pet it was brought to the new home and its wool was cut to make stockings for the Stone children. The family was four weeks and two days making the trip, and it rained every day but three. There was not a neighbor for miles around and Rev. Stone, when in a reminiscent mood, was wont to tell of the effect the solitude had on him as a child, and his stories of how they killed deer for food and protected themselves and their live stock from the wolves were thrilling to his listeners.

In 1820 the first settler located near the Stone family. His name was Samuel Clark. He located in what is now Pike county.

The deceased's father became a local preacher, and Abraham followed in his footsteps, when old enough, attended what was called Dr. Nelson's Institute. He taught school in Barry for a time and there he met Miss Mary Ann Lippencott, whom he married on Feb. 11, 1841, then setting on Stone's prairie and residing there for 17 years.

He was ordained a minister in the M.E. church in 1858 and for many years preached the gospel. He had been a superannuate for the long time.

He was a member of the legislature in 1849-50, and in 1857 he moved to Mt. Sterling, engaging in the grain and real estate business.

In 1859 he met Lincoln at Beardstown and drove him from there to Mt. Sterling, where he made a speech against Douglas. The deceased and Lincoln had become acquainted previously in Springfield and Rev. Stone knew the great emancipator well.

Deceased was connected with Gov. Oglesby's staff and was a member of famous "Blind Half Hundred." He moved to Quincy in 1866.

In 1876, in March, he was appointed agent at Ft. Peck by President U. S. Grant and afterwards was engaged as land commissioner and general excursion agent of the M., K & T. and Missouri Pacific, Iron Mountain and Texas Pacific.

His wife died in 1893, since which time he had lived a retired life. He leaves two daughters, Mrs. Putman, mentioned above, and Mrs. M.E. Strobridge, of Seattle, Wash.; also five grand children and five great grand children.

Dr. William Geiger was another student who went on to do important things. He left in 1838 to go west with a student named Benson. He had been appointed as a missionary to the Oregon Indians. His journal tells of working with Capt John Sutter in California and eventually becoming one of the early Oregon pioneers. I believe Benson was credited with introducing Greek Revival Architecture into the Northwest.

William and Jane Stobie Shipman attended Mission Institute in Quincy. William later studied at Yale and was ordained as a Congregational minister. He was eventually assigned a mission on the Big Island of Hawaii. Their fascinating story is told in the book, *The Shipmans of East Hawaii* by Emmet Cahill. Shipman descendants still live in Hawaii.

From *The Story of Oberlin: "One student, who passed six years in study at Theopolis, after fifty years testifies that life there seemed like a foretaste of heaven."*

Mission Institute is long gone. A few years ago the farmland where it stood was turned into a strip mall. This was the last corner of the foundation before it too was bull dozed.

At one time Mission Institute was comprised of 20 cabins and a chapel. There was a saw mill on the creek to the west.

These were some of the original rocks of the foundations at Mission Institute No 1 now the site of Kohl's on East Broadway in Quincy, Illinois

A tribute to the efforts of those who once lived on these grounds, the Deters decorate their flower garden with cornerstone rocks from building at Mission Institute No. 1.

A four and half inch solid iron ball with hole drilled through the center was found during the 1960s in the field behind Oakland where Mission Institute once stood. The ball would have been attached to the leg with iron brackets. The weight of the ball would have made travel difficult for the run away slave.

Chapter Six

THE NEXT JUNCTION: MISSION INSTITUTE NUMBER 2

A second Mission Institute was erected at 25th and Maine St. in Quincy. Mission Institute Number 2 was the scene of several historical incidents. In May of 1840, Rufus Brown and wife conveyed to Henry H. Snow, Edw. B. Kimball, Rufus Brown, Willard Keyes, and Moses Hunter, two pieces of ground. One is located at what is now 24th and Maine, which consisted of a little over eleven acres. The other piece of land was a forty acre tract in the southwest corner of Melrose township-- good for nothing except as a landing place for run-away slaves. This was Mission Institute #4. The question remains – where was No. 3?

Two years earlier, in *Appeal to the Church*, copyrighted in 1838, Dr. Nelson laid out his plan. He writes;

> *"Mission Institute" is situated within five miles of Quincy, Illinois; which town stands on the bank of the Mississippi. The students here board, clothe, and support themselves entirely, because they are willing to labor faithfully nearly three months out of twelve. They build their own cottages in which they live. To do this, they find wood on the land where they are. Each one gathers his own fuel from the woods around him. The course of education is the common course pursued in Colleges. Books are furnished by the Board of Trustees, without cost, to the careful student. Teaching is gratis to the student; but he is expected to spend an hour or more, per day, in teaching to others that through which he has passed; if teachers are wanted and cannot be procured. The average cost for a plentiful supply of plain substantial food, is from 40 to 50 cents per week. The science of medicine is taught gratis to those who may desire to go on foreign missions. "The Mission Institute," No. 1, is almost*

> *completed. From 30 to 35 students are all that are invited to occupy one point. A tract of land (80 acres) is offered gratis; on which No. 2 is just commencing. Tracts, for Nos. 3, 4, 5, 6, and 7, are already offered.*

Mission Institute #4 was located in swamp land near what is now called Turtle Lake. Turtle Lake Road is a southern extension of 24th St. Across the river from Mission Institute No 4 in Missouri was another river landing known as Marks Landing. Following a possible route would be to cross the river from Marks to Mission Institute #4. Students from Mission Institute #2 would check No #4 at regular intervals. A buggy or wagon with a fugitive safely hidden then followed a road north to Mission Institute #2 at 24th & Maine Sts., then north to the Turner homes and stations, continued north to Mendon area stations. Mr. Sam Bartholomew, another abolitionist, bought 180 acres of land next to Mission Institute No 4. Mr. Bartholomew's father D. F. Bartholomew was an abolitionist who owned a farm east of Mendon. It was in the Bartholomew cornfield, near Mendon, that a family of fugitives sought shelter when the buggy driven in front of them was shot at by slave hunters from Missouri, killing Dr. Eells' famous horse known as White Lightning.

Mr. Bartholomew also erected a steam mill (very innovative at the time) in Melrose Township on Mill Creek. Later it was sold to and known as Pape Mill.

Another route may have been to follow Mill creek to E. A. Humphrey's and then on to Oakland and north from there.

Mission Institute No. 2, or Theopolis as it was called, was established on the eleven acre tract extending from 24th to 26th and Maine, and north from Maine for two blocks to Vermont Street. This part of the school was presided over by Rev. Moses Hunter, who is said to have dressed in a long seamless robe in imitation of Christ. Actually, all the instructors lived a very modest life style, spending most of any income on religious and anti-slavery pursuits. Rev. Moses Hunter made his own clothes in a most unskilled way. Dr Nelson also taught classes there and was known to be unconcerned about his dress. I doubt he even noticed Rev. Hunter's attire. A chapel, a two story brick building used for recitation and 20 to 30 individual cabins were built by the students. Because of their anti-slavery activities, Theopolis became known as a "nest of dirty Abolitionists".

This home was part of Mission Institute No. 2. It was built by Benjamin Terrel in 1840 and was owned by the Oakley family at the time this photo was taken. It is one of the oldest brick structures in Quincy. It served as a four room dormitory for students attending Mission Institute. There is a hiding place upstairs in the floorboards between the ceiling and the floor. There was a room in the basement that had no doorway to it and had to be entered through a trap door. It has since been remodeled.

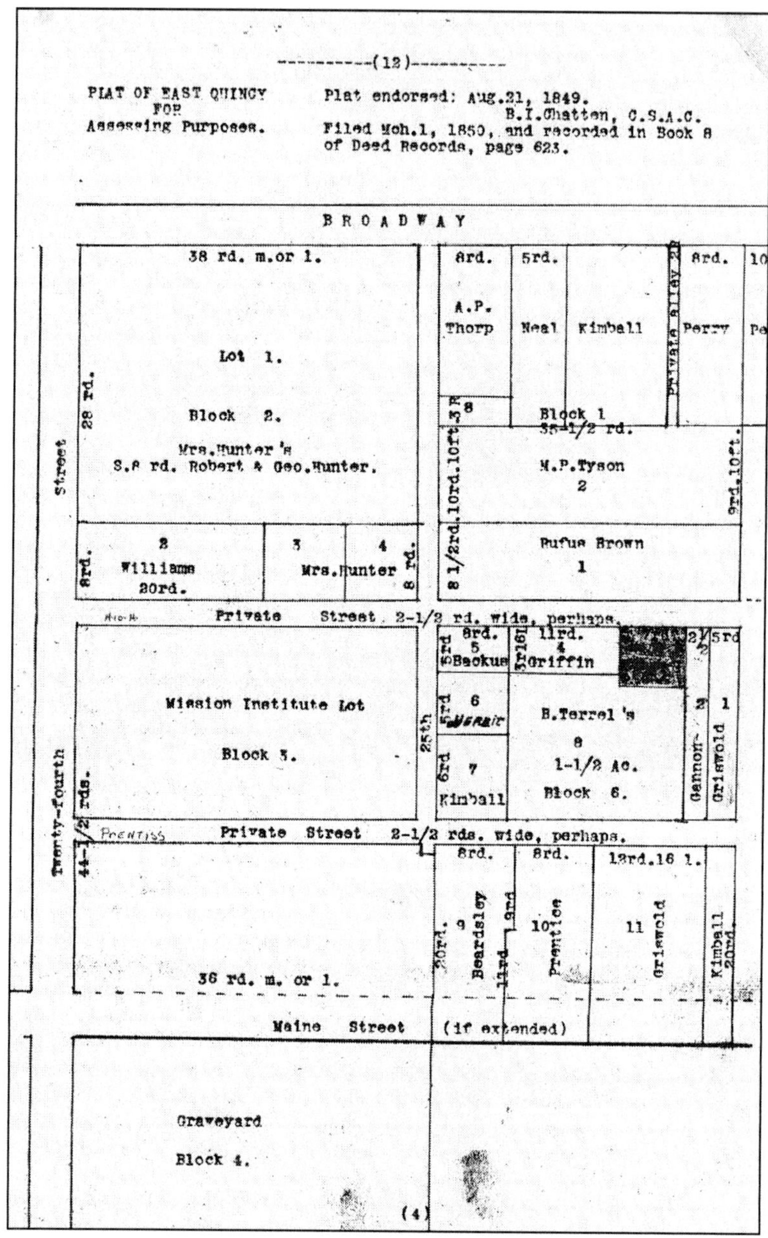

Early map of Mission Institute Number 2 – The graveyard is where Nelson was first buried.

Benjamin Terrel served as chairman of Mission Institute's Board of Trustees. Mr. Terrel's wife Electa was a student at Mission Institute. This simple statement seems insignificant to young women today but even through most of my life it was frowned upon for married women to do such things as work or attend school. Moses Hunter, the head instructor there, insisted that the school be coeducational and convinced a reluctant Dr. Nelson to include women students. In 1840 that thinking was certainly ahead of its time.

These women were involved in more than just education. In a later story a young lady by the name of Mary Terrel of near Newtown accompanied a young abolitionist on an Underground Railroad rescue.

The 1872 plat book shows a drawing of the George Terrel farmhouse. George Terrel, who I believe to be a relative of Benjamin, owned many acres near Newtown, in Adams County. Newtown is now called Adams, Illinois. Mention in Seibert's book is made to a prominent Underground Railroad station at Newtown – a large red barn (discovered in a later chapter). I believe these people were all connected in the clandestine activities. The George Terrel home is no longer standing.

Mission Institute Number 2 was known to have active abolitionists suspected of Underground Railroad activities. In one incident it all became very public.

In 1841, George Thompson, Alanson Work and James Burr of Mission Institute No 2 were caught in Missouri attempting to help slaves travel the Underground Railroad to freedom. No doubt this was an important 'catch' for the slave owners of Missouri because later in life Alanson Work claimed to have helped 4,000 slaves make their way to freedom.

This picture was given to me by Fr. Landry Genosky. It is the home where Alanson Work lived from 1836 to 1844 with his wife and four children at the time he was caught trying to help a slave in Missouri. He worked at Mission Institute No 2. This very humble home belies the aristocratic heritage of Work. His family, of Scotch descent, came from Auld Wark Castle and a distant cousin Frances Work Spencer was the great-grandmother of the late Diana, Princess of Wales.

The story of the capture and trial was recorded in the diaries of the three men. George Thompson published the diaries titled *Prison Life and Reflections*. In it, he writes:

> *About the first of July, 1841 James with another brother, made a tour of mercy into Missouri, which resulted in an agreement with two slaves. They were to meet them at a certain point on the river, on a certain evening to assist them across the river, on their way to freedom. On the day appointed, we went, arriving at the place about the middle of the afternoon. Alanson and James went into the country to view and reconnoiter, while I remained in the skiff to fish, and await their return. After dark, a number of slaves came to Alanson*

and James and pretended they were going with them. They had proceeded but a short distance, when on a sudden, the slaveholders arose out of the grass, with their rifles, and took them prisoners.

This swampy area just south of West Quincy, MO was the Mississippi river landing known as Marks, MO where Thompson, Work and Burr likely landed their skiff. Many other Underground Railroad operations likely took place here. When we visited, I felt like I wanted to listen for the tapping rocks, the signal that an Underground Railroad agent was here.

The slave holders found Thompson in the skiff and he too was taken prisoner. Thompson continues,

The next morning we were tied together and taken on foot to Palmyra– being led by slaves, and escorted by fifteen horsemen. We were taken to the court house, an warrant issued against us –witnesses examined, and we committed for <u>stealing slaves</u>(!)

From the following letter to a St. Louis paper, a Missouri resident rants about how he could have admired Work, Burr and Thompson if they had only been slave kidnappers for the purpose of selling them. As Abolitionists they were considered the worst form of man. It is almost difficult to read without one's jaw dropping. From *Narrative of Facts*, a pamphlet of information regarding the Thompson, Work and Burr case, prepared and distributed by the *Quincy Whig* paper:

The following is a letter by P.C.L., a member it is said, of the Episcopal Church in Palmyra, to the Editor of the *St. Louis Republican.*

> *Mr. A. B. Chambers:*
>
> *Dear Sir:*
>
> *From an editorial, which I observed in a later paper of yours, in regard to the Abolitionists which have been lately apprehended in this county. I perceive you have been led into an error in saying that they were Mormons. They are Presbyterians, and are the satellites of the notorious Dr. David Nelson, formerly of this county. Two of them are students of his; the other is a man of family. You will remember that this same Rev. gentleman was driven from this county some five or six years since for disseminating abolition doctrines. When these men were first arrested, I was under the impression that they were kidnappers, and that their object was to get the Negroes off and sell them, but I am perfectly convinced that they are dyed-in-the-wool abolitionists. They talk freely and openly on the subject, and say that the laws of God are superior to the laws of man. On Sunday I called on them, and conversed freely with them. They are quite conversant, and one of them is studying for the pulpit, as I am informed. They have prayer night and morning, and one generally gives a short discourse on the bible. I never have in the whole course of my life seen such poor deluded creatures. They say that they belong to a branch of the Institution over which the Dr. has no direct control. It may be interesting to those who read the Narrative, and have also read, or may hereafter read Dr. Nelson's celebrated work on Infidelity. To learn that the work*

was commenced while he lay in the woods secreted from pursuit of the Missourians, who were thirsting for his blood. The community, to a man, knew them to be Abolitionists, and invariably spoke of them as such.

Poor fanatics indeed! Surprising that they should think that God's law was superior to man's that in doing what they were about to do, they were endeavoring to set free a portion of Gods creatures who were in bondage, which is contrary to his will.

Speaking of the Rev Dr. Nelson, he says: But would you think he had the impudence to make an appointment at Philadelphia, a small place near Marion College, to preach, on last Sunday? News of this fact was brought to town in the early part of the week, when two or three large companies were formed in different parts of the county to go and take him out of the pulpit; but I am happy to say he left the county on Saturday, for had he remained and attempted to preach he would have been hung as high as Jaman. A large company however went to the College to make examination, but as I said he left the day before. In justice to Marion College, allow me to say, that it is in no way connected with these vile fiends. We are opposed to mob law in Marion, but there is a point beyond which lenity ceases to be a virtue. We are determined not to be harassed by this monster in human shape. We do not want to see one of our old and valued citizens stabbed and nearly murdered, as Dr. Bosley was a few years since, and that on Sunday, by the same gang, and that too under the guise of religion.

Respectfully yours,

P. L. C.

From the same Narrative of Facts is the following written on a margin cut from a newspaper. It appears to have been written by one of the student-prisoners from his Palmyra, Missouri jail cell.

3rd Heard the guard or someone without say, they came very near getting Dr. Nelson, and remarked, if they had got him, he never would have found the jail, but would have been strung right up.

5th Mr. Warren, Mrs. Work, and Mrs. Terrel called to see us. Mrs. Work was admitted. Mrs. T. stood at the door, wept and begged, but was not admitted. This is strange: their hearts seem made of steel; surely they cannot be flesh. Esq. Warren demanded admission as our counsel, but was denied!! They came near mobbing him. Poor deluded creatures. They act more like fiends than men.

Additionally Alanson wrote this in his journal:

Aug. 10. Last night, a Mr. Berry was confined here on the alleged crime of murder, committed in Kentucky, last November.

Aug. 11. Mr. Berry obtained bail and left us. He is a slaveholder.

Aug. 16. A few nights since, a woman of vile character spent most of the night with the guard overhead. The next day I wrote a letter to the sheriff, informing him that it was very unpleasant living so near a brothel.

Aug. 17. The patrols stand in the different streets at night; each armed with pistols, a club and cow-hide. If a white man passes he is hailed; if a Negro, his "pass" is demanded. If he has none, no excuse will answer; his shirt must come off and the cow-hide be applied to his back!

Aug. 20. Have been unwell. Looked at death. It does not appear dreadful, though I am so great a sinner. I love the Savior, his law and service; and though I would be glad to live to train up my children, and to help the slave; but "thy will, O Lord, be done," for which prepare me and my family.

Aug. 23. Last night, heard the guard say—"Since the d—d rascals have been here, more niggers have run away than ever before." They mentioned several, for whom $50 and $100 reward was offered. It makes our chain light to think that those of others are broken. We believe that our being here will spread the knowledge that there is a road to LIBERTY. Yes, yes, bless the Lord!

In his diary written during his time in the Palmyra jail, George Thompson writes about watching the slave women balance jugs of water on their heads, while walking back and forth to the Palmyra Spring to fill and return to their owner's big houses on the hill.

The water coming down by Mike's foot is from the same spring in Palmyra that the jailed students watched from their cell in 1841. Palmyra was founded because of this spring. The Indians said the water kept them young. My children, from left to right, Gerri, Susie, Kay and Mike are looking at the water coming from the spring.

In September, the three Mission Institute students were found guilty and sentenced to twelve years in prison. One of the jurors was Judge John Marshall Clemens, father of Sam Clemens, who became Mark Twain. Dixon Wecter in *Sam Clemens of Hannibal* writes:

Testimony of blacks against whites was not legally admissible in court, but since the prosecution needed such testimony to convict the abolitionists, in this case it was allowed. No doubt Judge Clemens and his Carolina friend and fellow juror Judge Draper, with all their schooling in the law, felt that the end justified the means. The chief abolitionist, Thompson, a deeply religious man who later wrote a book about his years in the Missouri penitentiary, in vain tried to justify himself by citing the Golden Rule. Hatred of the abolitionist who had begun to infiltrate northeastern Missouri in the ranks of the new immigrants—"the Eastern run," as it was contemptuously called—agitated for lynch law. But the good stiff sentence meted out by Judge Clemens and his neighbors was received with considerable applause.

The stiff sentence probably actually saved their lives as they would surely have been lynched by the mob eager for the opportunity.

Rev. William Beardsley, writing for the *Oberlin Evangelist* says, "*We have been assured by respectable people in Missouri, that there were many at the court, prepared and fully determined, in case they were not convicted, to assassinate them on the spot.*"

On the way to the Jefferson City Penitentiary, the Sheriff from Palmyra (a member of the Presbyterian Church where Nelson served as first pastor) told Thompson, Work and Burr that Dr. Nelson did not deserve to live.

Not all letters were negative however. Alanson Work received a letter praising him for his self-sacrifice written by a promising, young Illinois lawyer named Abraham Lincoln.

Joseph Smith and Dr. Nelson may have disagreed about religious philosophies but on slavery they seemed to share a conviction. The following is a letter written by Joseph Smith:

Editor's Office, City of Nauvoo, Illinois,
March 7th, A.D.1842
General Bennett:

Respected Brother:-I have just been perusing your correspondence with Doctor Dyer on the subject of American slavery, and the students of the Quincy Mission Institute, and it makes my blood boil within me to reflect upon the injustice, cruelty, and oppression of the rulers of the people--when will these things cease to be, and the Constitution and the Laws again bear rule? I fear for my beloved country--mob violence, injustice and cruelty, appear to be the darling attributes of

Missouri, and no man taketh it to heart! O tempora! O mores! What think you should be done?"
Your friend,
Joseph Smith
[History of the Church, 4:544]

Thompson and Work described the conditions in the prison as horrific. They felt they were able to endure the conditions better than the other prisoners because their missionary training prepared them to live with very little material goods. Mission Institute was a school for preparing missionaries to go into foreign lands. Not much has been written about the details of the training, but this quote from *Prison Life and Reflections* gives a picture. Talking about the food:

For this coarse fare we were prepared, by previous discipline while at liberty; so that the change affected us but little, in comparison with the other prisoners. Many who have been accustomed to the dainties and luxuries of life were immediately taken with diarrhea, loss of appetite, and were sick much of their time. Thanks to heaven for our Mission Institute training in this respect.

In May of 1842, Thompson was questioned as to the "slave route". He said, "There is such a route, but I do not know it, but a short distance." The slaves were escaping very fast, and the slave owners were able to retake only a few of them.

From the *Peoples History of Quincy and Adams County, Illinois* we know that about this time in Quincy, a meeting denouncing the abolitionists in the severest terms was held, presided over by W. G. Flood. A committee on resolutions was composed of Isaac N. Morris, Dr. Ralston, Samuel Holmes, (a neighbor of Mission Institute No.1) C. K. Bacon and Dr. H. Rogers. The meeting was addressed by Hon. O.H.P. Browning, afterward a prominent Republican and friend of Lincoln.

On March 8, 1843 at 3 A.M., the chapel at Mission Institute No. 2 was burned to the ground by a party from Palmyra. During this winter, the weather was severe and in March there was ice across the Mississippi. On that night a band of men set out from Roos's grocery of Palmyra, headed for Quincy. In the mob were some desperate men and hard case-gamblers, but also some respectable and prominent citizens. The college chapel was burned without much difficulty or resistance, and the party returned safely to their Missouri homes. No attempt was ever made to arrest any of them. The act was generally endorsed by the pro-slavery people of Adams County as a fair retaliation for the acts of the abolitionists in helping the slaves escape, and as precaution in preventing the establishment of an "abolition factory" as the college was nicknamed.

Because a light snow had fallen that night, the arsonists were readily tracked to the vicinity of the mills in the upper part of Quincy. From there the tracks led on to the river toward the Missouri shore.

Lewis County History gives this opinion of the incident. "Very many of the people of Quincy acquiesced in, if they did not endorse and approve, the burning, and no prosecution was ever made of the incendiaries, who openly acknowledged what they had done, and defied arrest or interference."

Nelson's son, William wrote that "although they were not stopped in this act, John Wood, later Governor of Illinois, did organize a party of abolitionists to chase the group home."

In *History of the Negro Race in America, From 1619 to 1880* George W. Williams writes, *"The Free Mission Institute at Quincy was destroyed by a mob from Missouri in ante-bellum days, because Colored persons were admitted to the classes."*

The loss of the chapel was demoralizing for the college, but when Dr. Moses Hunter, President of Mission Institute Number 2, died later in 1843, the college was devastated.

Mission Institute Number 2 also had a couple of famous alumni in the sons of Alanson Work who was arrested and served three and a half years in a Missouri prison for helping slaves escape. Alanson Work, Jr. was one of five men who founded the B. F. Goodrich Rubber Company. He and his son (B.G.) were both at times CEO of B. F. Goodrich.

Another son, Henry Clay Work became a famous musician. He attended music and Greek classes off and on at Mission Institute. He was inspired by the music at camp meetings (religious revivals). When his father went to prison David Nelson took him in and he later shared stories of singing in the pasture next to Oakland as he walked the dairy cattle to and from the pasture for their daily milking. He published approximately 80 songs; the most popular was "Marching Through Georgia" which sold over a million copies of sheet music. General Sherman supposedly said that if he knew Work was going to write the song, he would have marched a different direction! Other popular songs he wrote included "Brave Boys Are They!," "Grafted into the Army," "Little Major," "Babylon Is Fallen!", "Come Home Father!" A massive hit, "Grandfather's Clock," also sold over a million copies of sheet music. His first published song, "We Are Coming, Sister Mary," was sold to Mistrelman Edwin P. Christy and became a staple in Christy's Minstrels shows. His song, "Kingdom Coming!" is heard in the background in the 1944 Judy Garland film "Meet Me in St. Louis." He was inducted into the Songwriters Hall of Fame in 1970. The April 11, 1931 edition of *The Prairie Farmer* indicates that Work also invented and patented a knitting machine, a walking doll and a rotary engine."

Chapter Seven

RHYTHM OF THE TRACKS: NELSON WRITES MUSIC

"KNOW the songs of a country, and you will know its history for the true feeling of a people speaks through what they sing. During a period of great stress, the popular songs of the day invariably give the most accurate expression of the popular mind."

Bertram G. Work - 1884
(Grandson of Alanson Work and Nephew of Henry Clay Work – both were students at Nelson's Mission Institute)

Much has been written about Nelson's religious and anti-slavery impact on society during his lifetime, but little is known of his impact on music. This chapter enlightens the reader as to the remarkable and diverse intellect and interests of Dr. David Nelson. The following quote from *English Hymns; Their Authors and History* by Samuel Willoughby Duffield lets us know how important music was to Nelson's career as preacher as well as physician.

> *Dr. David Nelson, the great antagonist of infidelity, was a lover of English poetry, and especially hymns. In his practice as a physician he found that a bulk of the theological learning of the families whom he met consisted of what was contained in the standard hymns of the Church. Frequently he would sing one of these hymns, impressively and alone, as the prelude of, or the peroration to, a sermon. As a physician he has been known to read or sing to the dying some such stanza as:*
>
> *"Oh, if my Lord would come and meet,*
> *My soul should spread her wings in haste,"*
> *With the following triumphant stanza:*

"Jesus can make a dying bed
Feel soft as downy pillows are."

In previous chapters I have made references to Nelson getting involved with writing music beginning with his days at Centre College in the late 1820s. Here I will expound a bit further on this topic.

The Danville Kentucky area in the early 19th Century was at a geographic epicenter of the Second Great Awakening. This movement which emphasized the ability of an individual to amend his life, had a profound effect on Nelson. One of the significant outcomes of this religious awakening was an array of reform movements aimed at addressing social injustices and alleviating suffering. The rationale being that by getting involved in social injustices, one might put him or herself in a better light before God. One such social movement was abolitionism and, while Nelson did not fully embrace this movement for years, the seeds were certainly sown early in his life via religious and social awakening which was literally exploding all around him.

The Second Great Awakening also gave rise to another religious trend that had a significant impact on Nelson's life. This trend was the use of music as a tool for broadening the populous appeal of religious persuasion. A new breed of religious revival meetings known as camp meetings became an important piece of the movement to convert religious infidels in greater numbers. These meetings, typically held in a field or open prairie, were far more outwardly emotional and energetic in their attempt to convert non-believers than the more staid religious approaches which had been brought over from the European religious communities and traditions. And one of the most important ingredients for a successful revivalist camp meeting was music. Nelson was widely recognized as one of the most successful camp meeting revivalists of his time. It is also obvious as you study Nelson, that he definitely recognized the necessity for, and the impact of, music in both persuasion and conversion. This recognition would serve him well in his endeavors to convert souls, and later in life to free them.

Amazing History

In an earlier chapter it was reported that Spilman and Shaw accepted Dr. Nelson's challenge and in 1829 published their book of hymns titled, *Columbian Harmony.* It is unclear exactly how successful, from a financial perspective, *Columbian Harmony* actually was but it now appears that it was a huge success in terms of its influence on the history of American music.

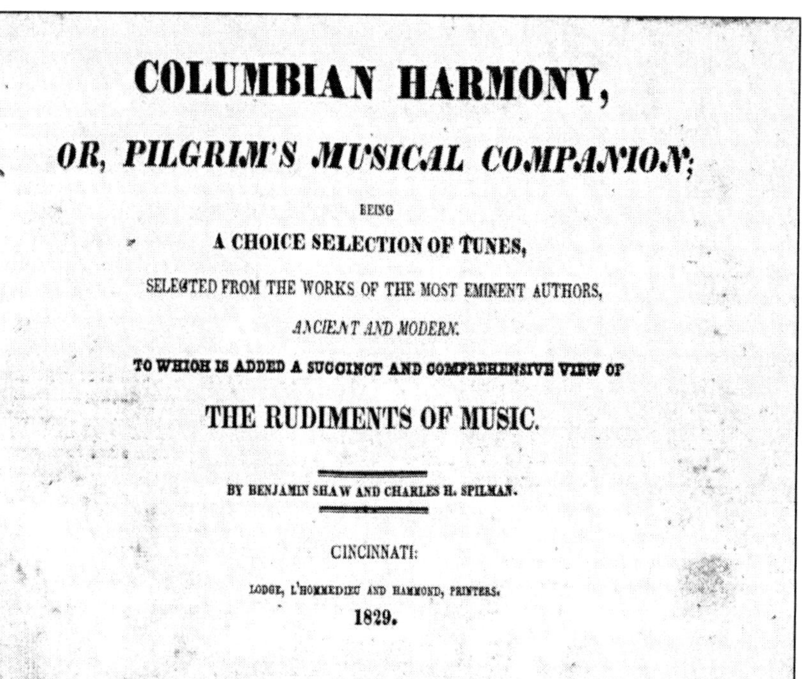

COLUMBIAN HARMONY,

OR, PILGRIM'S MUSICAL COMPANION;

BEING

A CHOICE SELECTION OF TUNES,

SELECTED FROM THE WORKS OF THE MOST EMINENT AUTHORS,

ANCIENT AND MODERN.

TO WHICH IS ADDED A SUCCINCT AND COMPREHENSIVE VIEW OF

THE RUDIMENTS OF MUSIC.

BY BENJAMIN SHAW AND CHARLES H. SPILMAN.

CINCINNATI:

LODGE, L'HOMMEDIEU AND HAMMOND, PRINTERS.

1829.

Returning to the historical significance of the hymn book, it is fair to say that from a historical perspective, until recently, very few people ever heard of or cared about *Columbian Harmony.* But then in 2002 Steven Turner released his book, "*Amazing Grace: America's Most Beloved Song*". The book details the history of "Amazing Grace." Originally written by an English slave ship captain, John Newton, "Amazing Grace" became an enormous hit in America yet it never achieved anything near that level of success in Newton's own country. The reason, as documented by Turner, was that the familiar music we now associate with "Amazing Grace" was not married with Newton's words until it arrived in America. But the long standing mystery surrounding the song is – where did the music or tune for "Amazing Grace" come from? For many years the answer to this question, while still not identifying who actually wrote the tune, was that the first known published book which contained the music for "Amazing Grace" was the 1831 *Virginia Harmony*.

However, in his book Turner documents, and further substantiates, a discovery in 1991 by music Hymnologist Marion Hatchett that the music to "Amazing Grace" was actually published two years prior to *Virginia Harmony* in a little known book comprised of various church hymns. That book, as you may have guessed by now, was the *Columbian Harmony* which, as we just presented, had been solicited by Dr. David Nelson to be written by two of his students, Benjamin Shaw and Charles Spilman. While it is still a bit of a mystery as to who actually wrote the music for "Amazing Grace," it is now widely accepted that the *Columbian Harmony* is the first known book to put the music down in writing.

I would have never guessed when I started researching Dr. David Nelson in this little town of Quincy, Illinois that I would eventually find him connected with a song so famous that it has been recorded by over 450 artists ranging from Elvis Presley to Rod Stewart to my favorite rendition performed by LeAnn Rimes!

As I read more about the life of John Newton, the author of "Amazing Grace," I couldn't help but to be amazed by the many interesting parallels between his life and the life of Dr. David Nelson. I suspect that Dr. Nelson may have been aware, if not inspired, by some of Newton's life experiences. In fact Nelson speaks of Newton and letters he wrote to his wife Mary in Nelson's famous book *The Cause and Cure of Infidelity*.

I think it is interesting, and perhaps beyond fate, that both Nelson and Newton shared so many life experiences. Both were prominent abolitionists in their respective countries, both found the basis for their abolitionist views from religion, both had been the benefactors of slavery earlier in their lives (Newton as a Captain of a slave trading ship and Nelson as a slave owner), both had fallen from their religion only to find it again in a more profound way, both became preachers, both became authors, and both wrote very famous songs.

Wishing for the Shore

A page from hymnal showing Nelson's famous hymn, "The Shining Shore"

Dr. Nelson knew that music could be used to move people, interestingly his most famous song was written while he was hoping that his friends would be able to come and move him – literally! While there are numerous accounts of the events surrounding Dr. Nelson's writing of his most famous song "The Shining Shore," I believe the following account from the *LaGrange Democrat* in 1882 is the most thorough and accurate:

> *La Grange Democrat: During a semi-centennial meeting of the Presbyterian synod of Missouri, in St. Louis two weeks ago, memorial services were held which brought out personal recollection of incidents full of local interest. Dr. J.J. Marks relates something of the early struggles of the church in northeast Missouri, among other things speaking of the difficulty which occurred at Greenfield*

camp ground, near Philadelphia, in Marion County, resulting in the stabbing of Dr. Bosley, by William Muldrow, and the subsequent flight of Dr. David Nelson to Quincy. Through fear of the mob Dr. Nelson and several others started for Illinois, but upon reaching the bottom found it flooded from a sudden rise in the river. His companions went to Hannibal to cross over and come up on the Illinois side to Quincy while he remained upon the river bank to wait until they could come after him with a skiff. For two nights and a day he remained there alone, and during the silent watches he composed a hymn which thousands hereabouts have sung without knowing anything of the local character of its authorship. The hymn will be found in all the old books and in many new ones. The first stanza and chorus are as follows:

"My days are gliding swiftly by,
And I, a pilgrim stranger,
Would not detain them as they fly,
Those hours of toil and danger."

"For now we stand on Jordan's strand,
Our friends are crossing over,
And just before the shining shore,
We may almost discover."

Dr. Marks thinks that the peculiarly pressing circumstances suggested the theme, and that the lights from Quincy flung across the dark waters to the minister in his forest covert, the fact that his friends had already crossed over, and the incidents connected with the dreary situation put into his mind the language found in the hymn and chorus. The disturbance and flight from the meeting was in 1836, and the hymn is known to have been in use since near that time.

Another account from, *My Life And The Story Of Gospel Hymns And Of Sacred Songs And Solos* by Ira D. Sankey and Theodore L. Cuyler also gives the reader a sense of just how perilous Dr. Nelson's situation was on the Missouri banks of the Mississippi.

> *This [Nelson's opposition to slavery] brought down upon him the wrath of his slave-holding neighbors, who drove him from his home and pursued him through the woods and swamps for three days and nights. Finally he came out on the banks of the Mississippi River opposite Quincy, Illinois. By signs he made known his condition to friends there, and then hid in the bushes to await the approach of night. As he lay there in danger of being captured every moment, the land of freedom in plain sight, with the swiftly gliding waters between, the lines of this hymn began to assume form in his mind, and he wrote them down on the back of a letter he had in his pocket. The voices of the vengeful pursuers were heard in the woods about him. Once they strode by the very clump of bushes in which he was concealed, and even poked their guns in to separate the branches; but they failed to notice him.*

As with "Amazing Grace," "The Shining Shore" may have never become as widely popular as it did if it were not for the proper marriage of great lyrics with great music. For "The Shining Shore" that music came from Song Writers Hall of Fame member, George Frederick Root. Yet while Root certainly gets the credit for writing the music and Nelson for writing the lyrics, it may be George Root's mother who should get most of the credit for bringing the words and the music together. The following account from *My Life And The Story Of Gospel Hymns And Of Sacred Songs And Solos* gives the reader a sense of how the two came together and how Root struggled to understand what drove the popularity of, in his perception, this relatively simple song.

> *"As to the music of this hymn "The Shining Shore" Mr. Root says: One day, I remember, as I was working at a set of graded part-songs for singing classes, mother passed through the room and laid a slip from one of the religious newspapers before me, saying; "George, I think that*

would be good for music." I looked at the poem, which began, 'My days are gliding swiftly by," and a simple melody sang itself along in my mind as I read. I jotted it down and went on with my work. That was the origin of the music of "The Shining Shore." Later, when I took up the melody to harmonize it, it seemed so very simple and commonplace that I hesitated about setting the other parts to it. I finally decided that it might be useful to somebody, and I completed it, though it was not printed for some months afterward. In after years I examined it in an endeavor to account for its great popularity – but in vain. To the musician there is not one reason in melody or harmony, scientifically regarded, for such a fact. To him hundreds of others, now forgotten, were better."

It is unlikely that the reader, or for that matter most people of today's generation, recognize the enormous popularity that Dr. Nelson's song enjoyed – and interestingly is still enjoying. In order to provide a better appreciation for the success as well as the historical impact of "The Shining Shore," I think it is worth sharing a few examples of the song's popularity and impact.

"The Shining Shore" became very popular during the Civil War. As a testament to this popularity noted American writer, Walt Whitman included it in his famous book, *Specimen Days.* The following scene described in his book took place in an armory hospital about a month and a half after the battle of Gettysburg:

44. Home-Made Music

August 8th- TO-NIGHT, as I was trying to keep cool, sitting by a wounded soldier in Armory-square, I was attracted by some pleasant singing in an adjoining ward. As my soldier was asleep, I left him, and entering the ward where the music was, I walk'd halfway down and took a seat by the cot of a young Brooklyn friend, S.R., badly wounded in the hand at Chancellorsville, and who has suffer'd much, but at that moment in the evening was wide awake and comparatively easy. He had turn'd over on his left side to get a better view of the singers, but the mosquito-curtains of the adjoining cots obstructed the sight. I stept round and loop'd them all up, so that he had a clear show, and then sat down again by him, and look'd and listen'd. The principal singer was a young lady-nurse of one of the wards, accompanying on a melodeon, and join'd by the lady-nurses of other wards. They sat there, making a charming group, with their handsome, healthy faces, and standing up a little behind them were some ten or fifteen of the convalescent soldiers, young men, nurses, &c., with books in their hands, singing. Of course it was not such a performance as the great soloists at the New York opera house take a hand in, yet I am not sure but I receiv'd as much pleasure under the circumstances, sitting there, as I have had from the best Italian compositions, express'd by world-famous performers. The men lying up and down the hospital, in their cots, (some badly wounded-some never to rise thence.) the cots themselves, with their drapery of white curtains, and the shadows down the lower and upper parts of the ward; then the silence of the men, and the attitudes they took- the whole was a sight to look around upon again and again. And there sweetly rose those voices up to the high, whitewash'd wooden roof, and pleasantly the roof sent it all back again. They sang very well, mostly quaint old songs and declamatory hymns, to fitting tunes. Here, for instance:

My days are swiftly gliding by, and I a pilgrim stranger,
Would not detain them as they fly, those hours of toil and danger;
For O we stand on Jordan's strand, our friends are passing over,
And just before, the shining shore we may almost discover.

We'll gird our loins my brethren dear, our distant home discerning,
Our absent Lord has left us word, let every lamp be burning,
For O we stand on Jordan's strand, our friends are passing over,
And just before, the shining shore we may almost discover.

Dr. Nelson, I'm sure, would have been very pleased that his words would offer comfort in such a way.

Further evidence of the importance of Nelson's song comes from studying the works of the famous American composer, Charles Ives. Ives is widely considered the first American composer of international significance. Mr. Ives apparently enjoyed "The Shining Shore" so much that he borrowed it for a large number of his music compositions.

Based on *A Descriptive Catalogue of The Music of Charles Ives* from the Irving S. Gilmore Music Library at Yale University (Ives was a Yale Grad) Ives borrowed the hymn "The Shining Shore" in many of his works including:

1. Symphony No. 1
2. Thanksgiving and Forefathers' Day (Fourth Movement of A Symphony: New England Holidays)
3. Orchestral Set No. 3
4. String Quartet No. 1: For the Salvation Army
5. Sonata No. 1 For Violin and Piano
6. On Judges' Walk
7. Religion
8. Rough Wind
9. The White Gulls
10. The World's Highway
11. Prelude for Thanksgiving Service
12. He even re-composed The Shining Shore in: Fugue in Four Keys on "The Shining Shore"

Interestingly, another famous abolitionist considered Nelson's "The Shining Shore" to be one of his favorite songs – Henry Ward Beecher. Henry Beecher was the son of famous abolitionist Lyman Beecher and the brother of Harriet Beecher Stowe, author of Uncle Tom's Cabin. Mr. Beecher may have been best known for providing guns to opponents of slavery in Kansas and Nebraska which became known as "Beecher's Bibles"!

One final example to illustrate the longevity of "The Shining Shore's" popularity; in 2007 the award winning classical music recording artists, Anonymous4, performed "The Shining Shore" on their latest album *Gloryland.* Apparently many people still like Dr. Nelson's music because the album debuted at #3 on Billboard's Classical Music chart and finished 2007 as the 16th highest grossing classical music album. I am certain that Dr. Nelson would be thrilled that he is still touching this many people with his music more than 150 years after he died.

Although much less popular than "The Shining Shore," Dr. Nelson did author other published hymns in his career. These include:

Rest In Heaven

1. Sleep not, the Saviour cries,
On this low, earthly ground;
Press on—above the skies,
There shall your rest be found.
Chorus:
Where the pilgrim reposes, the fields are all green,
There day never closes, nor clouds intervene:
O the forms that are there, such as eye hath not seen:
O the songs they sing there, with hosannas between,
While the river of life flows freely.
2. On earth cold storms arise,
And clouds obscure the sun;
For rest the pilgrim sighs—
But there his work is done. Chorus
3. My soul, be not dismayed,
But gird thee for the race:
I'll ask this hourly aid
To reach that happy place. Chorus:

A Fairer Land

"Twas told me in life's early day,
That pleasure's stream did flow
Gently beside life's peaceful way—
I have not found it so.
I thought there grew on earthly ground
Some buds without decay:

But not a single flower I've found
That does not fade away.
I wish to see a fairer land—
I've heard of one on high,
Where every tear by one kind hand
Is wiped from every eye.
Chorus:
Tis said the King of that bright place
Still welcomes travelers there
O come, then, let us seek his grace—
Unseen, he hears our prayer.

Before moving on from this discussion of Dr. Nelson's interesting musical history, I feel it is warranted to briefly discuss another great American song writer and composer who had close ties to Dr. Nelson – Henry Clay Work. Henry Work was the son of Alanson Work. The elder Work had moved his family to Quincy and was enrolled at Nelson's Mission Institute. He was also one of the three Mission Institute students along with George Thompson and James Burr who were imprisoned at the Missouri Penitentiary for soliciting slaves in Missouri to run away on the Underground Railroad to Canada. It was during this time while his father was in the Missouri prison that Henry Work started to gain an interest in music. I believe, given the following account which suggests that Henry Clay Work attended a music class at the Mission Institute and that he was certainly attending church on a regular basis (most likely with Dr. Nelson as the preacher), that Dr. Nelson would have been very aware of the young Work's interest in music and perhaps, like he did with his previous students Spilman and Shaw, may have mentored or inspired Henry Work in the field of music. Although it is also obvious from the following account that, while members of the church may have respected Henry's interest and ability to write music, some did not particularly care for the way he sang music!

From *Brainard's Biographies of American Musicians* edited by E. Douglas Boemberger:

Henry Clay Work was born in Middleton, Conneticut, October 1st 1832... and spent his early years in Quincy

> *Illinois. He received his first musical impressions while attending camp meetings. A few years later he took an irregular course (music) at Mission Institute near Quincy, Illinois, but was compelled to study much Latin and Greek rather than music. In the course of time, however, he acquired the principles of musical notation and took delight in joining in the hymns in church. To his amazement he was asked, privately, to desist from singing because he had "no voice". He desisted in church, but when the boy drove the cows to and from their pasture, his voice was heard far and near. Yes, he even went so far as to make up little tunes of his own while acting a cowboy.*

I have often stared out the back window of our house across the fields where the Mission Institute buildings once stood and tried to envision what things would be going on around me if I had been standing there 175 years ago. One of the things I think I would have quite enjoyed was listening to young Henry Work sing his songs while he drove the cows, as my sons Mike and Bill Deters III continue to do with their own dairy cows on this very land. I suppose there is something about that peaceful quiet solitude when you're walking alone behind those gentle animals which can bring out the song in anyone.

After leaving the Mission Institute, Henry Clay Work went on to become America's most prolific, and arguably most important, song writer and composer of the Civil War era. His famous songs include: "Marching Through Georgia," "Kingdom Coming," "Come Home Father" and "My Grandfather's Clock." In fact Work's "My Grandfather's Clock" holds two very interesting and unique distinctions – first, it is said to be the very first song in history to sell over one million copies and second, it is the source of the now ubiquitous term used to describe long case or floor clocks as grandfather clocks.

I hope this brief diversion from discussing David Nelson the abolitionist to discussing David Nelson the song writer and mentor to other song writers provides the reader with a better sense of how the life of this truly unique man touched, and continues to touch, the lives of so many individuals. I think he would want to be remembered in this light.

Chapter Eight

LITTLE LADY - BIG INFLUENCE

Dr. Nelson's grandson Harry Nelson told us that in the 1860's Eugene Nelson built the house in this photo for his mother. It is next to Oakland where she lived until her death on December 3, 1886 at Oakland.

Amanda's influence on Dr. Nelson's thinking should not be underestimated. Her children's diaries tell us that she was the first to encourage him to oppose slavery. Her grandson, Harry Nelson recalls:

> *During the Civil War, Grandma was a strong southern Sympathizer. She had no use for Abraham Lincoln until years after. Once she asked, "Emma who was it freed the slaves?"*
>
> *"Abraham Lincoln," Mother told her.*
>
> *"That man deserves an immortal crown"*
>
> *"Why, Mother, what has changed you? You never used to think so."*

"I don't know, unless the Lord."

Amanda was against slavery but she still had family and roots in the south. Her brother was a Chief Justice of the Tennessee Supreme Court and his six sons fought for the Confederacy. Most Southerners deeply resented the North for the devastation the Civil War brought onto the south.

By all accounts Amanda was a very small woman, not five foot tall. She was deeply religious and, although she came from a life of privilege and was the wife of a successful physician, she accepted the life of a frontier preacher's wife. Given her beliefs, she encouraged him even though it meant sacrifices for her and her children.

The students at Mission Institute and her large family would have benefited from her industriousness. Servants and a couple of adult children and grandchildren lived with her for most of her lifetime. An item of her hard work still remains. The old butter churn was still stored in the basement when we moved into the house. It was a rather large churn, but we know that there was a herd of dairy cows on the property based on the story of young Henry Clay Work driving the dairy cattle.

It would have been interesting to have lived there at that time to observe how caring for these people was managed.

Dr. Nelson spent his life caring for others with little concern for himself. Upon his death his family was left in dire straights financially. Owning the property alone was not sufficient to feed the children. Amanda began intensive work to bring the farm up to production sufficient to feed the family, servants and remaining students. The following notice gives evidence of the work she put forth. The following ad was posted in the *Quincy Whig* the spring after the doctor's death, April 16, 1845 which indicates the strong thrust for a working, economically viable farm:

> *Corn ground for a sixth, Buckwheat at the same price and wheat made into good family flour for a seventh in the horse mill at Adelphia, usually known as Mission Institute No. 1, near the residence of the late Dr. Nelson, and five miles east of Quincy. The subscriber would inform his friends and the public that the above Mill is now in first rate run of FRENCH BURR STONES and a good BOLT. He will grind for customers in all kinds of weather, with his own team at the above rates, and cheaper if the customer*

should find a team. All who find it convenient are invited to call and try the merits of the mill.

This is Amanda's industrial size 12 gallon butter churn, still in the home. It was listed in his will as one of the items in Dr. Nelson's estate. The large size was necessary to feed all her children, students and staff.

Earlier it was pointed out that Amanda excelled in botany while in school. Amanda had learned to adapt fruit trees. Harry Nelson, their grandson, wrote:

> *Her father kept an English gardener to beautify their grounds. From him she learned to bud fruit trees. This was most fortunate for in her days of adversity and widowhood she put the knowledge to practical use, and at one time had*

a fine fruit orchard. When I (Harry) was a child, the neighbors would sometimes send her some choice apples or peaches. She would send me back and ask for a branch to use for budding. When near 80 she would forget and put in plums, peaches, pears and apples of different kinds of the same tree.

When Amanda's orchard began bearing fruit finances in the fatherless Nelson home improved greatly. Year's later, the last remaining apple tree provided the Deters family with our fall supply of Jonathon's for many years.

Times might have been difficult for the family but young Eugene who was five years old at his father's death recalls his early years at Oakland this way:

Father's death when I was five years old left me with a vast stock of absolute freedom, restlessness, reckless impulse, tempered with considerable conscience. Plenty of swamp duck hunting, fishing, skating, logging with oxen, plowing, etc., together with cow's milk, corn bread, fat possum, 'hominy, and wild honey, brought me out to where I can truthfully say, I remember no prolonged sickness. First and last, my father turned his back on over $30,000 worth of slaves, when that sum stood for wealth out in the Southwest, and the jolt down from the odious pride, conceit, and sickly selfishness of Aristoi in the South prostrated some of the older members of our family, and they never quite recovered healthy environments. As for myself, I was born in and breathed the air of Demoi, and never wanted better; prefer spelling Character with a large C, and riches with a little r.

Eugene tells in his autobiography that he was raised mostly by his "black mammy." His mother had brought her slaves with her from the south, who were then her hired servants. A strong family bond existed with them.

By the time Eugene became an adult; two older sisters were living in the home with them. Rose Clapp was widowed about a year after her marriage. She returned home and never married again. Another sister, Emma, went to California in the gold rush and returned without her husband but with two young children. They also stayed at Oakland with the family. Eugene said his mother asked him to build the house in the photo (next to Oakland) for her. Probably she intended it to be used by some of the extended family.

Although her children reported that Amanda had a "sun stroke" late in her life which affected her speech, she appears to have been making business decisions up to the end. Before her death, Amanda sold forty acres in Missouri known as "The Sugar Camp" for one dollar to "her faithful servant Nancy Nelson, otherwise known as Nancy Shelton". The sale document lists Nancy Shelton as "Negro".

I learned something of Amanda from a neighbor known to me as Grandma Belker. She and her husband John had worked for Amanda and had lived in the servant's quarter, the room above the kitchen at Oakland. Amanda would sometimes sit upstairs by the balcony door and do needlework. She also remembered Amanda as a sweet little lady who spent many hours in her last years sitting in the cupola on top of the house smoking her corn cob pipe, which is in the possession of her descendents today. Her view from the top of the house stretched for miles. The lights of Hannibal, Missouri can be seen on a clear night. Perhaps she sat up their and remembered her days together with her beloved David.

As a woman and a mother of eleven children myself, I would often find strength pondering the life of the first lady of our house. It is clear that Amanda's husband was gone much of the time. It would have been up to Amanda to manage the day to day operations of the household, farm, and yes, the Underground Railroad station. How many times did Amanda open her doors for fugitives? How many times did she send food, blankets or clothing to the aid of fugitives? How many times did she meet with students of Mission Institute to advise them of Underground Railroad activity? We will never know because those were times when women were not expected to do such things. That is exactly *why* I think Amanda would have.

Nelson's Influence Up and Down the Line

While it is pretty clear that David Nelson did not seek out fame for fame's sake, I believe he was shrewd enough to recognize that he could leverage his fame as an author, preacher and educator in his quest to free slaves. While those of pro-slavery persuasion recognized Nelson and his colleges (Marion and Mission Institute) as one of the key centers for the national abolitionist and Underground Railroad movements, those on the anti-slavery side looked to Nelson as an inspirational leader for their cause. Thus, the Quincy area became not only a national hot bed of the abolitionist and Underground Railroad movements but also a target for pro-slavery mobs. It is interesting to imagine how many times members from opposite sides of these two camps must have met on the streets and surrounding roads of Quincy and Adams County without even knowing it. I'm certain the Underground Railroad conductors were often aware of the slave hunters as they made their way around the roads of the area looking for escaped slaves. But many of these conductors, as opposed to the more famous abolitionist figures such as Dr. Nelson, chose to remain, as would be expected, primarily anonymous – or at least more discrete in their abolitionist beliefs.

Much of the remainder of this book tells the stories of many of these lesser known Underground Railroad conductors. These conductors were, in many cases, working with, or inspired by, the more visible Dr. Nelson. As I researched Dr. Nelson I learned much about a number of these more anonymous conductors. I gained a tremendous amount of respect for their selfless willingness to put their lives, and the lives of their family members, at significant risk for the sake of a fellow human being. I hope my attempt to relate some of these courageous stories will leave the reader with a similar respect for these amazing Underground Railroad conductors. I know Dr. Nelson would want his fame shared with these brave individuals who took up his cause.

Chapter Nine

THE TURNER STATIONS

While I have no information that David Nelson actually met Asa Turner on any of Nelson's trips to the east coast, but it is clear that Nelson and Turner were working together on missionary schools and anti-slavery activities very soon after Nelson arrived in Quincy. After the Turner brothers got involved in the Underground Railroad they helped Quincy continue to make a name for itself as an anti-slavery town. Here is how it happened.

Around the time that Dr. Nelson was establishing Marion College in Missouri, seven young graduates of Divinity School of Yale University signed a compact to go to Illinois to establish a seminary of learning. They pledged to either teach or preach to the surrounding country. Members of the "Yale Band", as they were referred to, settled in the area from 1829-33. Although these men were not abolitionists before they came to Illinois, they were instrumental in arousing the anti-slavery feelings in the Quincy area. In November, 1830 Rev. Asa Turner, a member of the Yale Band, brought his bride Martha Bull to Quincy.

On Turner's way west, while staying in Cincinnati in early 1830 he met with Rev. James Gallaher (The same James Gallaher who previously wrote *The Calvanistic Magazine* with Dr. Nelson). Rev. Gallaher told Mr. Turner that in order to be successful he would need to have church camp-meetings. Turner began to attend some held by Presbyterians, and he said that "*all was orderly and quiet as in any country congregation in New England.*" It was at such a meeting that, in 1831, Asa Turner met with a "*phenomenal man and well-nigh peerless preacher, Dr. David Nelson.*" Mr. Turner wrote, "*His mere bodily presence was enough to inspire fear in a lesser specimen of humanity. They only needed to see his face: such meekness and benevolence shone through it.*"

From *Asa Turner And His Times*, written about Quincy, March 15, 1830:

This village has been settled 4 years, and now contains a population of about four hundred souls. Till lately we have never seen a Presbyterian preacher in the place. More recently we have had preaching six times in the course of 18 months. We are not destitute. Our people are new settlers, mostly from New England, and have little money: but provisions of every kind are abundant and cheap. If we could get a preacher possessing a missionary spirit, with a small family, who would be willing to settle here and become one of us, we could give him a farm and cultivate it for him, and support him as well, with a fair prospect of not leaving his family destitute.

Early in 1832, Rev. Turner reports: "*Our little church has now increased to 32.*"

Returning with Mrs. Turner from a long absence in the east after burying their infant child in Frederick, MD in 1833, he wrote:

Found our little church in a more active state than I feared; deprived almost entirely of ministration for the past six months, many of them possessed an unusual spirit of prayer." The cholera prevented special meetings on both sides of the river. (In Missouri it was even more severe." Out of 7 or 8 hundred people at Palmyra, more than one hundred deaths." …

The Methodist minister in Quincy was the first to die. In January, Mr. Turner reports that one tenth of the whole population was carried off. Nearly half left during the cholera epidemic. Sick himself and discouraged by this dreadful disease, he wrote: "The prospects of doing much at present are very unfavorable." However, the following November in some special services, it was thought, 15 or 20 were converted. He was aided by Rev. Mr. Hardy, who had been at Quincy in his absence the year before, and by Rev. David Nelson, M.D., of Missouri.

Asa Turner home taken in the 1960s

This home was known as Maple Lane and was also known to be an Underground Railroad station. The ice house had a false floor under which was a secret room.

An Association of Congregational Churches was formed in November 1834, at Rev. Turner's home in Quincy, called Maple Lane because of the long lane of maple trees. This group was solidly anti-slavery and used every means to support the abolition movement.

A member of the Turner family would usually carry the fugitives by wagon to the next stop, Deacon Jireh Platt's home. The home at Maple Lane was torn down to make way for Knapheide Manufacturing. The maple trees that lined the lane and for which it was named still stand.

All that was left at the time this picture was taken were the remnants of the icehouse, blown down by a tornado.

Like Nelson, Asa Turner was the target of angry mobs because he came to believe that slavery should be abolished. Once, at the Lord's Barn according to Asa Turner's memoirs, John Wood went among people from all parts of the county and said: "Don't touch Mr. Turner. If you do it will be over my dead body. I'll kill as many as Davy Crockett did."

Not only did Asa Turner face mobs and rioting around the Quincy church building, he faced them at Alton just before the assassination of the Rev. Elijah P. Lovejoy. Father Turner presided at a meeting which established the first antislavery society in Illinois.

Asa Turner left Quincy in 1838 and eventually settled in Denmark, Iowa. He founded Iowa College patterned after Illinois College in Jacksonville, Illinois, where his brother Jonathan Baldwin Turner taught.. Iowa College was later named Grinnel College. John Brown, the famous radical abolitionist was known to hide out there.

Asa Turner's sons, brothers, and nephews continued to live and help runaway fugitives escape in the Quincy area. Much about them is written in the *People's History of Quincy and Adams, County*.

Avery Turner and his wife Hannah Baker Turner moved to Quincy in 1835. They settled on land which had been entered by his brother, the Rev. Asa Turner. The Turner brothers developed a good farm. Avery Turner had at least two places to hide slaves on his farm. The ice house had a false floor under which was a secret room. He also had a hollowed out space in the hay mow at the top of the barn.

A fugitive who landed at Mission Institute No 4 need only follow the road north (24th St) to "Maple Lane." Miss Julia Turner, daughter of Avery's son Edward, related in an interview with Diane Cory Phillips in her unpublished thesis:

> *My grandfather was a type of the conservative, law abiding citizen who defied the Supreme Court quietly and courageously. He hollowed out a little space in the hay mow at the top of his barn where he hid runaways—at one time, four with a little baby, for a week. Grandfather would feed them secretly; expecting always that the hired man would betray them for the reward offered by the slave hunters, who would come riding up Maple Lane to track their quarry. Betrayal meant a raid some dark night, burned buildings and perhaps gunshots and death...*

Miss Turner remembers hearing stories about her cousin, Johnny Turner, who was a deeply religious youth, but not so scrupulous that he couldn't lie when the occasion demanded it. One fall evening Johnny started out for Mendon with a wagon partially filled with food, including a strong smelling ham. He had not even gotten out of the lane when a "Southerner" from Missouri rode up on horseback demanding knowledge of a runaway Negro boy that came that way. Johnny innocently denied any knowledge of his whereabouts and the man galloped away. In this manner young Turner proved himself an effective liar, since the fugitive was hiding directly under the seat of the wagon.

Avery Turner's two sons were Edward Turner II and Samuel B. Turner. In 1835 a frame house was built and in 1840 a house of brick was built. Edward's family resided on the old homestead for many years. In the *People's History of Quincy And*

Adams County on Ellington Township, Mrs. James Nielson writes that Edward Turner and his wife would go by wagon to the Mississippi River and smuggle the slaves to different "Underground Railroads"-- many times to their own home

Avery Turner's other son, Samuel B, was a boy when his family came to Quincy. He built a two-story brick home on his eighty acre farm in 1852, and married Catherine Savage that same year. They had three sons. It is said that they had an underground passage in their home. A small room near the kitchen sheltered the slaves. One time, slaves were caught hiding in the slave compartment and officers came with guns to take them to prison. The Turners reluctantly gave them up.

Samuel Turner home near Maple Lane, owned by the Bergman's when we were invited to check it out. It had a secret room it.

This house was empty when Ann Bergman gave us a tour. It has since been torn down. A creek runs behind it about a quarter of a mile from the house.

This secret room in the house was plastered.

A common practice of the Turners was to use their ice houses as Underground hiding places. At the time we took the pictures remnants of the hiding places were still visible.

The ice house served as a hiding place.

The entire ice house had a sub-space hidden beneath the wooden floor. In this picture you can see the remaining beam of the false floor.

Jonathan Baldwin Turner

Another brother, Jonathan Baldwin Turner, also from Templeton MA, was a Yale educated farmer. Sometime after meeting Dr. Nelson in Kentucky he came to Quincy and stayed with his brother for a time. He later moved to Jacksonville, Illinois where he became a newspaper editor and college professor at Illinois College in Jacksonville, Illinois. Prior to that he traveled a great deal, giving speeches and handing out pamphlets promoting the establishment of using land grants to help students work their way through college (similar to the way Marion College and Mission Institute were set up). He said, "At first I taught and did whatever came to hand, as we all did; from helping run the farm and the mechanics' shops up to the highest studies there taught." Meantime he had entered with energy into popular education, delivering, in 1833, a series of lectures in favor of a permanent common-school system.

In the following story from *Life of Jonathan Baldwin Turner* by his descendent Mary Turner Carriel, Turner tells of how he met Dr. Nelson and learning of their mutual interests of religion, education and agriculture:

The Osage Orange

"What can public schools do for families so widely scattered?" was the query that was ever ringing in Professor Turner's ears as he rode over the great, uncultivated prairies, with not a wagon or bridle-path to mark the way, not a bridge over creek or river. "How can they be peopled -- how can they be cultivated?" There was not enough timber to build fences, no way of protecting crops or corralling stock. What could be done to tempt the pioneer from his home in the East to settle upon the fertile lands in the West? The first problem was to get something for fences. It must be "horse-high, bull-strong and pig-tight"; it must be grown from the soil, for Illinois must furnish not only crops, by the material to protect her crops. He experimented with barberry, box, hawthorn and many other plants, even sending to England and other countries for varieties – a proceeding attended with no little expense. But not one of these would answer.

In the summer of 1835 Professor Turner attended a camp-meeting at Pisgah, {Kentucky} on Charles Drury's farm, where the first log church of Pisgah was built. Logs had been cut for benches, and a rude platform built for the speakers. The preacher, a man from New York, dressed in the clerical style of the time, broadcloth coat, white tie, and high silk hat, precise and formal, was addressing the people, but did not seem to interest them. The young people were wandering through the woods, picking blackberries while the older men stayed in the background, discussing the questions of the day. Late in the afternoon a man walked up the grassy aisle. His clothes were dusty and worn and his whole appearance so unkempt that Professor Turner put out his hand to stop him, thinking he must be some wayfarer who did not know what he was doing. To his surprise, the preacher stopped speaking and came forward to greet the newcomer. It proved to be the Rev. Dr. David Nelson who had for his circuit Illinois, Kentucky, Tennessee, Arkansas, and Missouri. No wonder that his clothes were dusty and worn, and that he wore one shoe and one boot, both of which had holes in them. He began to address the camp-meeting. Soon they gathered round until there was not one vacant seat, and for three hours he held this great audience.

After the meeting, Professor Turner, in talking with him, told him of his experiments in trying to find some plant that would make good fences, and asked him if he had seen anything, on his journeyings, that could be grown into a hedge. Dr. Nelson replied that he had seen a thorny plant growing on the banks of the Osage River in Arkansas and that he would bring some of the seed when he came again. Professor Turner said afterward:

"He gave such an interesting account of this plant that I immediately determined to send for it. I wrote to everyone in the Southwest I heard of that would be likely to give me any information about it; but, as the Doctor had failed to give me the name bois d'arc, by which it was known farther West, these inquiries were pushed for years without any satisfactory results. Finally an answer came from a correspondent, who sent me a few plants, which I put out, and found to grow well.

I now turned my attention to propagating from them, with pretty good success; but with a new supply of plants came a few seeds taken from the orange ball. The planting of these showed that from the seed it could be propagated with great ease and facility. I procured a quantity of seed, but the first proved worthless. The second time, however, I was more fortunate, and succeeded in growing some plants. Experience soon convinced me that the object of my search was found at last. But the preparation of the soil, the planting of the seed at what time and depth, how to cultivate the plants and how to take them from the ground, how to keep them from the frost until spring, all had to be learned by years of experiment and study. The return for all this was usually the incredulous laugh of the passer-by.

Even the Osage orange, for the first year or two, had the pretty appellation of "Professor Turner's Folly."

The cultivation by hand was too slow and expensive. The cost of raising prohibited their general use; so I invented and patented a cultivator to grind the dirt very fine by means of circular disks; also a drill and a planter to plant the Osage orange seed; and a corn-planter and wheat-drill where the driver could ride as well as drive.

In 1847 I issued my first circular to the people, offering the Osage orange plants for sale. In describing the plants the circular stated:

'It is a native of Arkansas and Texas, and will grow on any soil where common prairie-grass will grow. Overflowing the land does not harm it. It will live for weeks, even months, entirely under water. It endures all climates, from Boston to New Orleans, perfectly well. Prairie fires will not destroy it or often injure it. It is armed with a very stout thorn under every leaf. Its dense iron branches soon become so interlocked that no domestic animal, not even a common bird, can pass through it. Both its thorns and its bitter acrid juice prevent all animals and insects from browsing or feeding on its branches. Its seed is like the orange seed and its root like the hickory. Consequently it can never spread into the field. One hedge around a farm secures orchards, fruit –yards, stables, sheepfolds, and pasture-grounds from all thieves, rogues, dogs, wolves, etc. One good gate, well locked, makes the whole farm secure against all intruders. It may be trained so high as to afford shelter to stock and break the rough prairie winds.'

Eventually the hedge Osage-orange was used as fence in the region and now the hedge grows widely around the Quincy area.

Jonathan Baldwin Turner was known to be an abolitionist. Like his brother in Quincy, he was a conductor of the Underground Railroad. He had been influenced when he heard Dr. Nelson preach but they also shared an interest in agriculture and education. Nelson's oldest son, David D. Nelson was active in anti-slavery activity in Jacksonville and was no doubt affiliated with Turner. It is clear from the following reports that they had significant impact on the ant-slavery movement in Illinois.

In later years three runaway slave women credited Turner for helping them find their way to Canada.

A young law student from Turner's Illinois College named William H. Herndon was so moved by Elijah Lovejoy's murder at Alton that he encouraged his law partner Abraham Lincoln to accept his anti-slavery viewpoints.

In 1842 the following letter was received by Professor Turner, warning him of his threatened assassination and the destruction of his college on account of his opposition to slavery:

Louisville,Kentucky
September 10, 1842
J.B. Turner, Esq.

Sir:

Although a stranger to you personally, I am well acquainted with your character as professor and as a writer against the Mormons. I feel interested in you for these accounts as well as from the precepts of religion, and we were told that we should do to others as we should like them to do for us and now, sir, for the matter in view.

I have just returned from Missouri, where I was looked upon as a slave-holder, however. I had the entire confidence of some whose names I am honor bound not to name. But it is sufficient for me to warn you against the evil that hangs over your head and the heads of others; a hint to the wise should be sufficient. Be assured then the evil is determined against you, through an association of slaveholders in Missouri, and that the destruction of your college, the kidnapping of yourself and some others will be attempted; that, if that fails, a little poison, or a hemp cord on your neck, or a messenger of lead, or a bowie-knife will be certain in their time.

It is whispered that Governor T. Carlin is a hypocrite and connives at abolitionism, and might as well have a ball through him; they have determined the secret death of every abolitionist they can find. You may see that, should I

give my name and it be found out, I would lose my life but it; but you may depend on the truth of the above.
Hoping this may reach you in time, I am,

Your, etc.
FRIEND

P.S. The Quincy Institute is under the same threats as yours. Dr. Nelson is aware, I suppose, that his life is not safe. As to Carlin, I think they are mistaken about him; for from what I can learn, he is in favor of slavery; but he is rather two-faced.

The identity of the person who wrote this letter was found to be Kentucky newspaper editor, soldier and politician, Cassius Clay, cousin of Kentucky Senator Henry Clay. Cassius Clay attended Transylvania University in Lexington, Kentucky at the time Dr. Nelson was in the area and might have been teaching medicine with Dr. McDowell there. Also Spilman and Shaw were writing Columbia Harmony at this time and Spilman eventually got his medical degree at Transylvania University. Then Clay went to Yale where he was impressed by an anti-slavery speech given by famous abolitionist William Lloyd Garrison. Remember that Asa and Jonathan Baldwin Turner were Yale graduates. It is not inconceivable that Cassius Clay knew both Turner and Nelson personally-- hence the letter warning them.

An interesting story about Cassius Clay was that in 1854 he gave an anti-slavery speech in Springfield, Illinois. A heckler shouted, "Would you help a runaway slave?" Clay answered, "That depends on which way he was running." The speech was admired by Abraham Lincoln who was in the crowd that day.

(Muhammad Ali, the fighter was originally named Cassius Marcellus Clay, Jr. after his father, Cassius Marcellus Clay Sr. who was named for the emancipationist.)

His work on behalf of public higher education caused Jonathan Baldwin Turner to become known as the "Father of the Federal Land Grant System". The following article from the *Quincy Herald Whig* states:

A Builder Honored

When the new Jonathan Baldwin Turner hall on the campus of Illinois State Normal University was dedicated Sunday, honor was paid one of the most zealous builders of progress in pioneer Illinois.

It is proper that the building will house classrooms and laboratories devoted to teaching the practical arts, for

Turner, although a classical scholar, urged the teaching of things that would develop better farming and industrial practices.

Turner is termed the father of the land grant college act, under which federal aid was made available to certain universities in each state. It was the real beginning of public higher education. Now, more than a century after passage of the land grant bill,

Turner has been honored in new buildings at the University of Illinois and at Illinois Normal University. A plaque in the Griggsville High school building marks the site of Turner's appeal for low-cost colleges for deserving boys and girls.

The idea has grown into splendid institutions. In Illinois, alone; enrollment in the four state teacher training universities has grown from 6,400 to 26,000 in a little more that a decade, Royal Stipes, president of the teachers' college board, said Sunday.

Jonathan Baldwin Turner lived and worked in western Illinois. He was one of three young brothers who came west in the 1830s as part of the "Yale band." Jonathan settled in Jacksonville as a teacher in Illinois college. His brother Asa came to Quincy, became the first resident pastor and was for many years minister of the First Congregational church. Another brother, Avery, came to Quincy by covered wagon from the family home in Massachusetts in 1834 and settled on land entered by Asa Turner on North Twenty-fourth street.

There Avery Turner spent the remainder of a long life, a farmer. He built three homes, the last in 1852. In it lived his son Edward, whose daughters, Miss Julia and Miss Emily, also lived there in their late years. Miss Julia died in May, 1962, greatly loved and honored by the community.

The Turner brothers represented the best traits of the pioneers. Strong in body and mind, they stood fearlessly for their beliefs. They advocated the rights of man as opposed to Negro slavery at a time when abolitionism was unpopular. Jonathan worked for an educational system far in advance of his time, and won after many years of effort.

There were 42 of the Turner descendants in attendance at the services Sunday in honor of Jonathan Baldwin Turner. Illinois and the nation owe a deep debt to the brothers who lived and worked a century ago in Quincy and Jacksonville, but whose efforts now are felt all over the nation.

From this it is clear that our lives today are much better because of the sacrifice of these men.

Joseph Turner Home

Another Turner home, that of Joseph Turner in Ellington Township was said to have hiding places. When I visited the home, then owned by the Shriver's, they told how the hiding places, like one under the kitchen, had been removed when they remodeled. The hiding place behind the fireplace had been replaced by a new fireplace and mantel.

Chapter Ten

EELLS' CASE CHUGS ON TO THE SUPREME COURT

This is Dr. Richard Eells' home on 4th and Jersey in Quincy as it was in the 1970's. In the 1840's this house did not resemble this Italianate style. It was completely remodeled from its original Greek revival style including the entire roof slope and upper floor in 1871. The house was built of brick. I have noticed that several of the Underground Railroad stations in this area used brick in the construction. I suspect it was chosen in part because tapping on it would not echo a hollow sound indicating a hiding place.

When Dr. Nelson first arrived in Quincy he was associated with Dr. Richard Eells. Both men were physicians who had a common passion for stopping slavery. Eells was a graduate of Yale who came to Quincy in 1833.

In the late summer of 1842, the famous case of Dr. Eells began. It did not end until 1853 in the U.S. Supreme Court.

An unpublished journal of Enoch Platt, Underground Railroad conductor from Mendon, Illinois tells his first hand account of the events leading up to this famous case:

No. 6

The Doctor a passenger.

Among those who passed over this road was quite a variety of passengers.

A slave had escaped from his master, but was so closely pursued that when he came to the banks of the Mississippi and saw his pursuers coming behind him, he had jumped into the river and swam across, at a point where the river was more than a mile wide. The hunters saw him but not liking that way of crossing had waited to get a boat. This delay had given the fugitive time to reach the residence of one of the U.G.R.R. men in Quincy (Dr. Eells), who had furnished him with a suit of dry clothes, and taking him in his buggy behind a horse that had the reputation of being fast, had started for Mendon. By this time the hunters had arrived and given the alarm. A man had seen and recognized the Dr.'s horse and buggy as they passed out of town and reported the fact to the hunters. Reinforced by a number of the citizens of Quincy they mounted some horses and gave chase. The Dr. heard them coming and put his horse to his speed. He could keep ahead of them for a distance but soon found that with two in his buggy the race was too long to hope to win. Suddenly stopping by the side of a corn field he told the fugitive to jump and take care of himself giving him some direction where to go. Driving on he took another road and reached home before being overtaken.

The fugitive instead of going where the Dr. had directed him, attempted to get back to the Dr.'s house and was caught by the hunters. The wet clothes that he had on when he left his master were found and identified in the Dr.'s stable.

The hunters had caught their slave and had caught one of the abolitionists in the act of helping him away. This was their OPPORTUNITY TO PUNISH SUCH CRIMINALS.

Dr. was arrested, but though they were sure he was the right man, their evidence was defective. They could not prove that the Dr. had anything to do with the clothes found in his stable, or that the man who was riding with him was the fugitive; though one man (afterward sheriff of Adams Co.) swore that he saw a "Big buck nigger jump out of the buggy", but on his cross examination stated that he was more than a quarter of a mile away; that it was after dark with no light but the moon, and that the position of the buggy was such that it was doubtful whether he could see the buggy at all from where he was at the moment the man jumped out.

After a long and tedious examination the Dr. was discharged.

Though discharged by the officers of the law, the hunters determined that he should not escape punishment, and appealed the case to the court of "Judge Lynch" to try him by the "Lynch law".

A plan was formed to kidnap the Dr. and taking him to Missouri, kill him there, and a party supposed to be sufficiently strong was formed to carry out this plan. A boat load of them crossed the river, and just after dark sent a messenger to ask Dr. Eells to come to a house on the bank of the river to see a patient that was very sick. The party lay in wait to catch and gag him, and take him across to the court that "Always convicts". The Dr. asked some questions about the sick person and what was the matter. The answers aroused his suspicions, and he declined going that night. Enquiries the next day disclosed the whole plot. Having failed in their attempts to kidnap, they resorted to law.

This time they charged him with having committed the act in Missouri and brought it before the Grand Jury of Marion County Missouri, which brought in a true bill against him and got a requisition from the Governor of Missouri to the Governor of Illinois. (If I remember rightly Gov. Ford). The requisition was granted and the proper papers issued. It was not the intention to have the case tried in the regular courts, but he was to be taken from the officers and have the mob administer Justice (?) with certainty and dispatch. According to their code killing an abolitionist was no more a crime than killing a rattlesnake or a wild beast.

The Dr. heard of what had been done a few moments before the sheriff came to arrest him, and took passage on the U.G.R.R. for Chicago, where he remained in concealment until his friends could lay the facts before Gov. Ford. They proved 1st that the Dr. was in Illinois at the time he was charged with committing a crime in Missouri and 2nd that the docket of the officers before whom he was tried in Quincy showed that he had already been tried in Illinois, charged by the same parties with the same crime, claimed to have been committed at the same time that the requisition charged against him in Missouri. On these facts being presented the Governor revoked the order for his arrest and the Dr. returned to his home in Quincy. His friends took some pains to make a public demonstration of honor to him, and joy at his acquittal. Not long after this he died. Though an abolitionist he was greatly beloved and esteemed by a large circle of friends, and almost the entire city mourned his death.

When I was writing about the Underground Railroad for *People's History of Quincy and Adams County* I found additional information about the Eells story. The fugitive slave was brought to the Eells house by Barryman Barnett, a colored agent of the railroad, who lived along the riverfront. Barnett immediately notified Eells of the fugitive's arrival. The doctor got his buggy and fastest horse and started north.

By this time the slave owner, Chauncy Durkey, who had organized a pursuing party, had arrived in Quincy, determined to catch the slave valued at $800. One part of the group spotted Eells but he was able to out distance them. However, when a second squad overtook him, he hid the slave in a cornfield at twenty-fifth and Broadway and then managed to circle around to his home at Fourth and Jersey.

On the following day a warrant for Eells' arrest was sworn out by Durkey and a large crowd gathered at the courthouse (on 5th between Hampshire and Maine) to hear that the doctor was held on bail, but the case was not tried until 1843.

Six years later, Gov. Thomas Reynolds of Missouri alleged that Eells had fled to Chicago to avoid arrest by Missouri officials, but the Governor of Illinois, Thomas Ford, refused to assist or cooperate with the Missourians in capturing Eells on the grounds, that the indictment was probably procured to be found against him, not for the purpose of subjecting him to a fair and impartial trial but merely as a pretext and a means of letting Eells into the state of Missouri, so that illegal violence might there be inflicted on him by persons who believed that they had received an injury at his hands, which the law does not sufficiently redress.

Actually Eells was in Chicago attending the Sixth Anniversary of the Illinois Anti-slavery Society of which he was elected President for the ensuing year. When he did return to Quincy, he was tried in circuit court and fined $400. Eells appealed and the case dragged on. On a writ of error it was taken to the State Supreme Court which declared that the federal court alone had jurisdiction in fugitive slave cases. Finally in 1853 the United States Supreme Court confirmed the judgment of the original tribunal.

The case was important and got national attention because it settled the personal responsibility of a person in a free state who helped fugitive slaves escape after they left the state which considered them property. When the state courts maintained that the federal courts alone had jurisdiction in such cases, they lessened their authority in dealing with hired slave catchers who entered free states and used violent and forceful methods of recapturing fugitives.

The national attention that the Eells' case and the Thompson, Work and Burr case brought to the area as well as Dr. Nelson's active national participation in the Anti-slavery movement made Quincy a known activity center for the Underground Railroad. In my many years of researching the Underground Railroad I am always amazed by the people who were involved and in some cases, who their descendents became. This is one such story related by Allen Oakley in a letter to the Editor in the *Herald Whig*. The following is from a letter to the editor in the Sunday, March 25, 1990 letters to the editor:

Another twist to Quincy's Underground Railroad story:

To The Herald-Whig:

One good turn of the history wheel deserves another

Incidents related in last Sunday's Herald-Whig recall yet another chapter – one more obscure – in the story of Quincy's Underground Railroad connection.

It was just around the corner from the Eells house, subject of Sunday's story, that this chapter is centered.

In 1859, when the Civil War was brewing and abolitionist feeling ran high on the side of the Mississippi, two young easterners came to Quincy. Their lawyer-father was so committed to the anti-slavery movement that he purposefully moved in 1835 from Delaware to Wilkes-Barre, PA., then in 1852 to Skaneateles on New York's Finger Lakes, both key points on the route by which escaping slaves were helped toward Canada and freedom He was Henry Hill Wells, and after his death in 1856 his sons were drawn to Quincy, "another crucial focus of the Underground Railroad."

These sons were William Dagworthy Wells and Richard Jones Wells. They took jobs – as railroad freight clerk and express messenger – that gave them information useful in the cause. With some independent means, they resided at the Quincy House, the finest hostelry of its day, now the site of the renovated Newcomb Hotel. That was hardly more than across the alley from the Eells house where stirring events took place almost a quarter century before.

In later years, a second "e" was inserted into the Wells name and the grand-nephew and grandson of those two Wells brothers became famous for "Citizen Kane" and the panic of his radio invasion from Mars. Welles, with the extra "e," in fact used some of the family Underground Railroad experiences in an early, and failed, drama, "Marching Song." The story is told by Hollywood biographer Charles Higham in "Orson Welles: The Rise and Fall of an American Genius." It's at the library.

Allen M. Oakley

The Van Dorn Sawmill

In 1838 John Van Dorn moved to Quincy from Massachusetts and became a successful businessman, an active abolitionist, and a member of the Congregational Church. John K. and James Van Dorn and U. S. Penfield had purchased a saw mill and lumberyard from E. B. Kimball. It burned in 1858.The Van Dorn home was on the south side of State Street between Third and Fourth. From the *People's History of Quincy and Adams County,* he is quoted, "My location was such that I either had to ignore my principles or hide the 'outcast' and take the consequences of being persecuted as a despised Abolitionist." His sawmill was located near the river on Front St., between Ohio and Delaware Streets, and down the hill from Dr. Eells' house. This was often called "Station #1", because it was one of the first places runaways arrived after crossing the Mississippi River. From the Van Dorn Sawmill, the runaways could have traveled by land usually first to Dr. Eells then to other stations in the network.

Van Dorn alone helped 300 fugitives which averages at least one person every month for twenty-five years. It is said that few people knew of his activities until his death when several former fugitives attended his funeral. His story is told in a play entitled *Burnt Sugar*. Carl Landrum quoted this article from the *Quincy Whig* of May 11, 1875:

> *The colored people, whom he had befriended as he only had kindness and the courage to befriend them, were largely represented at the funeral. They asked to be permitted to throw flowers into the grave after the body was lowered to its resting place, but it was thought the crowd would make it inconvenient for them to do so. They secured a large supply of flowers, took them to the grave and one of their number, Mr. John Daniels, remained there after the crowd dispersed, to cover the grave with flowers when it was completed.*

Chapter Eleven

EXPLORING THE EVERETT MANSION

"You could have hid an army in there!"

An interesting thing happened at the time of the Eells trial. According to the abstract for the Everett property in court house records, the property on 12th and Elm Streets was owned by Richard Eells until he sold it to Charles Everett on March 29, 1843. (Dr. Eells was arrested in the summer of 1842 and may have needed the money for legal fees. Another possibility might be that Dr. Eells sold it to keep suspicion away from an Underground Railroad station – or to create a new one since his original one was discovered!) The house was built in 1843 by Charles Everett Sr. He was a brother of Edward

Everett who later gave the lengthy address preceding Lincoln's "Gettysburg Address."

Fr. Landry Genosky accompanied us when we explored the Everett mansion in 1968. The investigation was made possible by the graciousness of its owners, Mr. and Mrs. Tom Roberts and the guidance of its managers, Mr. and Mrs. Floyd Aucutt and their son, Gary.

All of our findings were later substantiated by Mrs. C. A. Brandt who lived in the house in the early 1900's. Mrs. Brandt was married in the mansion on June 9, 1923. Her grandfather, James Richardson, former Quincy post master, bought the house in 1891 and was told by the previous owners that it was a "station," hence the unusual construction.

With Mr. and Mrs. Aucutt leading the way we started our tour at the basement level. It is divided into many different rooms. We stopped first at a fireplace or open oven in one room. After checking every inch of it, we couldn't definitively say that it was a hiding place but it could have been.

From there we moved on to the room that was supposed to have had a tunnel to the river. The wood floor of the room had since rotted out and only the two feet by eight feet timbers were left covering the dark sub-basement. Because Mrs. Aucutt thought the open "hole" was much too dangerous for the children of tenants, she had the hole filled in with clinkers from the furnace. The only thing she could tell us about the "hole" was that it was dark as far down as she could see. Mrs. Brandt told us later that her cousin, Harvey Richardson, asked to be lowered through a trap door in the wooden floor below. He saw what appeared to be a fireplace, but this could very possibly have been the entrance to the tunnel. He didn't stay down there very long, Mrs. Brandt related, because it was so scary he fainted and had to be hoisted up limp!

After a short check of the grounds we proceeded through the first and second floors. Because these two floors were occupied by tenants we didn't spend too much time there. From the experience we had gained from checking other houses in the county we knew exactly what we were looking for.

With my husband, Bill, and Mr. Aucutt in the lead and Father Landry, Mrs. Aucutt and me double-checking everything, we pushed on. It wasn't long until Bill called out, "We've found it!" and, indeed they had. In the northwest corner of the house between the second and third floor was a room measuring 15 by 17 by 4 ½ feet that could be entered by a small hole in the floor next to the chimney in an attic on the third floor.

Mrs. Brandt explained that a small boy named Brison Stillwell tried to lower himself into the room to explore it but became hopelessly wedged in the small opening in the floor. With his feet dangling helplessly in the darkness below, a frightened little boy was finally extricated by a helpful coachman. Maybe Father Landry and my husband should thank these two for making the opening larger, because they were able to "shimmy" down into the room. With the aid of an extension light hastily furnished by Mr. Aucutt, they were able to examine the room closely. They said it would have hidden an "army" of fugitives.

It was a dusty but happy group that proceeded on to the cupola of the house. Mr. Aucutt opened the boarded-up windows and we were privileged to see one of the most majestic views of the Mississippi river as is possible to be seen from the east. Then Mr. Aucutt said, "Now that I know what you are looking for, there is another place…."When standing in the cupola you feel as though you are standing on the top of the roof. Actually the floor is about a foot below the roof and by sliding to one side a triangular panel in the wall underneath the windows, one can enter still another hiding place which would make a fourth floor if it were high enough. To further deceive anyone looking for hiding places, the ceiling on the third floor in many places is made up of wide roof boards. When one is standing on the third floor looking up, one would never suspect that they weren't looking at the roof of the house.

We went home that night elated with our findings and in awe of the men who went to such effort and expense to uphold their convictions. There are many more stations in Adams County, but this one is probably the largest and most famous. Regardless of the size, all the "stations" once stood as monuments to a political era in the United States that is unrivaled in romance and intrigue.

My husband said that there had always been rumors that a tunnel ran from here to the river. We believe it is more likely that a tunnel led to the carriage house. These pictures were taken when I toured the home. It has since been razed to make way for a Dairy Queen.

This is a picture of the sub-basement in the Everett home. All that is visible are the beams and the klinkers that were used to fill it in.

This area was camouflaged by a deceptive staircase. The room is four and a half feet high, 17 feet by 15 feet long and wide.

Chapter Twelve

MORE PICKUPS AND PULLS IN QUINCY

Hackberry Farm

This is all that is left of Hackberry Farm-- an Underground Railroad station run by E. A. Humphrey. It was named after the first hackberry tree planted in Adams County. The picture on the right shows one of the old majestic hackberry trees left on the farm.

Willard Keyes built the first cabin in Quincy in 1822.The first circuit court convened in Willard Keyes' cabin and the first steam ferryboat was brought to Quincy by Keyes. Called a strong abolitionist by historians, Willard Keyes signed a petition to have an anti-slavery convention in Illinois in 1837. Then in 1840 Keyes was one of several people who purchased land for the purpose of establishing Mission Institute No. 2. His daughter Mary Ann Keyes married E. A. Humphrey who operated this Underground Railroad station on Mill Creek, the creek that leads from the Mississippi River eventually to Oakland and Mission Institute No. 1.

Mrs. Chris Mast approached me after a speech and said that she grew up in an Underground Railroad station known as Hackberry Farm. Her father, William Pape, was the owner of Pape Mill along Mill Creek and Dyer's Springs, south east of Quincy. He told her the story about the house being a station. Its location and the connections of Keyes to Dr. Nelson support that this could have been a stopping place available on the Underground Railroad route. Those connections are made by the mill located nearby.

The Pape Mill originally built by Samuel Bartholomew.

The Pape Mill was originally built by Sam Bartholomew of the Bartholomew family that was actively involved with the Underground Railroad. The mill was powered by steam, which was very innovative at that time. As reported in an earlier chapter, Sam Bartholomew also owned 180 acres next to the Mississippi River landing known as Mission Institute No. 4 used as a landing place for runaway slaves. Willard Keyes and Sam Bartholomew were closely associated with Dr. Nelson in the planning and execution of Underground Railroad activities.

With her invitation Mrs. Mast accompanied Bill and I and Fr. Landry to Hackberry Farm, named after the first Hackberry tree planted in Adams County. The house was not safe to go in but she explained that there was a hiding place at the top of the stairs behind the closet. This station, like so many, is no longer standing.

Elizabeth Barr House Story

ROOM KEPT AS SECRET

This newspaper clipping resulted in a lifelong friendship with Carolyn Altenhein. After hearing of my research and being quite a history buff herself, Carolyn called me to share this newspaper article that she found in her mother-in-law, Emma Altenhein's scrapbook. Our resulting visit was memorable and we remain close friends. Carolyn is an amateur genealogist, an expert at research and helps me with the accuracy of information. From her I have learned how to research property titles and about such obscure things as 'swamp titles'!

This story is about a man who was a student of Dr. Nelson's at Marion College. Based on what they found in his house it is clear that Nelson's early influence affected his secret life in Quincy.
The story reported on Sept 23, 1913 is as follows:

ROOM KEPT AS SECRET

Hidden Chamber In Old Barr Homestead

Judge Epler Makes Discovery After Conducting Sale of Chattels of Mrs. Elizabeth Barr- What Was It Used For?

It was like listening to a romance of days gone by to listen to an account of the strange discovery made by Judge Carl Epler, as related by the judge himself in the circuit court today. A hidden chamber, the door to which was skillfully concealed and which at first baffled detection, was bared to the world by the judge, and while no lovely maiden prisoner was revealed when the door at last swung open, long shut away from the world, which suggested all sorts of romance and deeds of reckless daring.

It was after the sale of the chattels of the late Mrs. Elizabeth S. Barr, conducted at the old Barr homestead, north of the city on Twenty-fourth street, that the judge made his discovery. The household goods had all been sold and the people who had been attracted to the venue were leaving, when a lady living near the place, who had known of the old time days when Elijah Barr was living, and when his home was one of the finest in Adams county, came to the judge and asked him the startling question:

"What did you find in the secret room?"

A Secret Room

Judge Epler, who loves a mystery, especially if there is a flavor of romance attached to it, was thrilled by the question as is a battle horse at the sound of the trumpet ordering the charge.

"Where is the room?" he quickly demanded.

"In the library, behind the big bookcase, down in the wainscoting," was the reply.

The judge hurried into the library. There, against the wall, stood a towering old bookcase, heavy and massive. It seemed immovable when the judge put his own shoulder to it, and sought to force it away from the wall.

"We must take out the books," he said.

The old volumes were piled up in a large heap upon the table standing before the bookcase. Then again the judge put his shoulder to the corner of the bookcase. At first his effort seemed to be futile as before. Then the book case moved a little, and at last, reluctantly, as if loath to stir from the place where it had been a fixture for years, it was forced away from the wainscot behind.

Door Artfully Concealed.

The judge peered eagerly behind the bookcase. No opening or door seemed visible. But it is always so with true secret chambers. If the door was too apparent, the chamber would not by secret. So the judge continued his search, and at last he found a crack which was straight and seemingly unnecessary. He traced it all around the wainscot. It must be the outline of the door, he decided. But it was immovable. The judge exerted gentle pressure. Then he used force. But the door withstood his effort.

"Let's try a screw driver and pry it open," suggested the lady who had bared the secret of the hidden chamber's presence.

The implement was brought, and the judge inserted the blade in the crack. He pried several times. Then with a creak, which seemed somehow very appropriate under the circumstances, the door swung open a few inches. He pulled the door open. It was indeed artfully concealed. No hinges were visible. To one not knowing the secret, the wall seemed unbroken.

Chamber Is Discovered.

Behind the door was a chamber under an old stairway. It was large enough to enable a person to stand erect *therein, and in it was an old chair of the vintage of the sixties. A receptacle which looked as if it might have been used as a candlestick was also found, and another which might have been used to hold food. The dust of years had settled over the secret room, but that strange elusive odor still remained. Generations had sped since the room had perhaps been used, but the mystery still hung over it, thick and almost impenetrable.*

Downtown, the judge was speaking of his discovery. "Do you know what I think," he said. "I believe that chamber was used as part of the underground railway which existed here in Quincy and out through the county, in the days before the war. As I looked into the chamber, I could almost see the dark-skinned faces of the fugitive slaves who had perhaps sat there, while the sheriffs from over the river were searching for them. And all through these years, it has remained hidden. What a situation!"

A review of records for Marion College in Philadelphia, Missouri shows E. Barr of Allegheny Town, PA was a student there in 1832. It seems reasonable that such a student would join the cause and follow Nelson to Quincy. The Elijah Barr home stood on the ground now owned by Wilbur Mohrman along Holman Creek.

Thomas Ballard Station

And then there was the Thomas Ballard home! I remembered this home being there in my lifetime but when I looked for a picture I had to search for a long time. I think my daughter, Ellen, thought I was making it up until she too, researched this connection.

After one of my lectures, a lady whose name I don't recall, came up to me and told me a story which had been passed down regarding Mrs. Thomas Ballard. The Ballards would hide slaves hidden under a trap door in their kitchen. Once when Missouri slave catchers came demanding the slaves, a noise from a hiding slave's baby was heard, so Mrs. Ballard dropped her good china on the floor, and wailed and moaned over the loss of her best china, all the while declaring she had no hidden slaves in her house. She did this all in an effort to muffle the sounds so the slave catchers wouldn't hear the baby. The guise apparently worked as the slave catchers left without discovering the hidden slaves. This story always impressed upon me the precarious position of the Underground Railroad conductor and his family. It also impressed me as to the quick thinking and ingenuity that it sometimes required to be successful on the Underground Railroad.

It turns out that the Ballard family who operated an Underground Railroad station was active in the antislavery movement in Quincy and their names come up in a variety of places related to anti-slavery.

When George Thompson wrote his book, *Prison Life And Reflections*, he included this extract from a letter to Mother Ballard, who visited him in his Palmyra jail cell.

> *We do not feel to murmur or repine, because we are here confined, and deprived of former privileges. No. It is not for us to say what we will do-where we will go, &c.,-all this we leave with our Father, to direct as will most glorify his name....Although our chain is a very large one, yet it feels very light. I sometimes forget I have any chain on my leg. I hardly think of it. Mother, come and pray with us in our palace. Come and see how we keep house. We are highly favored. We not only have a cook, but our victuals and drink are even brought to us, so that we are not obliged to step a foot out of the door.*
>
> *Yours truly,*
> *George.*

The son of Deacon Jireh Platt tells how he helped a fugitive escape while the Ballard daughters accompanied him in the buggy to disguise the real purpose of the buggy ride. Platt writes that it was the "*pleasantest*" buggy ride he ever took.

In 1843 Deacon Ballard was arrested for harboring a slave. Harriet Holford Vacek lived in the home as a child and remembers the trap door in the kitchen floor. Harriet provided me with the photo of the Ballard house. More activities of Deacon Thomas Ballard are mentioned in the Platt journal entries later in this book. The house was on the southwest corner of 36th & State in the area now known as the Holford subdivision.

Henry Kemp Station

Cellar and porch were used to hide slaves at Kemp home

The Henry S. Kemp home in Ellington Township on what is now Koch's Lane was noted for the Kemp family assistance to the slaves. The slaves were smuggled and cared for in the cellar and on a porch which is the only information I have regarding this station. Henry married Miss Margaret Franklin. In pre-civil war days they built this beautiful home on their land. In front of the home is the Kemp family cemetery which remains as a landmark on the property.

Chapter Thirteen

FUGITIVE FREIGHT FROM QUINCY TO AREA STATIONS

Abolitionist Charles Brown

The old section in back had a hidden room accessed by a tunnel

Recently I came across this home on the official Quincy, IL website, *Quincy Landmarks and Historical Districts*. This house was built for Charles and Samuel Brown about 1850. The back, one story section was built in the 1830s. Apparently the website author of this website was unaware of the anti-slavery activities of Charles and Samuel Brown. Charles and Beulah Cleveland Burns were married in Rockport, Massachusetts. Their eighth child Lucinda was born June 2, 1831. They moved to Quincy, IL in 1834 (around the same time other anti-slavery advocates moved from Rockport, Massachusetts to Quincy, among them Capt. John Burns – possibly related to Beulah

Burns). Charles Brown was among those individuals who attended and signed the roster at the first Illinois Antislavery Convention in Alton in 1837. We also know that many references are made of "Deacon Brown" helping slaves escape to Mendon. We do not know which Brown this refers to, as several "Browns" were involved in Underground Railroad activities. Charles Brown's daughter Lucinda later married Andrew Haines Allison in 1851. Andrew, his brother Harmon, and father William were active on the Underground Railroad in McDonough County, Illinois. The Allison children had a private teacher because of the family's abolitionist position caused such animosity in the community. The Allison family did not talk about their activities until many years later.

Bill and I knew Charles Brown was an abolitionist because he signed the petition for an Anti-slavery convention to be held in Alton in 1837. We also knew that the house on North 12th St. was built by Charles Brown in the 1830s. Recently I called Linda Boden, present owner of the house and asked her if there were any hiding places in the house. She replied that indeed there was. Her sons found it and had great fun sliding in and out of the small crawl space under the summer kitchen. The crawl space led to a secret room under the kitchen. It was completely plastered and the only entrance was through that crawl space.

Wilbur Seibert wrote a most comprehensive book on the Underground Railroad in the 1890s. He obtained much of his information by writing letters to descendents of persons he knew to be connected with the Underground Railroad, asking each of them the same series of questions. The following is a copy of a letter written to W.H. Siebert in response to questions about the Underground Railroad. In it the writer refers to a family by the name of "Ellison". I believe the family name was really "Allison", the family that Lucinda Brown married into. The writer has other spelling errors and likely only knew the family name as he heard it orally. This personal account gives of a glimpse of the daring adventures of these people involved in the Underground Railroad:

Galena, Ill
March 6th, 1896

Mr. W. H. Siebert
Cambridge, Mass

Dear Sir,

Yours of the 2nd is rec'd & reply would say 1st that I lived in Mendon, Adams, Co. Ill from 1834 to 1856-My father was one of the practical Abolitionists- Mendon being the first station from Quincy- here the start was made.

My Elder brother, Henry, guided many a runaway to the next station which was Round Prairie about 25 miles from Mendon this was usually the 1st nights trip- the next station was about 3 or 4 miles from Macomb- in McDonough Co- Known as Ellisons's. Mr. E had two sons & two daughters all very nice kind hospitable people their home was a refuge for all who were fleeing from Oppression- & they had a great faculty for keeping dark & no one would think they knew anything about what was going on- thus far on the line - have traveled- & then so far as I was concerned the U G – R R ran into the ground again.

2nd The period of activity of the Road was I should think between 1840 & 1848-

3rd Quincy is about 16 miles from Mendon. Sometimes word would be sent by some safe person coming that way or a special Messenger to let us know when travelers would be along & where to meet them- if all was quiet on the road & no pursuers had been seen & the runaways were all men- we would meet them with fresh horses which they would mount & be off in a minute & sometimes if the pursuit was hot we had to hide them away- in the cornfields or barns, & keep them until it was thought safe to go on & though we had some narrow escapes I do not know of a single slave who was captured & taken back to slavery-

I remember one bright mulatto slave whose name was George who made 4 trips to Canada & back to Missouri- the first time he went to try to get his wife but not successfully, he brought with two or three other slaves & every time he went back to Mo he brought some one with him- I saw him several times on three different trips & fed him in the cornfield when they were hot after him.

The hatred of the Missourians toward the abolitionists in Mendon was intense frequently often some slaves had taken flight for Canada some twenty or thirty mounted men fully armed would prowl around the neighborhood- threatening to burn barns stacks & we have to watch the Barns & Premises of those farmers who were thus threatened- we boys rather liked the sport we were oftened (sic) dammed with hard words but never with anything more serious than that-

Dr. Eel(l) s of Quincy had incurred the _____ of some people of Mo- & they succeeded in obtaining a requisition from the Gov of Illinois to arrest & take him to that State- which of course would have resulted in his being lynched- one of the friends got wind of it & got him out of the way- I think it was one of the coldest nights I ever knew I was called out of bed about 11 o'clock at night- & found O. K. Van Dorn of Quincy (one of the most active & fearless men I ever knew) & Dr. Eel(l)s they had just heard of the requisition & were getting out of the way in haste- I put up their horses & put in a fresh one & the next day they were safe at Elison's where he was perfectly safe- & where he remained until the requisition was withdrawn as having unadvisedly granted.

On another occasion I was called up about midnight during a fearful thunder storm- to put up a horse for a traveler- when within about 2 miles of our place they had been attacked by a party of negro hunters- The wagon containing the slaves was some distance in the rear & two men in a buggy ahead- a slash or flashes of lightning revealed the condition of things & Mr. Van Dorn's buggy was fired upon- the people in the wagon behind took refuge in a cornfield and the wagon turned round & went back to Quincy-

I put the horses in the stable that night (by the way the horse belonged to Dr. Eells) and he seemed to be all right- In the morning I led him out of the stable & he seemed to want to roll- he lay down stretched himself out & was dead in two minutes- upon examination I found he had been shot with a bullet through the groin.

I presume you have a better list of the men of Quincy who were prominent in this matter- I can remember Dr. Nelson from 1834 have often heard him preach on the Prophesies & he was sometimes a guest at my Father's house-

I knew Mr. Work of Burr, Work & Thompson who were incarcerated in the State Prison at Jefferson City for going into Missouri to help slaves to regain their liberty. Mr. Work was My Sunday School Teacher- & a very good man but I think he went too far, he should not have crossed the river-

I am sorry that I can not give you more valuable information with regard to this history- very few who took an active part in it survive.

John & Mr. Van Dorn, Edward Lunur, Dr. E(e)lls- Mellen & others in Quincy- Col Chittenden- Levi Stillman- Erastus Benton – Jirah(sic) Platt- N. Clark- Weed- E Fowler of Mendon- all are gone.

S. O. Stillman

The horse mentioned was known as White Lightning because of his remarkable speed such that pursuers were unable to keep up and re-capture the fugitives.

Enoch Platt, in his journal reported in a later chapter, refers to a conductor as Mr. A. Could Mr. A. have been Mr. Allison receiving the "freight" on the "train"? We may never know, but it certainly seems plausible.

Stillman Station

Original homestead of Levi Stillman. It was the longtime homeplace of Sydney Wright family, located at the current site of Duanne Cramm home. Photos courtesy of Barb DeWeese.

Original homestead of Levi Stillman, located northeast of Mendon, Illinois, showing barns and stable in back where White Lightning died.

Chapter Fourteen

PLATTS OF MENDON: DARING CONDUCTORS ON THE LINE

Hazel thicket hiding place behind Jireh Platt's house as seen today

Twelve miles north of Quincy a community was developing that was made up of another courageous group of citizens opposed to slavery. First called Fairfield, later renamed Mendon, this community began by establishing a Congregational church and building farm homes in the area that could be used to usher runaway slaves to freedom. In *Past and Present of the City of Quincy and Adams County, Illinois* Mendon is described this way:

> *Mendon helped to make real history in the days of the UGRR. It was from an early day, a well-known station, many of its best men being faithful agents of the company. In the days of Dr. Nelson and until the result of the Civil War put an end to traffic in human beings, the route via Mendon to Freedom was*

a trunk line, in constant use. If the escaping slave was Posted beforehand and had the right start Quincy, Mendon, Plymouth, Galesburg etc., all receiving stations never failed of the desired result. No one was ever known to be captured and returned to slavery if he had a through ticket on this route. Mendon was known as an abolitionist town and prices were set for the capture and delivery in Missouri of certain of its citizens.

The reason for such success lies in the efforts of one remarkable family – that of Deacon Jireh Platt and his wife Sarah Duncan Platt.

Deacon Jireh Platt

Sarah Duncan Platt

Back left - Luther Hart Platt (1835-1896)

Back right - Jeremiah Evarts Platt (1833 – 1899)

Front left - Henry Dutton Platt (1823-1903)

Front right - Enoch Platt (1825 – 1891)

Photos provided by Luther Platt's great granddaughter Zona Platt Galle.

The following picture and story were published in the November 26, 1931 *Mendon Dispatch Times*:

Memorial of Trying Times in Nation.

"Mendon's Underground Railroad Station"

Scene of Stirring Events in Slave Days, Is Included in Historical Tour of State

Old House Hides Many Secrets

Landmark on Route 36 Has Secret Recesses In Its Walls -----

In seeking for scenes of interest in Illinois, to be pictured in a book to attract tourists and show them places where history was made, the Illinois Chamber of Commerce has secured a photograph of that old, abandoned, weather beaten home, one mile east of Mendon on Route 36, once a station on the "underground railroad".

Motorists of this generation who dash past the old house, without a thought of its history, may wonder what the underground railroad was. They know about the Burlington which has a branch line hard by, or the Wabash tracks they see at Clayton, but the underground railroad is puzzling indeed. Yet there was a time in history when the term was a household word. Traffic on the underground –illicit traffic it was— commanded public attention as liquor running does now.

Slip back along the road of years for nearly a hundred milestones. Go back when the house was new, to the time when Deacon Jireh Platt damned the slave owners in Missouri with every nail he drove into its clapboard roof and the operation of the underground railroad was big news.

Old, old homes hide many stories they never tell. Deacon Platt's new mansion in the '30's, was the first station on the underground railroad out of Quincy. For the underground railroad was organized and fanatically maintained exclusively to handle ivory-black ivory, a term used to denote the slaves across the Mississippi. There were many of these black men and women in bondage there-working in the corn lands of Marion County, the hemp fields of Lewis. In and near Mendon and in many other Illinois communities there were secret, well organized groups of Abolitionists sworn to assist these Negroes to become free. They planned to bring the Negroes into Illinois and secretly pass them from one station to another until they reached Canada, where they would become freemen under an alien flag. It was an illicit program and secrecy was needed to evade the laws. Negroes were moved at night, when darkness created a pall safe as moving underground- hence the term.

Joseph B. Frisbie, postmaster at Mendon, says that his father, J. B. Frisbie, was a "conductor on the underground." Men who helped the Negroes escape were called conductors. He names other Mendon citizens prominent in the '30's, who were either active conductors or who gave moral and financial support to the "underground". He says his father often told him how the men of the underground evaded the Missourians who came searching for their escaped Negroes.

Three Marion county men came riding up one day when father was digging potatoes in the garden," he said. "With rawhide boots clattering over the clods, jean pants and slouch hats, they, were a hard-looking trio. 'We want our niggers and we are gwine to git 'em,' one cried.

'If you don't skeedaddle almighty quick I'll brain you with the potato fork,' Father Frisbie replied. His eyes were burning and he started after them. They skeedaddled." The old deserted house's walls may have echoed to the curses of this same trio, for it is altogether probable that they knew it was an underground station and doubtless they stopped to ask Deacon Platt about their "cattle."

What strange and marvelous stories the old house might tell if only its strong walnut timbers were as resonant as they are enduring. They have trembled under the fervor of Deacon Platt's fanatical prayer, "O Lord, how long, how long," when he poured out in supplication his curses of that iniquitous system that made one man the property of another. Those walls have been warmed by the touch of the black flesh lying hidden in secret nooks that are there today-hidden niches made to safely shelter the cowering, cramped passengers for the underground. In the bitter war days they echoed to the deacon's triumphant song when in bursts of ecstasy he shouted;

"mine eyes have seen the glory of the coming of the Lord. . . as He died to make men holy let us die to make men free."

The old house, like the terrain about it, is vastly different from what it was a hundred years ago. Lilacs still bloom there and soon the old locust trees will hum with bees, as a hundred years ago. The tall cedars that overshadow its crumbling chimney were saplings then. The cleared farm lands about it were dense with oak and walnut, the ravine that runs almost to the yard was thick with sumac and hazel, a jungle where many a black man slipped away to safety when the pursuers were nearing the door. Then a slave crept away into the corn and was hidden there while he was waiting to be transported to another underground station.

There are four rooms on the first floor and four on the second. An attic is above the upper rooms and in the center of the building is a huge square rock chimney with a great oven opening into the kitchen and two Dutch ovens beside it. A section of the kitchen wall has fallen away, revealing a space back of the chimney that well may have been a hiding place for a slave. He would have been cramped in that space, but the chimney rocks would have kept him warm through the bitterest night. No slave hunter could have found this hiding place unless all the boards were removed, and Deacon Jireh Platt was not the man to let a Missourian beat a tattoo on his kitchen walls.

It is not improbable that the Rev. David Nelson, a famous Abolitionist of the pre-war period, met his comrades of the underground there and the old house trembled when his mighty preaching voice implored God to aid the bondsmen and confound their owners. It was in 1836 that David Nelson, fleeing from the slave advocates of Marion County, sought safety in Quincy. Strange, indeed, if he did not seek the companionship of his co-workers in Mendon. . .

This is a photo of the Frisbie house in Mendon where Father Frisbie threatened to stab the Missourians with a potato fork if they didn't leave.

Joseph Frisbie was born in Branford, Connecticut and came to Mendon with his family on June 5, 1837. If his name sounds like a familiar toy it is because he was no doubt related to the Frisbie family that ran the Frisbie Pie Co. from Branford, Connecticut. The game of throwing the Frisbie Pie tins originated the game of Frisbie (later trademarked as Frisbee) as we know it today, when college students would warn bystanders to watch out by yelling "Frisbie"! A plastic version was created by former WWII pilots Walter Frederick Morrison and Warren Franscioni of California. In 1958 Wham-O bought the rights to the toy and trademarked the name Frisbee. Although named after them, the Frisbie family did not gain from this business.

His descendents report that, as a conductor on the Underground Railroad, Joseph Frisbie's life was threatened on several occasions by Missouri slave owners.

Both Frisbie and Jireh Platt worked together in Mendon, Illinois as conductors on the Underground Railroad. Dr. David Nelson visited the Jireh Platt home on a number of occasions. The Platt's were honored by the visits from the influential preacher and fellow anti-slavery activist. Jireh Platt was believed to be the only station-master in this area that kept a diary of slaves, including names and numbers, who went through his station. This blue book was last known to be in possession of one of his sons in Nebraska. When Wilbur H. Siebert wrote his comprehensive book, *The Underground Railroad*, first published in 1898, he quoted excerpts from Platt's diary. Letters to Mr. Siebert, written by Deacon Platt's sons J.E. Platt and H. D. Platt in 1896 describe harrowing adventures experienced by these two brothers when they were quite young. They wrote their stories down as responses to questions presented by Mr. Seibert. Their stories were summarized but not detailed in Siebert's book. Because their story is so powerful in their own words and pertinent to Underground Railroad story in the area, these personal accounts of what the Platt boys experienced as children and teenagers demonstrates not only the high drama but the risk and sacrifice; not just by the adult males but the women and children as well.

Their account of personal experiences told in their own words is more powerful than any attempt that might be made here to retell it. (The personal accounts quoted in this book by Platt's and others often refer to people by a first initial. We can only assume the full name of the person referenced.)

These first quotes are excerpts from letters typewritten to Mr. Seibert and were responses to specific questions. I do not have the exact questions, but they can be assumed by the responses.

Here are some of the excerpts written by Rev. H. D. Platt:

> *(1) Route, from Quincy & vicinity to the N. E. toward Chicago. I was intimately acquainted with the line for 45 miles, through (or near) Mendon to Plymouth or Augusta, Hancock Co. In a general way, I know that beyond these last two points, it passed thro' or near Macomb, Farmington & Galesburg.*
>
> *Quincy on the Mississippi, was a noted Station- with "Keepers", and Conductors, Dr. Eels, Rasselas Sartle, J.C. and William Van Dorn and others less noted.*
>
> *Two miles E. of the public square of Quincy, was Mission Institute, (a school for the education of Missionaries), whose students and villages near were nearly all ready to help in any way. I was a student there constantly from December '41 to May '47. Few fugitives stopped there – prominent conductors were Alanson Work, Burr, George Thompson, Lewis Andrews,*

John Rudyard, George and Andrew Hunter, Edward Griffin, William Mellen and myself. A couple of miles further East were Deacon Ballard, Mr. Safford, and Deacon Brown – all farmers."

Mendon, 15 miles Northeast of Quincy, was a very prominent Station – not so much the village itself as the farms in the vicinity. As "Keepers", or Conductors, or both, were Erastus Benton, Levi Stillman, Nathan Clark, Darwin Bartholomew, William Battell, Deacon L.A. Weed, Deacon Jireh Platt and Sons: & some others.

Augusta, where Strong Austin and others were Keepers and conductors.

Plymouth, was 4 miles North of Augusta, with L.A. Cook, and ____Adkins, & sons, as Keepers and Conductors. Plymouth received and forwarded nearly all who passed that way. In dangerous times, detours were surveyed and followed for safety. These Stations were not always taken in a trip. Sometimes the trip would be made, in one drive, 45 miles, from Quincy to Plymouth or the fugitives might not touch Quincy, but pass directly through the neighborhood to the East of there. There was another Route from Alton, Ill. & a little South of there, of which I knew but little, nor can I give the names of Keepers and Conductors.

I do not know how the fugitives knew where to find their nearest friends and helpers. How did the Negroes learn 1000 things? I think that after the Burr, Work, and Thompson affair, no effort was directly made to entice them away. They all knew "The Method of Operation" was imply to receive, hide, feed, & guide or transport to another Station. They were taken on foot, on horseback, in buggy or carriage, in open or covered wagon, any way which promised at the time most real speed and safety, mostly by night. But when completely hidden disguised in open day. Sometimes on the principal roads, but often through the woods by infrequented bridle paths.

The "members", in a community, all knew each other thoroughly – and they each knew the members, & their locations, at the next Station. Each one knew some neighbor, who could be trusted in an emergency, and who would not be suspected of Sympathy with the cause. Such furnished good places for hiding.

There was no special "System of Communication" – No cipher language – very little letter correspondence. The communication was mostly personal and verbal. The Keeper was never startled by a rap at his side door at any unseasonable hour, and was always ready. There were some understood signals, and forms of expression.

Late in 1842, or early in 1843, Dr. Eells of Quincy started for Mendon with a fugitive slave in his one-horse buggy. Near Mission Institute, on leaving the open prairie, coming to where the road was fenced on both sides, he was confronted by several slave hunters, from Missouri. He turned S. instead of N. – drove like Jehu, passed out of their sight, sent his passenger into a cornfield, drove rapidly back home, put up his fleet mare, (which the Missourians christened "White Lightning,") and was in bed and apparently fast asleep before the hunters got there. They found an old pair of trousers, which were identified as belonging to the Negro. The Negro got away, but the Dr. E's residence was surrounded and watched, he escaped through the backyard and a Barber's Shop on the next street, took passage on the U.G.R.R. to "Father Dobbin's" in McDonough Co., where he was in hiding for a long time.

In the fall of 1845, Dea. Brown, rode horseback & piloted 4 Stalwart fugitive men from his farm E. of Quincy, to Dea. Jireh Platt (my father) near Mendon. They had gone through the forests and by unfrequented roads till they came into the main road, ¼ of a mile west of father's house. Dea. Brown started for home on the main road at 3 a.m. and about daylight met 4 armed men, on horseback, who did not molest him. These hunters saw the track of the big coarse shoes, one of which had the sole worn off at the toe and leaving at every step the point of a big toe in the dust. They followed the tracks into our front gate. Father had gone to the village to get promises of help, if it should be needed. He had hurried the slaves down into the pasture into the hazle [sic] -thicket so dense that you might pass within a yard of a man and not see him. Mother and the younger children only were in the house, when the hunters came and declared the "niggers" were there, and they w' d search the house. When asked for their Authority, they pointed to their shotguns and two searched inside, while the other two stood guard outside. Finding no one, they galloped down through the pasture in a path not 40 feet from their "Niggers", to some old building ½ mile away, at an old camp-meeting ground. The rewards offered were very large, and in a short time 200 men or more, were searching the farm. To tell how the ex-slaves were fed, and finally removed 1 ½ miles to the premises of a queer old man, whom no one would think of suspecting, where they were concealed for a few weeks, till the hunters had given up the chase, and then were carefully forwarded to Canada, would require a volume to give details. The pursuers never could see how it was done!

Sometime in the Autumn of '44 or '45, Andrew Hunter took nine fugitives, men, women and children, in a farm wagon, by night, on a road 5 miles east of the usual road to Mendon. Rasselas Sartle and another conductor, with Dr. Eells' "White Lightning" and buggy, were to keep some distance ahead of Hunter's team to see if the road was clear. About 2 ½ miles S.E. of Mendon, in a road fenced on both sides, a dozen men rose out of the fence corners and began firing on them. The mare was shot and ran against the fence and over turned the buggy. Sartle rose to his full height and shouted, "Is this the way you treat gentlemen traveling peaceably along the highway?" and they slunk back into a fence corner again. One of Hunter's horses had balked in a mud hold and refused to pull. Hearing the guns, the darkies scattered like quails into Mr. Bartholomew's cornfield and next morning one of them found Mr. B. and they were cared for. Mr. Sartle and his friend drove on to the Mendon Hotel, and finding it full of men from Missouri went on to Levi Stillman's for the rest of the night. In the A.M. the beautiful fleet, plucky "White Lightning" was dead. She deserved a Monument. After discharging his live freight, Andrew Hunter drove home. In the morning 50 men were searching in that region for those 9 fugitives and did not find them.

A little before this time, one Jerry, a very large strong slave, swam the Mississippi, a little below Quincy, and after drying his clothes in the sunshine, he appeared at Mission Institute at dusk, and asked for food. He carried nothing but a green hickory cane, as large as a baseball bat. He was concealed and fed, and the next night, Lewis Andrews walked with him to a dark ravine, 3 miles South of Mendon, where I met him, as agreed on, at 1 a.m., I having gone on horseback, & managed with another party to receive him at 3 a.m. As I left he bro't down that heavy stick with great force, and hissed thro' his teeth, "They don't cotch this chile alive!" I learned from a white man from Mo., who knew him well, that he had been offered his freedom if he would go thro' to Canada, on the U.G,R.R. and report all names & places. His reply was, "I likes my freedom mighty well, but I scorns de act." He was too daring and careless, but got through.

A black "Baptist Preacher", who ran away 3 days before, was handed over to me, just long enough to make traveling dangerous, I put on a work suit, got a team and farm wagon, covered the preacher with enough hay for 2 or 3 days rations for the horses, and drove quietly to Mendon, with him, to Erastus Benton's. It seemed the safest plan just then.

Another big stout fellow I took from Dea. Ballard's, in Mr. Safford's nice two-seated carriage. He wore bonnet, shawl, & a spread over his knees, and two of the Deacon's daughters went along to complete the blind. It was the pleasantest trip I ever took to Mendon!

Edward Griffin and Mary Terrell, one winter's day took a fugitive from Mission Institute to Plymouth, under the seat of a one-horse open buggy, with his head and shoulders in a trunk that fitted nicely behind the seat, the back wall of the trunk having been sawed out sufficiently for the purpose. A warm buffalo robe concealed everything in front of the seat.

In 1850 my oldest brother and I took a young man and woman, from father's farm to Strong Austin's at Augusta, nearly 30 miles, one night, all on horseback, taking the four best horses on the place. The two darkies rode the horses that followed us home the next morning.

I make now a few quotations from a sort of diary and farm record of my father's, which came into my hands at his death. There was a "blue book", which had vastly more in it, and some very exciting records.

"May 19, 1848. *Hannah Coger arrived on the U.G. Railroad, "the last $100.00 for freedom she was to pay to Thomas Anderson Palmyra, Missouri – the track is kept bright, it being the 3rd time occupied since the 1st of April."*

November 17, '48. *"John Buckner arrived in a car- had been "acquainted with Thornton and others that have traveled this way." Had been sold to a trade, and was to start South Next Monday morning. He had spent most of the time for a week in sawing off his chain with an old casa-knife." (Here follows a cut of the knife) (no date, but between September 5 and September 14, 1849.) "It is rumored that John escaped, not long since from the [steamer] Kate Kearniey." December 5 (year not given) within a month past, there has been a great stir, advertising, telegraphing, and hunting property from Missouri. Oh, what a spectacle! Eleven pieces of property, walking in Indian file, armed and equipped facing the North Star! $3000.00 offered for their apprehension, after they were safe in Canada! The hunters say they must have gone from Mendon to Jacksonville on a new track.*

July 1, 1854 – *Henry Edwards took passage on the U.G. Railroad, for fear of being sent South, report says. From St. Louis, and within a few weeks past, William crossed the Mississippi river in a dugout paddling with a shingle-board after having been shot at. Also one other, who had been taken to Pike County Jail, and the sheriff commanded them to let him go. He had a bullet hole through his left arm.*

November 9, '54. *Negro hoax stories have been very high in the market for a week past.*

November 2 ' 57. *Freedom progressing. Within a few weeks 10 tickets have been disposed of at the U.R. Depot and among the passengers were Harrison, slave of the Free State Governor of Missouri, Caroline, Bonaparte and Stephen. I was informed last fall by neighbor Metcalf, that one of his old Kentucky friends had lost 5.*

October, 1859. *U.G.R.R. Conductor reported the passage of 5 who were considered very valuable pieces of Ebony, all designated by names, such as John Brooks, Daniel Brooks,*

Mason Bushrod, Silvester Lucket and Hanson Ganes. Have understood also that 3 others were ticketed about mid-summer. This is the last record of the sort in the book. These are among the least thrilling of many which I know occurred.

A great number, first and last, took passage on that route, and my father assured me that only one of them all was ever recaptured, and that one, at or on high bridge over Crooked Creek, several miles Northeast from Plymouth. There was no other crossing for vehicles for miles either side of the bridge. A new route had to be planned from Plymouth. I think no arrest or fine was put upon any Keeper or Conductor along that line, except in case of Dr. Eels of Quincy, which, considering the business done, was very remarkable.

I must mention two remarkable cases on the route from Alton, Illinois, where Reverend E. P. Lovejoy was martyred in 1838. In 1853 or 1854, I think, a fugitive came to some colored people living in the woods, on Wood River, having an iron collar on his neck. It was of iron one inch wide, and between 1/8 and ¼ inch thick, hinged on one side and riveted on the other. It had 3 prongs of heavy iron, equal distance from each other riveted to the collar. These prongs were perhaps 12 inches long, and at the end of each a bell had been attached. The negro had crossed the Mississippi, somehow, had twisted off those bells, and reported to those free darkies. Friends took him to a blacksmith shop where they cut the rivets of the collar, with a cold chisel on the Anvil! I have seen and handled that heavy iron collar. It is now (or at least 10 years ago it was) in the possession of Mr. Michael Brown, of Brighton, Illinois, a good Christian man of some 84 years of age.

Our curiosity piqued, Bill and I and Fr. Landry traveled to Brighton to check it out. A Quincy College history student originally from Brighton, Joe Dickman, invited us to Brighton to explore the area as it was a hub of the Underground Railroad. We checked out these homes and then discussed the area's Underground Railroad connections over a generous meal prepared for us by Joe Dickman's mother.

The Michael Brown house in Brighton-- Originally built by his ancestor, a Dr. Brown, who was an active abolitionist believed to be the person who sawed off the iron collar.

An Underground Railroad station near the Brown home was torn down and a new home built on the foundation.

This house near the Michael Brown home had a tunnel out of the basement under the street to another home across the street. The family used the hole to put a sump pump in it.

The Platt letter continues:

Later, perhaps in '57 or thereabouts, one Smith, a colored man, was taking several fugitives in a wagon with a white cover, a little east of Chesterfield, 30 miles or more Northwest of Alton, when a group of men, armed, ordered him to halt, that they might search his wagon. He turned out into the prairie toward an open grove, with thick hazel [sic] bush around it, and drove on full run, till the harness reins were shot off close to his hands, and the horses ran into the brush, and all the darkies got out and hid and were not found. The pursuers caught the tired horses, and brought them to the house and Dea. Josiah Whipple, & were about to tie them there, when the Deacon forbade them and frightened them by telling them they were liable to arrest as horse-thieves! The hunters did not catch the slaves, nor identify Smith.

Jireh Platt born at North Milford (Orange) Ct. 1798, removed to Plymouth Ct. to care for himself at 10 years of age. Had hard time, with little schooling, as "boy of all work" with a crusty old couple till 14- Served apprenticeship & worked as *house-joiner till he was 24 – Married Sarah Dutton in 1822- Worked for Eli & Henry Terry, clock manufacturers till 1833. Removed to a farm near Mendon, Ill. where he died in 1870 aged 72. He acquired most of his education after his marriage. He had 4 sons & 3 only (1896) survive. He became a Christian soon after his marriage, & was an earnest faithful member of the church to the last, & a Deacon in the Congregational church at Mendon for his last 35 years. Three of his sons became Congregational ministers. He was frugal, industrious, benevolent, honest, & thoroughly conscientious- One of the first to espouse the Temperance cause- one of the earliest of the Anti-Slavery men, when it cost something to be an "Abolitionist" – Was very active in his Service on the "Under Ground Rail Road," in which he was both shrewd & fearless. Was subjected to many annoyances, as a friend of the Slave, and at one time a reward of $1000.00 was offered for him delivered in Mo. "Dead or Alive" !*

He ended his life in peace, rejoicing in "the consciousness that he had been on the right side, in all the great practical questions which have agitated Society." The funeral address was on "The Faithful Soldier." & all the great crowd felt that it was a fitting topic.

It was very affecting, after all the "White folks" had looked at the familiar face, to see two Freedmen, lean over the coffin, & look reverently & lovingly on one known to be eminently a friend of their race.

H. D. Platt
Franklin Nebr.
March 20, 1896

The following are more excerpts written on March 28, 1896, as answers to questions by J. E. Platt:

Mr. W. H. Seibert
Cambridge, Mass.
Dear Sir,

In answer to your request for information in reference to the Underground Railroad I will make the following statements.

1. *The route of the road from Quincy Illinois to Chicago, lay through Mendon, Plymouth, Macomb, and Gaylesburg,.(sic) on to Chicago. My Fathers house was at Mendon the first station from Quincy. The second lay 30 miles N.E. of Plymouth, and the station Keepers were Marcus Cook and Mr. Adkins, I am not acquainted with names farther on,*
2. *About 1840 to 1860.*
3. *Runaways crossing the river near Quincy somehow found friends, who would escort them to some of the Conductors, of which there were several, A Mr. Van Dorn being a prominent one, and Mission Institute two miles east of Quincy was full of them. Some of those Conductors would lead them in almost every conceivable way, usually in the night to my Fathers, who by some member of the family, or a neighbor, would escort them to Plymouth the following night. Sometimes a carriage would drive into my Fathers barn in the day time with a colored man dressed up in fine clothes, and a Stove pipe hat, for a driver, with the conductor on the back seat. Sometimes a person with a lady's cloak, hood and veil on would alight from the back seat of a carriage, with the conductor driving. Fathers barn no the haymow used to be the place for refreshment and retiring. In the summer time, the hazel thicket in the pasture was used for the same purpose.*
4. *One night in Aug. of 1843 when I was a ten year old boy, a man came to my fathers escorting four strong hearty*

Negroes, who had walked all the way from Quincy. Father gave them something to eat, then took them to the hazel thicket. Their pursuers were so close behind them on horseback that the Quincy conductor met them a quarter of a mile from our house on his return trip.

The hunters stopped at the Mendon Hotel a mile further on, and early in the morning were again on the road looking for tracks. It was very dusty. One of the colored men had a shoe a little too short, and he had cut off the toe of it, and as he walked in the road, his longest toe made a mark in the dust. His master knew that mark right well, and tracked it to our gate, and not farther. He was positively certain that his four colored men, worth $1000 apiece were upon our premises, and he was determined to catch them. He asked permission to search the house, which was granted after which the party mounted their horses and rode down through the pasture within a stones throw of where his darkies were concealed.

That night they were spirited away somewhere and somehow, the particulars of which I never learned.

That master hired some fifty men to help him, and they hunted night and day for two weeks, watched all the roads, and could not understand why they could not find them, hence the name Underground R.R. They watched our place with great vigilance, blacked up a white man, and sent him there as a runaway slave, caught our chickens, to draw father out at night. Whet their knives on our front fence, and called out to us to be up and saying our prayers for we had but three minutes to live. They caught me {Jeremiah Evarts Platt} one day about a ½ mile from home and a dozen of them surrounded me and threatened to shoot me, and hang me, and cut my throat from ear to ear if I didn't not tell them were the Negroes were.

It was well that I did not know where they were at that time, for I thought surely they intended to kill me, but they got nothing out of me. After two weeks incessant search the master returned to Missouri and offered $1000 for fathers head, dead or alive, and five hundred dollars for my older brother's head. A singular fact connected with this case is that about nine years ago in Comanche County Kansas I organized a Sunday School in the private house of that very man's son, who had *been born since the war, and had made a new home in Kansas. I did not tell him that his father once offered $1000, for my father's head.*

I could spend a whole day in writing up remarkable incidents, but time will not permit. One man came to our house with a bullet hole through his arm, which his master had shot so closely was he pursued. A runaway was being taken to the house of Erastus Benton, another Mendon Conductor, and they were so closely pursued that the horse was shot which drew the vehicle in which the slave was riding, but they escaped through a corn field and were not captured.

When about 14 years of age, my father started me off on horseback at nine o'clock one evening, with a colored man on another horse by my side. We made the thirty mile trip all night and I led the horse home the next day. When I was about 17 years old, eleven slaves came along at one time some of them women. We put them into two tightly covered wagons, and I drove one of the teams. It was not practicable to stop at the Plymouth Station, so we had to drive to the next sixty miles from home, took the day time for the last thirty miles. Keeping the darkies well covered with hay in the wagon body. Did not reach home until the fourth day, and you can well imagine that our folks were pretty well frightened about us. I suppose that nearly one hundred slaves passed the Mendon Station of the Underground R.R. and I never heard of but one being captured. That was near McComb, McDonough County Illinois.

Father's given name was Jireh. He was born at Plymouth, Conn. Litchfield County in 1798. Married Sarah Dutton, brought up seven children, I was the fifth. He moved to Mendon, Illinois six months after my birth in 1833. Bought a farm one mile west of Mendon, the first farm he looked at, and spent the rest of his life on that farm, dying in 1870, leaving in his will, $1000, to each of three Missionary societies, and $1000, to each of his five living children. He was Deacon in the Mendon County Church from by babyhood until his death. So many people are dead, and others scattered...A Man by the name of Strong Austin used to be Conductor, living at Augusta, Hancock County Illinois five miles south of Plymouth, I took a Passenger to his house. He died many years since.

Cordially Yours,
J. E. Platt

The previous quotations are from letters written by two Platt brothers in 1898 in response to questions by Wilbur Siebert who wrote the most comprehensive research on the Underground Railroad entitled *The Underground Railroad From Slavery To Freedom.* Another son, Enoch Platt, wrote an extensive journal that is now in the possession of the Kansas Historical Library. Copies of the journal were given to me by Jireh Platt's descendent, Zona Platt Galle. He begins his journal with an obvious error in the dates as he writes that the route from Quincy to Chicago began 1845. I don't know why he used the year 1845 except that he wrote his journal later in life and made a mistake. His own journal gives stories that pre-date 1845. I cannot account for the error. The stories he tells, however, are wonderful recollections of authentic stories as he lived them:

> *The route from Quincy to Chicago was organized about 1845. My earliest recollections of it were, seeing four strangers ride up to our house very early one summer morning. They stated that they were hunting stolen horses, and after making inquiries rode away.*
>
> *In a few moments they returned and said, "We might just as well tell our real business. Four slaves ran away from Missouri night before last. We have tracked them to the fence in front of your house; can track them no farther; we know they are here and are going to have them."*
>
> *Their friendly advice was to quietly give them up and save farther trouble.*
>
> *When questioned about the tracks, they said that one of them had a shoe too short for his foot. He had cut open the end so that every track made with that foot, his big toe left a mark in the dust. A fifth person was with them when they came but had gone back. The tracks were fresh and must have been made that morning. This was all true. The fugitives were at that time secreted in a little thicket just a quarter of a mile away and from their hiding place could see their masters at the house, and my mother gave them leave to search the house. I can well remember the wonder with which we children saw those strange men search the house.*

Not finding their missing property in the house they began a search of the farm, and every place near where they thought it possible for them to be secreted. This hunt continued three weeks, not less than fifty different men were engaged in it, many of them our neighbors, who were induced to engage in it by the hope of reward, and by their hatred of "the nigger." Repeatedly some of the hunters were within a few steps of the fugitives, and a number of times they saw and recognized their old masters.

Day after day, men with guns on their shoulders, and dirks or bowie knives in their pockets or belts, might have been seen riding in every direction through the "Deacon's timber," with upturned faces rising into every tree top; or carefully looking into every ravine and thicket, eagerly watching if possibly they might find "a nigger loose." During that hunt there was hardly a night that they did not make some disturbance around the house; sometimes firing guns; sometimes going to the chicken roost, catching some of the chickens and making them squawk. One night a crowd of them gathered around the house, and shouted to us to "Be up and saying your prayers for you hain't got but fifteen minutes to live," at the same time noisily whetting their knives on the fence. I think that the excitement against any man who would "help steal niggers" was so intense that, if they could have got my Father into their hands at night, he would have been murdered. But with daylight their courage and bluster passed away, and they either kept at a respectful distance, or treated him with outward respect. During that hunt a lamp or candle was rarely lighted in our house. To encourage the family some of whom were very much frightened, Father told us that is there was not light in the house there was no danger of their break in, unless they had a light with them so that they could see what they were doing after they got in. In those days, he advocated in a general sort of way, the principles of the "Peace Society," and was called a "Peace man," but in my opinion if one of those hunters had broken into the house, he would have run a great risk of going out "a piece of a man."

This much I know. The floor in the front hall was each night taken up; the ax and crowbar were brought in and placed handy; while the "old revolutionary musket," that had been bought before he left New England to use on "Muster days," (the only firearm of any kind that he ever owned) was kept loaded to kill.

One day they caught my brother, a boy of about twelve years old, who had been sent to a neighbor's on an errand and by threatening to hang him; cut his throat from ear to ear; skin him alive, and many similar threats, tried to frighten him into telling what he did not know, where the fugitives were secreted. To make their threats more terrible they brandished their knives, and one of them taking hold of his ear drew his knife across it so that he could feel its edge. They would not let him return home, and kept him with them a prisoner until Mother becoming alarmed, asked Father and an older brother {Henry} to go in search of him. Though more than a dozen of the hunters well armed were surrounding the boy, they let him go and all ran away as soon as two unarmed men came in sight.

Day after day passed, and still the question "Where are those darkies?" was as much of a hidden mystery to the hunters as at the first. Having failed in their search, and in their attempts to frighten, they resorted to strategy. One of their number (we afterward learned that it was a neighbor) conceived the bright idea that if he could pass himself off for a runaway slave, he would be put with the others, and in that way ascertain where they were. One night he blacked himself, and came to our house, claiming to be a poor black man running away, and asked to be let in. He was told that if he were a poor black man he would be a great deal safer somewhere else. He gave a deep groan, turned on his heel, and went back to his companions telling them, "The old Deacon's a leetle too smart for me."

He usually wore very heavy whiskers when most men shaved their faces clean. Some years later he was passing and stopped for a few minutes chat. He had shaven off his whiskers and Father did not at first recognize him. On ascertaining who he was Father told him "Now that your whiskers are off no one would know but that you had always been a white man."

Gradually those who had been assisting in the hunt became discouraged and gave it up. Finally the masters concluded that their four slaves were lost property; that it was useless spending any more time or money in searching for them, and returned to their plantation in Missouri, sadder, if not wiser.

Where all this time were the fugitives? As soon as they came to our house they were taken to a little thicket in the pasture in plain sight of the house. The bush was so thick that a horseman could not ride through it and the thicket so small that they did not think it worth while to get off from their horses to examine it. Again and again, the masters rode within a few steps of their slaves, and were seen and recognized by them.

But they needed something to eat and drink as well as shelter. How to supply this while the hunters were closely watching every movement was a difficult question to answer. At that time we had no well. All of the water used at the house was hauled from a spring in the pasture. For this purpose we used a barrel on an old fashioned Yankee stone boat drawn by a yoke of oxen. After breakfast Father filled his pockets with biscuits, and taking a bridle in his hand, caught a horse that was grazing in the pasture. Mounting the horse he attempted to drive up the oxen. They were usually very quiet, and well behaved (as any Deacon's oxen ought to be), but this morning they acted as if possessed of an evil spirit. They would not go toward the house; and they would keep running around that thicket, in every direction, while Father riding bare back on his horse was close at their heels shouting and yelling like one mad. The hunters all this time were looking on taking great pleasure in seeing the cattle bother him; but every time the horse came to the edge of that thicket a handful of biscuit would come down among fugitives; literally "Bread rained from above." When the supply of biscuit was exhausted, the cattle became more quiet and were driven into the yard and yoked up. A bucket of water was placed in the empty barrel and with my brother driving he started for a barrel of waters. A path but little use led by a circuitous route past the thicket to the spring. This was the road taken this time and the boy was so sternly reproved for any carelessness in driving that his whole attention was taken up with the team. So dexterously was the bucket of water transferred to the thicket that not only did not the hunters see any thing suspicious, but "The lad knew not any thing." As soon as the barrel of water was at the house Father went to his daily work, just as though nothing unusual had occurred.

But the danger was too great to keep them there. A plan of greater safety must be provided. They were told that if in a thicket in an adjoining field they heard a rooster crow just at dark, they were, one by one, to stealthily crawl over the fence, and keeping in the tall weeds and grass in the fence corners, to come to that place. Something rather unusual attracted the attention of the hunters at that hour in an opposite direction. When finding the coast clear, {Father} went to a thicket in another part of the field, and there by a man who had never been suspected of being an abolitionist, who had consented to secrete and feed them. Some oats in the sheaf had been packed in the barn, which setting left a space about two feet deep below the floor of the loft. Into this space they were put, and some additional sheaves of oats crowded into the front to give it the appearance of a solid mow. Provisions were handed in by removing two or three sheaves.

That was their home until the hunt was over, when they were sent forward and safely reached Canada. One of them afterward returned to get his wife. His life of danger and adventure deserve farther notice, and will be the subject of the next number."

It seems that in spite of the seriousness and danger in 'conducting' fugitives, those involved seemed to manage it with a sense of humor – even to the point of flaunting their Underground Railroad activities at times. The term "hidden in plain sight" seems to apply here. Such seems the case in the following story from Enoch Platt's journal":

No. 7
The Quincy Lawyer.

The proprietors of the U.G.R.R. were not so prejudiced against any class, that they would forbid any one who needed their assistance the privilege of riding on their trains, because of color.

At one time Mr. A. living near Plymouth, was taking a fugitive in his wagon, in daylight, and the disguise was not as complete as it ought to have been. A man whom he passed on the road suspected his business and followed him. Seeing that he was followed A. whipped up his horses, and while passing through some woods, at a turn in the road that for a moment hid him from sight, his passenger jumped from the wagon and "Took to the brush". When he had driven some distance farther he allowed the man following him to overtake him. Of course nothing "Contraband" was found in the wagon, but he was arrested, and though nothing could be proved against him he was bound over to appear at the next term of the District Court in that County. The fugitive in the woods was found by friends and carried safely through.

Before Court time a fine looking man with light sallow complexion and wavy hair came through as a passenger. His manners and address were those of a polished gentleman, which his clothes were not only in the latest fashion, but were of finer and more costly material than common folks could afford to wear. He claimed on his father's side to come from one of the "First families of Virginia". On his mother's side by tracing back far enough he had some African blood in his veins; though she too on her father's side claimed kinship with the "Southern Aristocracy". Everything in his appearance, speech and manners indicated that he could well claim to be a peer of the proudest of them.

Yet he was a fugitive slave, running away from a man who claimed to be his master, though in reality greatly his inferior.

My brother took him to the residence of Father B. who was living near {a} neighbor to the man bound to court. Wishing to learn more of the particulars of the case they went to see Mr. H. (father-in-law of A.) Father B. loved a joke and introduced the fugitive in such a way that H. thought he was a lawyer from Quincy, who had come up to inquire about the case.

They met with cordial reception. Mr. H. was greatly pleased to see so much interest manifested by the friends in Quincy; insisted on their stopping until after dinner, when he would go with them to Macomb. The invitation was accepted, and his wife soon prepared for them an excellent meal, which was also shared with some other guests who would have felt highly insulted to be invited to sit at the table with a "Slave", but thought it an honor to dine with a "Distinguished lawyer." They would have returned the fugitive to his master, and prosecuted all those engaged in helping that slave away, if they had known anything about it.

Though in dress and manners well fitted to sustain the assumed character, he was a stranger in Quincy and did not know anything of persons and things there.

To prevent embarrassing questions, Father B. took the lead of the conversation, and was even more jovial than usual, always ready with a story or joke to turn the conversation, whenever it seemed likely to lead in a dangerous direction. On their way to Macomb, as they passed the place where A. had been chased, Mr. H. proposed that they play a joke on those people. He wanted one of them to play the part of a runaway and the rest of them act so as to excite their suspicion and get them all arrested. As they had a lawyer along they would be all ready for a trial, and could show up this slave hunting to ridicule and thus create public sentiment that would help in the coming trial. Father B. objected but Mr. H was so earnest in his desire to carry out his joke that finally he was told that there would be no joke about it. They really had a fugitive with them who was trying to escape, and their lawyer friend was "A runaway slave",

To say that H was astonished does not begin to do justice to his feelings. He had entertained this man at his table as an honored guest. He had introduced him to other guests as a distinguished lawyer. He had left his work to bring him up to Macomb to study his son-in-law's case. He had been conversing with him for several hours and yet he had all this time been deceived. He, a fine Yankee, had been so imposed upon; and without knowing it was assisting a slave escape. He was an abolitionist, but the joke cut too deep and he never quite forgave father B. for passing off on him "That runaway nigger" for "A Quincy Lawyer".

As I read the stories of these brave lads I am amazed that their parents put them at such risk at such an early age. The parents,

U.G.R.R. conductors, may have resorted to using their children when they themselves were being closely watched for U.G. R. R. activity. And yet, these young men handled it with adult composure. The following story unfortunately is missing the first two sections but it demonstrates some of the young men's bravery:

No.10

Search on the Prairie

"During the hunt mentioned in the last two numbers, the three fugitives were in a good deal of danger. No convenient barn, where in safety they could be hidden until the hunt was over, was available. The hunters were not so sure that they were on the right track, as when they had tracked fugitives to our gate within an hour of the time that they had arrived; and kept up the search over a much larger scope of country. The ruse of the blacksmith had only given time to move them a short distance, and it was finally decided to run the risk of sending them forward while the hunt was still active, taking as great precautions to avoid the hunters as possible. A young man by the name of Frank C. (whose father lived at the next station, thirty miles above) {probably L. A. Cook at Plymouth} and my brother {Henry or Jeremiah Evarts} volunteered to act as conductors. It was thought safest to make the journey on foot, but one of the fugitives was a woman, and they feared that she would not have strength to walk that distance in one night, so a saddle horse was taken along. A dark misty night was selected, and, as they were both familiar with the country, they attempted to make the journey without following the commonly traveled road.

They had traveled about two thirds of the distance and were congratulating themselves on their success thus far, when, as they were crossing a large prairie, they heard the sound of horsemen approaching from an opposite direction, and so close they could not turn from the road without being noticed. Not knowing what else to do they stopped.

The horsemen who were a party of the hunters searching for those same fugitives were surprised at meeting any one at such a time and place, and being in doubt whether they were the parties for whom they were searching, also stopped. For some minutes they stood but a few steps apart, each waiting to see what the others would do, "each anxious to avoid a general engagement".

After a time the hunters turned aside and passing came into the road behind the fugitives. Finding the road in front of them clear the boys cautiously moved forward but soon found that the hunters were following close behind them. To get away from them they left the road and traveled quite a distance across the prairie, only to be closely pursued. If they stopped their pursuers halted. If they moved forward in any direction, the hunters were only a few steps behind them. After an hour spent in this way Frank turned to brother and said, "This will never do. They will follow us until morning, and then we shall all be taken. We must get rid of that horse and they will follow you. When they are gone I will make my way to father's as best I can." He {Platt} handed him the compass, but forgot to give him the matches. Frank and the fugitives lay down in the grass, and brother mounted the horse and rode away. The hunters followed him a long distance, until they were satisfied that he was alone when they gave up the pursuit. Though he was free from the hunters, the situation was not an agreeable one. He was alone that dark misty night, on one of the great uninhabited prairies of Illinois not knowing where he was, with no road, no land marks, nothing to indicate which way he ought to go. Giving his horse his own way he kept on riding. At daylight he found that his horse had been going towards home, and was much nearer the place from which he started than that to which he intended to go. As soon as he knew where he was, and could see which way to go, he turned and rode rapidly to Mr. C's but Frank was not about. Full of anxiety for him and his party, he only waited long enough to feed his horse, and get his breakfast, when he was again in the saddle, to learn if possible what had become of the party which he had left on the prairie, but at night returned to Mr. C's with no news of them.

After brother left them they had lain still until some time after the sound of the horses feet had died away in the distance, when they rose and tried to find their way back to the road they had left. They succeeded in finding a road, but by this time Frank had become confused, so that he could not tell which way the road ran, and it was so dark that he could not see which way the compass pointed, and had no match to strike a light. Thinking it safer to do nothing than go wrong, they sat down and waited for the coming of day.

Frank knew that it would be impossible to reach his father's in daylight without being seen by someone who would report it, even if he succeeded in avoiding the hunters. His companions must be secreted and fed. As soon as it was light enough, he found a hiding place for them, and then "Went out foraging". He succeeded in finding an acquaintance who was willing to give Frank all the provision that he wanted, but did not want to tell him just who he was going to feed. He was sensitive to anything that looked like "Abolitionism", and wanted him to be able truthfully to say to the hunters that he did not know anything about their fugitives and to his neighbors that he had never helped or fed a runaway slave. Of course if Frank fed them with provisions that he had given, that was none of his business. The next night he reached his father's with his company. From there they were safely sent forward.

The hunters finally became tired out and gave it up. This was last systematic and long continued hunt ever occurred around our station. We very often saw hunters, but after that, they never gave us any trouble. All that we had to do was to watch them when they made their appearances, and keep the fugitives out of their way, or use such a disguise that they would not detect what we were doing; but the class of people called in the dialect of the time "Nigger hunters" deserves more particular notice than I have space to give in this number.

After reading some of my research, my granddaughter Yvonne who is now a teacher, commented that it was amazing to realize that so many people were involved in the movement. From an age when communication is electronic, she also commented that *word* traveled so efficiently and far by means such as a *horse*! She also commented that the movement was larger than she realized and was surprised that they were not caught. That may have been partly because of the obvious appearance of those coming to catch them as you will note from the following journal piece:

No 11
The Hunters

Hunting runaway slaves was in some of the slave states a regular business: those engaged in it, keeping blood hounds trained to track them. The "Professional Hunters" did not do much in the free states. As soon as the fugitives got among friends who would assist them their dogs were useless, and I shall only speak of such hunters as we met with in our experience. Though the slaveholders had given the name of Under Ground Rail Road on account of the secrecy with which its work was carried on, they in time learned the route taken, and the name and residence of all of the more prominent abolitionists at every station for more than a hundred miles from Quincy, and an accurate general knowledge of the entire route to Chicago. After the morning when they tracked Charley Duncan and his companions to our house it was one of the first places watched.

It was customary for masters who had lost slaves to offer a reward for their return. I do not remember any reward offered of less than Fifty dollars. Sometimes as much as three hundred dollars was offered for the return of one and in one instance when ten escaped the reward offered was twenty-six hundred dollars. The reward was a strong inducement to men who for money would do anything that did not involve personal danger to try and secure it. There was little danger in hunting slaves. The law was on the side of the masters, and the abolitionists always preferred running to fighting. Nearly every community had some men who would skulk around a neighbor's premises by night, or hunt squirrels through his timber by day, in the hope of finding the lost property and securing the reward. These were one class of the hunters.

Then there were those who came from the south, whose sympathies were with the masters. They were always ready to assist their friends in hunting for lost or stolen property.

Another class was always ready for any excitement. If some one would furnish the whiskey they would hunt anything. It mattered not to them whether deer, wolves, or men were the game.

But primarily "The Hunters" were the masters, or those sent by them, to advertise the loss and organize and direct the search. They always came horseback: good horses, generally wore broad brimmed hats tilted a little down over one eye, and as they rode up and down the road were looking into every corn field, orchard or thicket which they passed, as though they were every moment expecting to see "A nigger loose". One at all familiar with them would recognize them with unerring certainty as soon as seen, quite often the first intimation which we had of any business on the line was seeing them ride by. In fact the appearance of persons who engaged in hunting was so different from "Common white folks" that we could recognize the hunters by their looks and actions, almost as certainly and quickly as they could tell a black man from a white one. Our recognizing them was of great assistance to us. While they were watching us we were watching them, and while their backs were turned we would forward the fugitives, or adopt such a disguise that they would not know them if they saw them; or if unexpectedly we met them it helped us greatly in evading them."

There was a ferry that crossed the river near Marblehead, Illinois, south of Quincy. Marblehead was called Millville, named for the mill there. It may have been there that the following adventure took place.

No. 12

Ben's Knife

We used to hear it said, by the advocates of slavery, that the slaves were contented with their lot, and would not leave if they had an opportunity, unless someone persuaded them to. There was some foundation for this statement. The Africans, as a race, have a strong love of home; and when leaving their slavery involved breaking away from all of the home they had ever known, it required a strong love of home; and when leaving their slavery involved breaking away from all social and family ties, and bidding goodbye, perhaps to wife, children, friends and all of the home they had ever known, it required a strong inducement for them to go, especially when running away exposed them to very great danger. The motive that influenced a great many to undertake the perilous journey is illustrated by the story told by one of our passengers, called Ben, who came along some years after the events occurred recorded in the foregoing numbers.

When asked what made him run away he answered: "I found out massa was goine ter sell me to da trader to go down south. I wouldn't have run off if dey had let me stay on de ole plantation; but when I hear massa tell dat trader 'What you give me for Ben?" I thought dat if I had to go I'd ruther go whar I could be free dun to go down do river. Ide ruther die dan go down onto dem sugar plantations."

The story he told in answer to the question "How did you get away?" interested me very much. I wish I could give it all in his own words. He did not know where to go to find friends; did not know where he could find freedom; but had heard that on the east side of the Mississippi river, was a free state and he thought that if he could get there perhaps he could find out something about it.

So one night he left home and crossed the river in an old "dug out' (canoe) that he found on the bank. But the next day the hunters got on his track, and overtook and caught him in the river bottom a short distance below Quincy. While taking him up to the ferry to cross, on their way home, they passed a mill. "A man was crossin de road wid a sack on his shoulder, and saw dat I was tied. He ask 'What de matter?' Dey say 'We have caught our run away nigger and are takin him home.' Den dat man just throw down dat sack right in de road and stepping right in from of us he say 'You cant do dat here. I have you know dis is a free State and dat you cant take him back widout de law." The man carrying that sack was one of our prominent abolitionists, and insisted on their taking the {significant portion missing here}

log chain. He dared work at it only at night when everyone else was asleep, and kept the knife hidden in the dirt under the floor during the day. It took him a week to

accomplish it. Each morning he filled the crease he had made with dirt, to prevent anyone from seeing his work.
A day or two before the three weeks were up he was again at the mill, found the man who had before befriended him, and was by him put on board the train bound for Canada. He had with him the knife which had been the means of his release, which father tried to buy; but he said that he should keep it as long as he lived. Father laid the knife down on a page of his account book, and drew his pen around it, giving a profile view of it notches and all. If you will call on my brother who now has that book, he will show you this picture of
Ben's Knife.

'Generic' books on the Underground Railroad say that fugitive movement is greatest in the summer time when the weather is nice. Many of the hiding places I have found have been built near fireplaces as if to keep the fugitives warm. This next section tells that, indeed, slaves escaped when it was cold.

No. 13
Christmas Passes

How so many of the slaves were able to learn of the existence of the Under Ground Rail Road, and how to find the right persons to assist them, was a matter of surprise to the masters, and perhaps greater surprise to us. In many cases I could only call it a special providence leading them in a way which they knew not. The following incidents will show how some of them obtained their information.

"The Holidays", from Christmas until New Year, was the great festival time among the slaves. In the border states, on most of the plantations, all work was laid aside, except such as was necessary to provide for the eating and drinking, which was the order of the day. During this week all of the masters who hired out their hands by the year, made their new contracts. The ordinary restraints thrown around the slaves were greatly relaxed, and sometimes the entire week would be spent in going from plantation to plantation attending all sorts of gatherings of the colored people, not

being at home at all during the entire week. It was a custom in the slave states if any one found a slave away from his master's plantation without a written permit to arrest him and take him back; sometimes administering a punishment.

To keep up this custom, and at the same time to grant them a degree of liberty during the holidays, the masters wrote and gave each one a "Christmas pass".

One day during the holidays I saw two colored men on horseback pass our house. One of them had a bundle of wooden trays, strapped behind his saddle. In the evening a colored man living in the village, came to our house and calling father out, told him that these men were runaways and asked him to assist them. They had with them their Christmas passes, of which we took a copy. Since father's death the book in which they were copied has been lost and I cannot recall the names of either masters of slaves. They read about as follows:

"Dec. 25th 18—Let the bearer----"(here was written the name of the slave) "pass and repass until the first of January. (The master's name) ...

The names signed t these passes were those of two brothers who owned adjoining plantations in Missouri some distance west of Quincy. The boys were mounted on good young horses which they claimed that they had bought when they were colts, and raised, feeding them on grain which they had grown in the "Patches" which their masters allowed them to cultivate "Sundays". They had brought with them to sell some wooden ware which they made nights, a part of which they had sold in Quincy. Father bought what they had left, and some pieces were still used in the family when I left to make a home of my own.

The boys had concluded to use their passes to pass without repassing, and wanted a nights lodging and directions as to the road to take to get to freedom. Of course it could be no crime t comply with the written request of the masters, but father advised them to get away as fast as possible. Their horses were fed, they were given their supper, and a guide was provided who conducted them thirty miles on their way before daylight.

Before the time mentioned in the passes had expired, the masters became uneasy about the use their boys were making of them, and came in pursuit. They had no difficulty in tracing them to our place, but heard nothing more of them until they reached Farmington. On inquiring in that village a man tole them that he had not seen or heard anything of them, but, (pointing to a farm house on a hill south of town the residence of Dea. B.) said "The man that lives in that house will know if they have been anywhere around here." To the Deacon's they went. After some conversation they accepted a cordial invitation to stop and spend the night. Their hunting runaway slaves naturally suggested the subject of slavery as a topic of conversation, the Deacon telling them in plain words what he thought of slavery and slave holders. After supper his daughter sang some stirring abolition songs. Before retiring they had family prayers. A passage of Scripture was read which condemned the sin of oppression and then the Dea. prayed. He prayed for the slaves, that they might be freed, and especially for the two that were now hunted that they might safely escape, and then he prayed for his guests,, that they might see their sin in holding slaves, and repent of it, and show their repentance by freeing all they had. In the morning when they asked for their bill the answer was, "Night before last your slaves were here. They sat at the same table that you did; they slept in the same bed that you did; they fared in every way just as you have; I did not charge them anything and I shall not you."

The impression made can hardly be imagined by one not familiar with the way in which slavery and abolitionism were looked upon in the south. They had always been accustomed to consider slavery right, as a matter of course, and an abolitionist was considered one of the lowest and meanest of criminals. To meet with such treatment at the hands of a well to do farmer who had the respect and confidence of his neighbors was an entirely new experience. They gave up the hunt and returned home. The day after their return they met at the country store a number of their neighbors who wanted to hear all about their trip. They gave an amusing description of the night they spent in Farmington. One of them said, "To think of that old reprobate abolitionist praying for us I felt like killing him. But boys" (he added with an oath) "I tell you one thing. I'll never hunt niggers in that state again. If they once get across the river they may go for all my going after them."

Their story was listened to by one whom they did not notice. A colored girl had been sent to the store by her mistress, to make some purchases. Hearing the men around the stove talking about that hunt, she managed to be so long doing her errand that she overheard enough to know that in Illinois there were those who would help the slaves to escape. The result was that not long after this Deacon had another guest in the person of that girl.

A few days later her master received by mail a letter bearing the postmark of Farmington, Ill. On opening it he read:

"Farmington Ill. Feb. –18-

Dear Sir,

Betsy is here and on her way to glory."

No name was signed to it, but those who had enjoyed the Deacon's hospitality a few days before had no trouble in guessing who was the writer.

In a great many cases the first, and sometimes the only knowledge which the slaves had of the U.G.R.R. was overhearing the masters cursing about it. In more than one instance they made good use of the knowledge thus gained.

When we think of the Underground Railroad we think of desperate fugitives on the run. The following love story is material from which romantic adventures and novels could be made.

No. 14

The Wedding Trip.

On coming from my room one morning I was very much surprised to meet in our sitting room, as its only occupant, a fine looking young lady apparently about eighteen years of age, who was an entire stranger. She was a beautiful brunette with a heavy head in the yard a tall well dressed mulatto man, a tall silk hat on his head and a massive gold chain and seals dangling from his watch pocket. We had a number of guests at our house, but none such were there when we retired, but when I saw one of the "Mission Institute boys" I guessed, what proved to be true, that a train had come in on the U.G.R.R. during the night. The passengers were a couple on their wedding trip. I believe they had married according to slave custom, but no legal marriage was possible for slaves in any slave state. I felt some anxiety about their showing themselves so publicly, but soon learned that the man had his "Free papers", and the woman would pass for a cultured white lady. She had been from a child the waiting maid of a wealthy aristocratic lady in St. Louis, who had taken great pains to have her maid accomplished in her manners.

This was their story. He was a barber, residing in Chicago, and the owner of some valuable property there. Being in St. Louis on business, he had met this young lady. The result was a mutual attachment, and a wish to marry. Not liking to have his wife the property of someone else, he had offered her mistress one thousand dollars for her. This was refused. After a time finding his love growing stronger he called again upon her mistress and asked her what she would take? Her answer was "She is not for sale. If you keep coming here you will get such notions into her head that she will be spoiled for a waiting maid, and I will sell her down south. But you can't have her". He went away saying to himself "My lady, you had better take one thousand dollars than nothing, for I am going to have her. I offered you a good price, and now see what you will get." He did not go near the house again, but communicated with her through a free colored family of her acquaintance. She obtained permission to go to church Sunday afternoon, and came to the house of this friend where he met her. He had purchased tickets and secured a state room on a steam boat which was to leave that night for Quincy, and had provided a suit of boys clothes which he thought would fit her. Dressed in these she made a fine looking boy, except her hair, which was very luxurious, and hung down to her waist. He wanted to cut this off, but she objected. Her beautiful head of hair was her pride. So it was rolled up on top of her head and put under her cap.

When all was ready they passed into the alley, and keeping on the back streets were making their way toward the levee, when her hair came down. A boy who was playing marbles in the street saw it, and pointing towards them called out "Look there. There's a gal trying to be a man." Said he, "I tell you my heart jumped. I thought it was all over with us, but nobody beside the boys noticed it, and they were so busy with their game that they did not follow. As soon as we could we turned into an alley and the hair was put back under her cap. As soon as we reached the boat, I hurried my brother, Jo" (her name was Josephine) "into the state room and put him to bed, telling those around that he was sick. As soon as I could I borrowed a pair of scissors to trim the captain's whiskers, and I tell you that hair came right off."

When they reached Quincy the brother was so much better that he was able to walk from the boat to a carriage which he hired to take them to a friends, and the next night they were brought to our house. In the morning father detected the disguise and told them it was not necessary to keep it up any longer. The clothes she had on when she left her mistress had been brought along and when dressed in them, she was the handsome young lady whom I had so unexpectedly met that morning. A gentleman and his daughter were visiting at our house on their way to visit friends near Galesburg. They had room in their carriage for another passenger and, though they had never connected with the Under Ground Rail Road, consented to let the "White girl" ride with them. Another conveyance was provided for the man, who having his free papers to show could travel as safely as any other citizen would. Our friends were to start after early dinner, and were just ready to get into the carriage when an acquaintance, who was a strong pro slavery man, stopped at the gate. The colored folks (if those so near white could be called colored) were placed in the hall. If he came to the front door he was to be invited into the parlor. If he came to the sitting room door (the entrance generally used by the family) they were to go into the parlor. He came to the sitting room door, where he was cordially welcomed, and as we had just risen from the dinner table, invited to dine. While he was eating our friends passed out at the front door and drove away without his noticing anything unusual or suspicious.

The happy couple continued their wedding trip and in safety reached their home in Chicago."

This couple spent the night in Quincy before being brought to Mendon by "Mission Institute boys." Did they perhaps stay at Oakland? We will never know.

Knowing the cruelty of slavery it is hard to comprehend the fact that so many righteous, religious people were so openly in favor of it. This next section of Platt's journal relates a story of a preacher's runaway slave:

No. 16

The Preacher's Loss

Soon after our return from Kansas I attended a republican rally in Quincy. It was a short time before the presidential election of 1856 when Fremont and Buchanan were the rival candidates. One of our abolitionists said to me, "Have things ready for business on the U.G.R.R. up at your station. A party of fugitives is in the woods below town. We expected them in last night, but they did not arrive, and this morning some friends are searching for them. A party of hunters is close on their track. If we find them and can, we want to send them to your place tonight. I heard nothing more from them until the day after election. The hunters having returned home to vote: the fugitives were brought to our place.

It was a strange party to be running away. A middle aged man, a woman with two small children, and a woman so afflicted with inflammatory rheumatism that she could neither walk nor stand. They had been owned by a popular minister residing in one of the border Counties of Missouri and were the only slaves he had.

By some means they had made the acquaintance of a colored man who lived in Illinois and was familiar with the U.G. R.R. He agreed to help them across the river if on Sunday night they would come to a certain point, and build a fire on the river bank as a signal. When the day arrived, one of their number was so sick that she could not walk. What should they do? If they gave up going now it might be years before they would have another such an opportunity, and liberty was sweet. If the rest of the party went and left the sick woman, her situation would be a trying and critical one. If she betrayed them and gave warning to the master, they would be captured and punished. If she did not give warning, they would say that their leaving the same room, she must have known it and was an accomplice in what in the slave states was called a great crime, assisting slaves to run away. This she dared not meet. When even a preachers righteous indignation was thoroughly aroused on the subject of the "Divine Institution", it was not always safe for one so entirely under his control as his slaves were, to brave it. They finally decided to all try to escape together.

The preacher had an appointment to preach Sunday night and did not get home until eleven o'clock. Of course the man must be at home to take care of the horse, besides they wanted to borrow the horse and carriage to take the sick woman to the river. Then it was considered wise to let the good man of the house get sound asleep before starting lest he might hear them when they left and object to their going.

The night was far spent before they kindled the signal fire, and anxiously they watched to see whether their friend with his boat was still waiting, or had become tired and left. If he were gone their only hope was to drive home if possible before morning without their master ever knowing the use to which his horse and carriage had been put.

When they saw the welcome boat approaching they unharnessed the horse and turned him loose to go home, while the carriage was left standing on the river bank.

After safely crossing the river they had to decide what to do next. They could not hope to reach Quincy by boat, rowing against the current. They had no conveyance in which they could ride. The guide had planned to have the men carry the children and the women walk, thinking it safer that way. He knew of no friend near to whom he dared apply for help. But something must be done, and that before daylight. They first tried carrying her in their arms, but this caused her great pain. They then laid her on a blanket and tying the corners together they passed a stick through it and placed it on their shoulders, while the other woman carried the two children.

This was very hard work and they soon found that they could not continue it long; while to add to their difficulties a fog arose that made it very difficult finding their way. They finally decided to hide the sick woman, and the rest of the party try to reach a place of safety. A pile of drift wood was opened and she was placed in it. They gave her a little bread which they had with them, and with the promise that if they escaped they would send some one for her, they buried her under the drift wood, taking pains to place it so that it would not hurt her, and left her alone.

The rest of the party made their way as rapidly as they could, but day light overtook them as they were passing through a proslavery settlement some distance below Quincy, when the guide concealed them under a small bridge in the carriage road, and they hurried to the residence of one of the prominent abolitionists and reported the situation in which he had left his party. As soon as possible a party was made up to go to their rescue.

A few moments later a messenger from the master arrived at Quincy and organized a party to hunt for them and if possible capture them.

In the morning the preacher was very much surprised to find his servants, horse and carriage all gone. Arousing some of his neighbors a messenger was started in haste to Quincy to head them off, while the rest of the party followed the carriage track. The carriage and harness were found just as they had been left, and in crossing the river they soon found where the boat had landed, and from there followed the fugitives track to the pile of drift wood where the woman was hidden. Here the great number of tracks made while they were hiding attracted their attention but finding nothing suspicious they again followed the trail, and of them saying, "There's just as many tracks going away as there was coming."

As soon after the guide returned as possible, a covered hack with three men went to the bridge where the fugitives were concealed. A sentinel was placed a short distance on either side to give warning if any one approached. When no one was in sight one at a time they were conveyed to the hack, while that stood innocently by the road side while passers went by. Before the hunters following the tracks reached the bridge they had been taken to a place of safety. A carriage was then sent for the woman in the driftwood, and as it did not arrive until sometime after the hunters had passed they had no trouble in getting her safely away.

When the election put an end to the pursuit, they were sent to our place, and a family, where there were no small children or hired men, received them as their guests. A pair of mules were harnessed to a covered wagon, the man and children were seated on the floor in the back part; the two women with gloved hands and thickly veiled faces, sat on a seat before them, and a young friend H. and I family moving. Knowing however that we would be suspected if seen too near home we started at three o'clock in the morning, as sat in front. Altogether we seemed a very respectable we were particularly anxious to be beyond the settlement at Fletcher's Mill before people would be up.

I asked the woman "How did you feel while you were buried there alone?"

"I was some lonesome at first" she said "but I pray de Lord, and de bressed Jesus was wid me, and den I wasn't afeared. Bime by I hearn somebody comin, and when I look through de cracks, I see massa and some mo of de neighbors dat I knowed, jous so as plain as day. Den I heerdem talk bout finding de carriage, an crossin de ribber, an follerin up de tracks. One of um stan on de logs right ober my head, and when he spet his backy juice come through de cracks on my dress. But de good Lord

he kep der eyes from looking dat way, so dey didn't see me, an when dey was gone didn't I bress de Lord."

About daylight we passed a settlers cabin, and saw the proprietor (a democrat we were very sure from his looks) leaning over the fence watching some pigs while they ate some corn he had just given them. He looked cross and sour as though just getting over last night's drunk. To divert his attention so that he would not notice us too closely, I did what I had never done before and never have since. I shouted "Hurrah for Buchannan". Instantly a change appeared. A broad smile spread all over his face as he enthusiastically responded "That's right, and he's elected too". As soon as we were out of his hearing H. turned to me with the remark "That was better to relax him than a box of pills." Before noon we reached a place which we sometimes used as a station. They could not conveniently keep them, but furnished a fresh team and a man who was familiar with the roads, and was acquainted with a family that were always ready to assist but did not live directly on our usual route. This place we reached that evening, left our company there, and the next day returned home. During our absence Father met one of our neighbors, a Kentuckian, who at that time or soon after was the democratic representative from our county to the state legislature. He said that he had recently received a visit from an old friend living in Missouri, the Rev. Mr. Bird, who had met with a serious loss. All of his slaves five in number have run away. They were worth twenty five hundred dollars. He said that Mr. Bird was a good man and a useful preacher, and as he was not very well off he could not afford to lose them. He felt very sorry indeed for him, and wished that something could be done to prevent such good men from suffering such losses. So did we."

Even though their house is no longer standing these accounts recalled firsthand incidents experienced by the Platt family of Mendon Illinois. Such a perspective is difficult to find about the

Underground Railroad because of the secrecy involved in the project. I thank the Platt descendents for sharing them with me.

Chapter Fifteen

SAFE HOUSES AND SECRET DEPOTS

When Bill and I were researching stations for *People's History of Quincy And Adams County, Illinois* we found very interesting hiding places in the Mendon area near where the Platt family was conducting the railroad. We knew that the design of the Underground Railroad was such that each station had alternative routes and hiding places to confuse the slave hunters. Examples of such alternatives were used in the stories told in the previous Platt letters and journals. The following hiding places were near the Platt home and would have been available. We were fascinated by the fact that each of the following stations had a unique design based on optical illusions in architecture.

Chester Tallcott

The Mendon Township history written in the *People's History of Quincy And Adams County, Illinois* as reported by Gerald W. Finlay tells how Abigail Tallcott came to settle here with Chester. It seems that two young men were smitten with Abigail who remained in the east. Colonel Richard William Starr and Chester Tallcott competed to get settled here and bring her back as a wife. It soon turned into a race and Tallcott was the first to arrive east and secure Abigail as his prize! The women who came here at that time shared a rugged life of hardships with their husbands. In addition, Abigail Tallcott had to share her house and husband with the rigors of the Underground Railroad.

Built in 1834, the Chester Tallcott Home east of Mendon, was located near a tributary to Bear Creek.

Chester Tallcott home

When we visited, Burt McClelland owned this house, northeast of Mendon. Built in 1834, it was a much older home than it looks. Most of the stations are very square and simple on the outside, but when you get inside they become intentionally confusing. They have jogs, turns, and landings that you wouldn't expect of a square house like this. In this home just beyond the front door there is a stairway that circles upward to the second floor. There, walls jut out for no apparent reason.

There was a 9 by 12 room in this house that had no door. The only entrance was through a window. They would keep a ladder there and the fugitive slave would go in and pull the ladder up inside and be safe. If the Missourians came into the house and up the stairs they would actually miss the area where the room was. We talked to the woman who bought the home in 1927. They discovered they had a bedroom with no door to it. They talked to some of the old timers in town and they all seemed to know that the house had been an Underground Railroad station and the room was where they hid the slaves. Then owner Mrs. Mary Evans put a doorway to the room in 1927. The room in the photo is pictured through that doorway.

Upstairs window to the left opened to a room with no door

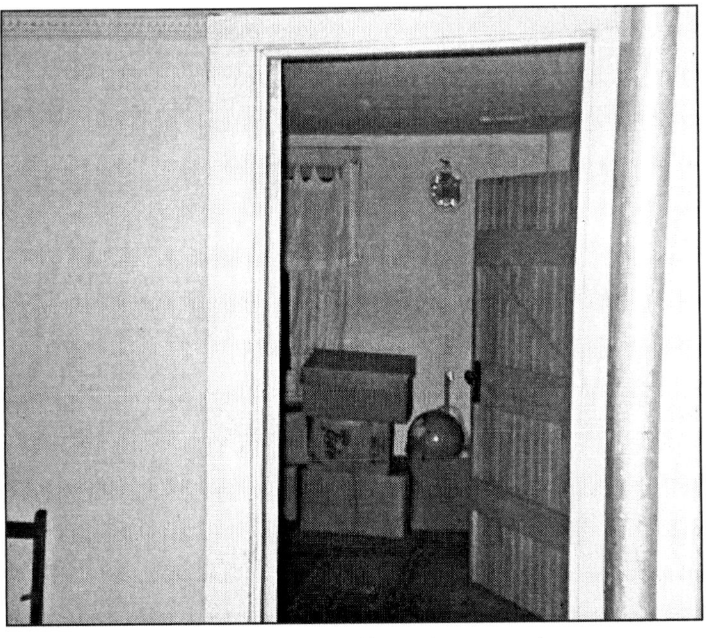

Room originally built without a door to enter it

Jonathon Hubbard

The Jonathon Hubbard home south of Mendon, Illinois is located in Section 14 of Mendon Township, near a tributary to Ursa Creek. This home is owned by Mr. and Mrs. Tom Kuhn.

Mr. Tom Kuhn came up to me after one of my speeches and wondered if his house could have been part of the Underground Railroad. He was doing some remodeling on his old house and found what appeared to be a secret room under the stairs. With his invitation we loaded up the family in our station wagon for yet another "history outing". His children and ours got a lesson in history as we explored and took these pictures of the hiding place.

Just having a hiding place was not enough to substantiate a home as an Underground Railroad station. It was necessary to determine *who* built the house and their religious and political persuasions. In our area Underground Railroad stations were built prior to 1850 partly because after the passage of the Fugitive Slave Act of 1850 the punishment for harboring slaves became much more severe. In most cases the stations were built as the area was settled in the late 1830s and 40s. We asked Mr. Kuhn to check his abstract to find out who built the house and when it was built. He visited the bank to see the abstract and generously brought a copy of it to us. Jonathan Hubbard built the house! That was exciting because Wilbur H. Siebert listed Jonathan Hubbard as an Underground Railroad Operator in his landmark book on Underground Railroad in 1898. This house was definitely part of the Underground Railroad route.

From the outside the steps look like any other. But two steps lift up and allow access to the hidden room. The next pictures show what it looks like from the inside. Looking up there appears to be coat hooks installed. My daughter, Kay remembered as a child when we discovered this hiding place.

From the opening in the step, looking up into the hiding place – coat hooks are on the wall.

From the inside you can see the stairs that allow the access to this room. All the walls in this room were plastered, probably so that it would not sound hollow if someone knocked on the wall.

Henry Hoffman

Hoffman home

This home, near Marcelline, Illinois was owned by the Warnings at the time we visited. Several years ago they had a fire in this house. They had to tear out the wall and were surprised that the fire got between the chimney and the brick wall. The fireplace was built similar to our house, with the room around the chimney. It was remodeled after the fire.

This property would have been the first building one would see after entering the mouth of Bear Creek from the Mississippi River. The land from the river to this area was swamp land at that time. County recorder Henry Snow was the first to record this land in 1827 to Henry Hoffman on a "swamp deed". Both men were present at the Antislavery Convention in Alton, Illinois on September 27, 1837. Elijah Lovejoy was the secretary at that convention.

Edward Fowler

The Edward Fowler home is no longer standing.

Mr. Edward Fowler built this home just east of Mendon. Mr. Fowler left Mendon and began the village of Fowler in 1857. This picture was provided me by Ruth "Kak" Finlay Carwile who was born in the front bedroom of this old Fowler house. Her brother always teased her about getting to be born in the front while he had to be born in the back bedroom. When asked, Ruth's mother said she was born in the front bedroom because it was winter and too cold to have a baby in the back bedroom. The house was heated by a chimney in the center with individual flues for two fireplaces and a bake oven. She said the house was so poorly sealed that once her doll clothes were ruined when rain water dripped in through the flue hole for the big fireplace in the center of the house. The big fire place was in the dining room with a closet beside it. One step under the stairway lifted up to enter a hiding place. Carwile remembers the rickety old ladder in the basement that a runaway slave could climb up into the closet under the steps.

The Fowler barn had a false floor in the hay mow. The runaway slaves were placed in there and the opening was covered with hay. This is likely the barn that hid a family for a week as told in the Platt journal. It is no longer standing.

Erastus Benton

Erastus Benton of Mendon was such a significant person in Anti-Slavery activities that more attention needs to be spent telling about this Mendon resident. Benton was named repeatedly in the Platt letters as being a person assisting in the Underground Railroad. His home was just northeast of Mendon, not far from Levi Stillman's farm where White Lightning died. Unfortunately, it is no longer standing and I was not able to discover any pictures of it. At the Illinois Antislavery convention in 1840, it was decided to support an Abolition ticket for president. Erastus Benton was put on that ticket.

From the 1872 Plat Book we are given a brief family history of Erastus Benton who we know was very active in anti-slavery activities:

Erastus Benton was born in North Guilford, Connecticut in April, 1804. At the age of 24, he was married to Miss Cook. She lived only 2 years after their marriage. After her death Mr. Benton married a sister of his first wife, Miss Caroline J. Cook. They had a family of three children and D. C. is the only one living in 1872, Mr. Benton moved with his family to Mendon in 1832 where after purchasing several large farms he engaged extensively in agriculture and milling. In 1846 he moved to Quincy for four years in the lumber business. In 1850 he purchased a farm on Section 8 Melrose Township, where the balance of his life was spent. He succeeded in accumulating a large fortune. He early identified himself with the anti-slavery party, and was among the many exponents of these principles. As it is well known, the gentlemen who entertained those views had to bear the most violent opprobrium of party feeling, but Mr. Benton happily lived to see those principles triumph in the emancipation of the slaves. He was a Republican and among the most earnest supporters of the Union Cause.

It is evident from the previous stories that the little community of Mendon had several active Underground Railroad stations and that the entire community seemed to support their anti-slavery activities. This account from *Past and Present of the City of Quincy and Adams, County, Illinois* gives a feeling for the attitude of the majority of the citizens of Mendon at the time:

> *The Illinois Black Laws, prohibiting the immigration of Negroes was in effect, when three black boys came to Mendon and worked for two farmers. After they had been here beyond the law limit, they were seized by armed men and run into the village of Marcelline. The law took its course and finally resulted in the following notice being posted. The notice in short said that it was a misdemeanor for slaves to stay in Illinois for more than the set number of days. The boys were fined fifty dollars, then they were to be put up for auction to a buyer who could pay his fine and give him proper care. The day of the sale came and only one bid was made for the boy being sold.*
>
> *The boy was sold to work ninety-nine years and six months to pay the fifty-dollar fine. During the progress of the sale the purchaser had been knocked down, kicked, and choked, by a Methodist minister who was present at the trial, and the six foot son of the complainant, who attempted to interfere with the ministerial work, was given a broken nose, with accompanying side dishes and desserts, which necessitated the use of a big wagon to carry him home, where he remained contently for*

several weeks. The Negro boy went home with his purchaser, whose wife persuaded the boy under promise that he should not be pursued, to run away before morning, which he did. He afterwards worked about Mendon without molestation. The other boys, who had also been fined for the same high misdemeanor and had been advertised to be sold two days later, were offered to the public, but the market seemed overstocked and no bids were received. They were discharged and admonished not to cause any further trouble in this line, although the infamous "Black Laws," to the disgrace of the state, remained on the statute book for years afterward; but their enforcement was never attempted in Mendon.

Chapter Sixteen

ANTI-SLAVERY WINDS BLOW OVER PAYSON

Drawing of the windmill by Gary Butler with his permission

Many residents of Payson, Illinois, twelve miles southeast of Quincy would be surprised to learn a grand windmill such as this artist's depiction was once Payson's most identifiable landmark. It was erected on high ground on the northeast edge of town. Captain John Burns (You will remember that it was Capt. John Burns who rescued Dr. Nelson from the Missouri side of the river and brought Nelson to Quincy) moved to Payson to construct the mill and procured the partnerships of Albigence Scarborough and David Prince. Construction began in the summer of 1836 and was completed in 1838 after experiencing many delays and problems with those hired to build it. *A History of Payson, Illinois 1835 – 1976* gives this description:

The mill was to be built circular and pyramidal in shape, with the foundations to be 3 ½ feet thick, and the diameter 25 feet. The superstructure was to be 42 feet, 7 inches in height, or the equivalent of five stories, with openings for 16 windows and 4 doors. The completed windmill was 7 stories high. The top was to be made of brick, the foundation and the first story was to be constructed of stone. The wings of the windmill were to be 30 feet long, making the total diameter of the wheel 60 feet.

John Burns was chastised by the Congregational Church for operating the mill on Sundays. When he continued to operate the mill on Sundays the management of the mill was taken from him. In 1841 he joined the Payson Methodist Church. The windmill was very expensive to build and to operate so it was assumed that Capt. Burns ran the mill on Sundays if the wind was blowing because he couldn't afford not to. Burns probably also didn't mind the fact that runaway slaves could have seen the rotating blades for miles around. Slaves often escaped on Sundays while their masters were observing a "day of rest," so the sight of the windmill high on the prairie as a sign to follow on the Underground Railroad would not have been viewed negatively by Burns.

This picture, taken from where the mill once was, looking to the east, shows how it would have stood out on the landscape.

This is the view Burns would have had from the mill on Mill St between Fulton and Main facing east towards Adams, Illinois. The Pottle station would have been directly in line with this view. The Pulman station would have been to the left of this angle. Beyond the first row of trees the view extends for many miles towards Adams, Illinois.

From this location, Main Street in Payson runs directly south culminating in the Mississippi River bottoms.

At the time I was writing the history of the Underground Railroad for the *People's History of Quincy and Adams County, Illinois,* Helen Shelton of Payson was writing the History of Payson section for the book. Through our research we met and became friends. Another Payson historian, Dorothy Jacobson shared much of the Payson history with me. Although these lovely ladies are no longer with us, their stories of Payson's place in the history of the Underground Railroad and their enduring friendships helped to make this book a reality.

From early Payson history we know that the area near Payson now known as Plainville was called Stone's Prairie after Samuel Stone who settled there in 1822. Stone's son Abraham later attended Mission Institute Number 2. (Abraham Stone's lengthy obituary is reported in a previous chapter.)

Albigence Scarborough arrived in Quincy from West Hartford, Connecticut in 1833. With the help of known abolitionists Dr. Eells, Capt. Burns and Asa Turner, Scarborough set out to find land to settle on. He traveled to Rushville and Lewistown before spending the night in Mendon with John Chittendon originally from Guilford, Connecticut and anti-slavery advocate and founder of the Congregational Church in Mendon. The next day he traveled with John Wood to what is now Payson. Urged to move to Illinois by Dr. Eells, he returned to Connecticut to bring his family back to Illinois. The first of his friends to follow to Illinois were Charles Whitman, Daniel Scarborough, a nephew of Albigence, and Joseph Fielding. All three had homes built in Payson by 1836. This is important because the Fielding home was since identified as a possible Underground Railroad station. Albigence Scarborough was known to have been staunchly anti-slavery.

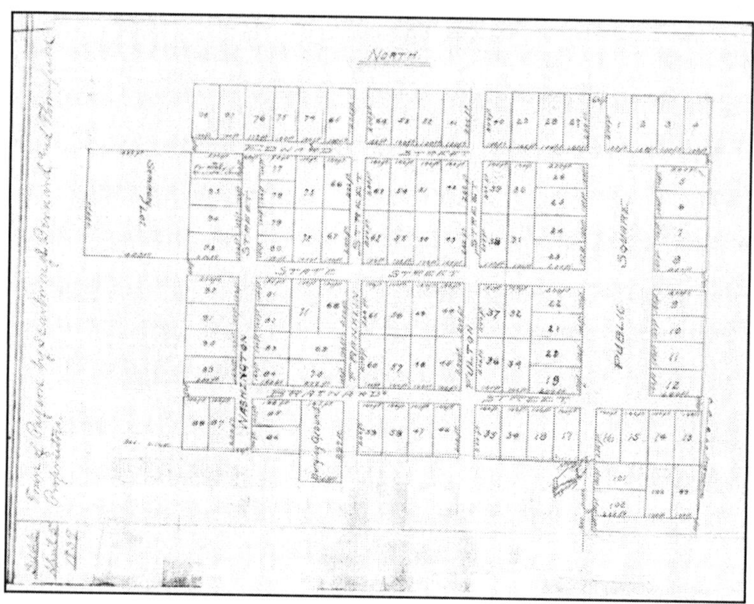

Early city plan for Payson, Illinois

This early plan for Payson in 1837 shows that a planned lot was set aside called a Seminary Lot, intended for a school. It has always been my belief that Mission Institute Number 3 was planned for Payson. Could that Seminary Lot have been the planned location for Mission Institute Number 3? This plan was drawn up by early settlers Scarborough, Burns and Thompson, all active abolitionists. We know from Dr. Nelson's book, *Appeal To The Church,* that the land for No 3 was designated somewhere and all of the early settlers of Payson had been influenced by Nelson's preaching.

Payson parsonage

Albigence Scarborough first lived in a log cabin. He removed it and began the construction of this grander home in 1838. The Mormons having been run out of Missouri in 1838 were given work on the construction of the foundation and chimneys. At one time the house served as a day school. Since 1912 it has been used as a parsonage. It has been remodeled such that no evidence of a hiding place, had there been one, exits. Certainly much discussion about abolition and slavery took place here.

George Hunter Home

This was the home of George Hunter on the edge of Payson, Illinois.

On the north end of Fulton Street, not far from the windmill that Capt. John Burns managed on the corner of Fulton and Mill Streets is a home often called the George Hunter home. You will recall that his father, Moses Hunter, was the head teacher at Mission Institute Number 2.

Most homes built in the area in the 1830's and 40's were of the simple lines of the Greek revival style. The photos were taken before the extensive remodeling done by the Kenneth Meyer family. This home identified as an Underground Railroad station was a puzzle until I read its story in *A History of Payson, Illinois 1835 – 1976*:

Located in section 7, on the northwestern edge of the town of Payson is the home of the Kenneth Meyer family. The Meyer's purchased the home in 1970 from Iry Scott and have extensively remodeled the farmhouse. The house and land had been in the Scott family for over 90 years. Mr. Scott's great grandfather, Edward C. Scott, settled in Adams County in 1840. … Mr. Scott bought the home from George Hunter in 1882 and added to the Hunter home a room, used as a parlor by the family, on the southwest corner of the house and a cupola which gave a panoramic view of the surrounding area.

George Hunter, as his father before him, was active in the Underground Railroad. It is thought his home in Payson was a station used by slaves on their way to Canada.

During the time he resided at this farm he stated his occupation as fruit grower, but no doubt he was a highly educated man. The Hunter family belonged to the Payson Congregational Church with Mr. Hunter serving as Sunday school teacher. For 17 years he served as deacon of the church after the death of Albigence Scarborough in 1865.

His first wife was Elizabeth Ann Francis who died on February 3, 1860. His second wife Julia Dean Hunter read Latin, Greek and Hebrew fluently. She served as a missionary to Jamaica for 10 years before her marriage to Mr. Hunter in December on 1860.

The Hunter property had been planted as an orchard by a previous owner, Jesse Fell, who called the farm "Fruit Hill". Mr. Fell was a lawyer and real estate dealer. During the panic of 1837 he lost all the wealth he had been able to accumulate while a resident of Bloomington, Illinois. He came to Payson and purchased 60 acres in the northwest one quarter of section 7. He sold this land in 1853 and returned to Bloomington, where he again accumulated another fortune. Mr. Fell being a personal friend of Abraham Lincoln was asked to publish a biography the President had compiled. A man of many accomplishments Mr. Fell was founder of five towns and the University at Normal.

George Hunter was mentioned in the Platt letters as one of the conductors transporting fugitives to Mendon in the 1840's. By now the reader knows that Mission Institute taught men and women to be proficient in Latin and Greek. I wonder if George Hunter and his second wife became first acquainted at Mission Institute.

It is also likely that Jesse Fell was associated with Dr. Nelson and Jonathan Baldwin Turner. All three were passionately interested in agriculture, education and abolition.

In the Hunter home there is a hiding place behind the closets upstairs. This is the view looking into the closet that shows yet another smaller doorway into yet another small room.

This closer view is looking into the second doorway showing a hidden room behind the closet.

From the outside looking into an opening from one of the rooftops on the Hunter house.

Seymour Underground Railroad Station

Martin Seymour station in Payson, Illinois

Martin Seymour moved his family from Hartford, Connecticut to this farm one mile west of Payson, Illinois in 1836. (The same year that Dr. Nelson escaped to Quincy from the mob in Missouri). The family would eventually be linked to the Nelson's by marriage, but first was linked by the desire to work against slavery.

The Seymour house just west of Payson, IL, was built with a hiding place in it. The house is not far from the George Hunter house and within visual sight of the imposing windmill mentioned earlier. Grant House, a descendent of the Seymours, gave us a tour of this house while he was living in it. The Seymours, members of the Payson Congregational Church, were acquainted with Mission Institute and records show that they attempted to visit Thompson, Work and Burr in the Marion County Jail, but were turned away by the authorities. Martin Seymour's granddaughter, Ellen Greene would later marry Eugene La Fon Nelson, youngest son of Dr. David Nelson. Eugene's son, Harry Rowland Nelson visited us and shared memories of visiting his Grandmother Amanda at Oakland.

In 1904, a newly remarried Lyman Kay Seymour desired a new home. He divided the old house in two sections. The front section, seen in the photo of Martin Seymour's home, was moved by logs and mules 150 feet south, and the back section was moved across the road about 250 feet from its original location. A new house was built on the original site.

Hidden door in closet

In this angle, you are looking up into the ceiling of the closet.

A curious interior space in the Seymour house.

Brackett Pottle

On May 6 & 7, 1836, a meeting was held to organize a Congregational Church in Payson. Asa Turner, Capt. John Burns and Willard Keyes from the Congregational church in Quincy and Payson resident Rev. Anson Hubbard were present. Brackett Pottle was approved for the congregation on the spot by profession while his wife Mary was approved by a letter from a church in West Hartford, Connecticut. Brackett Pottle came to Payson in 1833 from New Hampshire. The 1872 Atlas lists him as a retired farmer. Family history tells that he witnessed the martyrdom of Lovejoy at Alton.

Bill and I were thrilled with an invitation from Mr. and Mrs. Russell Altoff to visit the Brackett Pottle home which they owned in the 1960's. The house was empty and in the process of being torn down.

Brackett Pottle house

Hidden area behind stairs

The stairway from the first floor to the second floor had a large curve at the top that allowed a hidden area behind the curve of the stairs that could be entered from the third floor. The risers between the second and third floor were made of etched glass with a design on them. A person could see someone coming up the stairs though the glass risers.

Mrs. Pottle's granddaughter told us an interesting story. She said her grandmother told her that one day a Missouri mule-farmer knocked on her front door and when she opened the door, he 'haughtily' asked, "Where are my slaves?" My grandmother said very *sweetly*, "I don't know anything about your slaves!" The mule farmer grudgingly left. Then my grandmother said *sweetly*, "All the time, they were in my attic!"

Fielding – Elliott House

Did slaves haunt this station?

This house as seen in the 1872 Plat Book was built by Joseph Fielding who came to Payson with Albigence Scarborough. Fielding first built a log cabin and as so many others did in those years added on in time. The house had ten rooms. Fielding made his living raising silk worms. He sold it to Joseph Elliott in 1849. Signe Oakley, daughter of Dorothy Jacobson, owner of the house across the road from here told me that the Elliott house had a hiding place in it. She suggested that I talk to the Butler family who had lived in it for several years. After they moved away the owner tore it down.

Savina 'Cookie' Butler confirmed what had appeared to be a hiding place, existed in the home. In the third floor attic were marks on the floor that clearly indicated that there had been a false wall creating the illusion of less space up there than had actually existed. The hidden room would not have been large – perhaps wide enough for a person to stand behind. The attic had windows on each end so that a person could see out side and slip in the hidden room if the need arose. The door leading to the attic was in a second floor room known to have been the servant's quarters.

Cookie said that one night when she was sleeping downstairs in the living room, because of the difficulty heating the upstairs when cold, she awoke to see a young girl standing in front of her. The girl appeared to be holding a floppy, cloth doll. As Cookie gasped in fright, the child turned and seemed to *float* away. Cookie said that she was a person who was not accustomed to report seeing ghosts. She had not seen one before or since that time, but she recalls that experience quite vividly. Since she was so upset by the experience, she researched the history of the past residents and there was no mention of a little girl ever dying in the house, so she wondered if it was, perhaps, a little slave girl, since there would be no record.

Dorothy Jacobson lived across the road. Mrs. Jacobson had lived there for a long time and had researched local history as a hobby. Mrs. Jacobsen confirmed that the house was known to have been an Underground Railroad station but no records were kept during that time because of the need for secrecy.

Around that same time, Cookie's brother was staying with them for a time. He was sleeping in the bedroom across from the room which would have been the servants' quarters. He reported waking in the middle of the night to see a large man standing with arms crossed at the doorway looking seriously at him. He thought at first it was his brother waking him for an early morning shift. He asked him, "Is it time?" The man turned and *floated* out of the room.

Neither Cookie nor her brother told each other of the apparitions fearing what others would think. Years later when they spoke of it to each other, they were amazed at the similarities in their stories.

The room that was known as the servant's quarters had an eerie effect on the Butler family. It was decorated as a playroom but the Butler girls aged 3, 7 and 10 would not play in the room. They would drag their toys into the hall rather than play there. When asked, the girls would say, "I don't like that room." They would never go up to the room at night. Even Cookie said that she felt uncomfortable in the room. When her husband was gone and the girls at school she painted the walls. She said she would get an uneasy feeling in there and it took a *long* time to finish those four walls. Cookie points out that she would go into the basement or anywhere else without that feeling. She has lived in several old homes and lives in a 100+ year old home now but has never experienced that feeling there. While she was telling about the room, her now adult daughter, Trudy said she remembered still how uncomfortable it felt in that room – like somebody was watching –but only in that room.

The Mary Pulman Station

Joseph Pulman Home

Heading northwest between Payson and the village of Adams, (called Newtown in the 1840s) is the Pulman Underground Railroad station.

This is the first Underground Railroad station I found. I was writing for the history of Adams County and knew that the Congregationalists were active in the abolition movement. My mother and step father lived near Payson (between Payson and Adams). They introduced me to a neighbor, an older gentleman in the area by the name of Delbert Haire, (spelled Hare in the 1872 atlas) who said he'd never heard anything of the Underground Railroad around there. I asked him to call me if he did. We weren't home for longer than fifteen minutes when he called. He said, "I called my cousin who lives across the road and she said her house was one!" He said, "I've lived here all my life and I never knew that."

I called his cousin then. She said that she was 75 years old and her father told her about it when she was seven and told her not to tell anyone. She had not told a soul all those years until the day I talked to her on the phone. My husband and I met this remarkable woman, Mrs. Louise Callahan, when she showed us the hiding place and explained it to us. She said there was a long narrow place along the sidewalk between the house and the sidewalk that kept sinking in. She asked her father what it was and he told her it was a place where they hid the slaves, "but don't tell anyone." Until I called her, she never did! When she went to high school, she boarded in Payson. There was an elderly man named Uncle John Nichols. He told her the same story. Aunt Mary Pulman was the woman who ran the Underground Railroad Station.

The Joseph Pulman home west of Adams, Illinois and north of Payson had a trap door in the kitchen floor which opened into a tunnel that led to the barn.

One thing we know about the woman who ran this station is that she was not afraid to defend herself and her station. One day, Aunt Mary Pulman shot a man who intruded into her house. She then bandaged him up and told him to leave and never come back. He was last seen slowly walking down the road.

In later years, the owners of the home needed space for a fuel tank so they put it in the entrance to the tunnel.

Fuel tank in tunnel opening

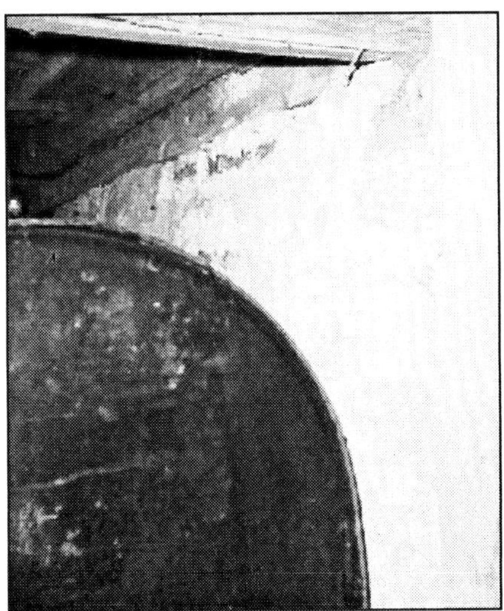

Close up of rock wall along the side.

George Terrill Home near Newtown (Adams) IL

From the 1872 Plat Book – a drawing of the Terrill house

Dr. David Nelson told his student N. A. Hunt to take the fugitives to a station identified as a big, red barn near Adams. For years I have wondered about the actual location of that station. I speculated that the barn may have been on the George Terrill farm a short distance from the Pulman station.

The Terrill (sometimes spelled Terrell - in the same document referring to the same man) family was actively involved in the movement. Benjamin Terrel was on the board of trustees of Mission Institute No 2. He had a nephew named George. The1872 Plat book indicates that this property was in the ownership of George Terrill.

Mary Terrel from Payson was along on one of the rescues reported in the Platt letters. I have been unable to determine Mary Terrel's exact relationship to the family. There is nothing left on the home site to confirm or exclude its existence.

Josiah Read Station – Newtown, Illinois

Present day view of Josiah Read home

As I was completing this book I still did not know the location of that large red barn at Adams. So many references had been made of it that local amateur historians were beginning to say that it was at Oakland. (probably because of the reference to Nelson.) Oakland was only five miles from the river and the barn was said to be sixteen miles away. Then Carolyn Altenhein gave me a copy of the obituary of Josiah Read and the clues started falling in place.

His life was summarized in his obituary printed in the *Quincy Herald Whig* on May 18, 1882.

Josiah Read was born Jan. 6, 1822, at Swansea New Hampshire. For eight generations his ancestors, as far as traceable, had been farmers from John Read of Beheboth. The ancestors of the American Reads were three of that picked company of men, women and children that came over in the ship that bore Gov. John C. Winthrop to the Massachusetts shores in 1680. That company consisted of about 800 families, mostly pious and intelligent Puritans. Among these families was Edward Garfield, the ancestor of President Garfield.

Prior to his life as a farmer Josiah Read taught school most successfully many years in New Jersey, New York and Illinois. He has been twice married. His first wife, Miss Amy Roe of Orange county New York, died within a few years of their marriage. His second wife, Mrs. Caroline A, Roe survives him, at the age of 69 years. By his first wife one son survives him, Frank Read, a deaf mute teacher in the Illinois Institute for the deaf and dumb and editor of the *Deaf Mute Advance.* He had four sons by his second wife, all of whom are actively engaged in business.

In religion Josiah Read was a ruling elder in the Presbyterian Church during many years of his life. In politics an old time abolitionist, and as a matter of course an active member of the Republican Party since its organization.

Another corroborating piece of information was court documents that indicated that Josiah Read was arrested for harboring slaves on September 24, 1845.

Josiah Read was buried in the family plot in Newtown Cemetery. The cemetery also has Eells' burial plots from the Civil War.

The village of Newtown, later named Adams, was identified as a place of Underground Railroad activity and Josiah Read may have been responsible for that reputation.

For years I knew that at Adams, Illinois was the site of an Underground Railroad station identified by a large red barn. Seibert's book mentions it and includes Adams, Illinois in his country wide map of Underground Railroad tracks. As I was completing this book I still did not know the location of that barn. As I was preparing the information for this chapter I believe we came across the location of that infamous red barn.

Melvin Sims grew up in the home on the farm originally owned by Josiah Read east of Adams, Illinois. He told me that the house was there when his grandfather John T. Sims bought the farm. He remembers that his grandfather raised bees on the farm but was not aware of the farm's Abolition connections.

Today the Josiah Read home is owned by Caroline Schenk who has lived there for the past sixty years. Bill, Ellen and I visited her and learned what she knew of the history of the home. She grew up just south of the property and her mother remembered when John T. Sims built the existing house in the early 1900s. She remembered watching him move the original kitchen from the Read home and attaching it to the new house. The kitchen we were meeting in was the same one that so long ago must have been the setting of anti-slavery discussions. She had been aware that the history of the area suggested abolition activities but was unaware of specifics.

We shared with her Hunt's letter about secreting the runaway slaves to a large red barn and asked her if she knew of one existing in the neighborhood a long time ago. She pointed out the window to the one story white barn outside. "It used to be a two story red barn." The top story of the barn used to be a large hay mow. (pronounced hay mau) When she was younger she participated in harvesting the hay. To pull the hay up into the barn, a horse had a rope tied to his harness and it ran through a pulley at the top eaves of the barn near an open door at the second story. The other end was hooked to the hay mound. Caroline, a petite woman, remembered being frightened of the large horse as she led it away from the barn. This would lift the hay up to the level of the door and the hay would hit the track; then go into the barn. Then a trip rope was pulled to release the hay to the hay mow. Only a very tall barn would be used this way because of the height needed for the set up. Eventually the large hay mow upstairs was no longer needed and Caroline's husband wanted to start a dairy so they cut the top story off and roofed it with tin and painted it white. No wonder we couldn't find the large red barn!

When Bill and Ellen went around the building to photograph it they saw the original back wall of the barn, still painted red and the old standing beams now cut off to make room for the more modern metal roof.

This looks like the barn that Dr. Nelson would have had his students bring runaway slaves to and he surely was a visitor here himself as well.

I spent years looking for the red two story barn. I didn't know that the top was removed & it was painted white.

Chapter Seventeen

THE TRAIN ROLLS ON TO THE NEXT AREA STATIONS

Collins station was an old hotel in Columbus, Illinois

I was told that this house in Columbus, Illinois, owned by Charles Brant had been a station in the Underground Railroad. I called Mr. Brant and he invited us to the house. Mr. Brant was a lifelong bachelor who wrote poetry and tended to keep to himself, although he did belong to the Quincy Exchange Club and went regularly to those meetings. Mr. Brant had maintained the house just as it was when his mother was alive. He was very knowledgeable of the history of the home and seemed to enjoy sharing it with us. We became friends, and I took him along to my presentation in Pittsfield, Illinois. After that, he wrote the poem, "*Friendship*" and gave it to me. This home of the late Charles Brant was built by Frederick Collins in 1837, who, along with his brother Michael, had a mill in Naples, Illinois. They also had a steamboat in which they used to take their grain down to St. Louis. Being men of temperance, they called their steamboat the "Cold

Water." When they got to St. Louis, some hooligans gave them a rough time, so they decided to give up their mill. Michael returned to his Liberty, Illinois farm and Frederick Collins settled in Columbus, Illinois. In 1837 he built this home and store in Columbus. The Frederick Collins home was an Underground Railroad station, with a hiding place on the third floor. Charles Brant told me that Lincoln held court in an upstairs bedroom of this home. It probably happened when Lincoln was traveling the circuit court while the home was a hotel. At that time, Columbus was very active and vying for county seat because it was the center of the county.

Carl Landrum told me that a *Quincy Whig-Journal* of Feb. 11, 1923 carried a story that indicated that Lincoln stopped overnight at the old "Lincoln" Inn in Columbus the night of Oct. 14, 1858 after the debate in Quincy with Stephen Douglas. Frederick Collins always said that Lincoln spent the night in a corner room on the second floor, right side.

Frederick Collins also organized a Presbyterian Church, was an elder, and for many years its leading supporter. He was an active abolitionist. He was hanged in effigy at one time by pro-slavery sympathizers along side of an effigy of a Negro slave woman after assisting a runaway female slave on her way toward freedom. A candidate of the Free-soil Party for Lieutenant-Governor of Illinois, in 1834 he made a speech in commemoration of the act of emancipation in the West Indies. A man significantly ahead of his time he said these words, "For me thinks the time is not far distant when our own country will celebrate a day of emancipation within her own borders, and consistent songs of freedom shall indeed ring throughout the length and breadth of the land." He was also a trustee of Illinois College.

The home has two brick hiding places in the upstairs bedrooms that are above dropped ceilings in the closets. There was another hiding place above a six foot brick oven in a summer kitchen. Another hiding place was above a false ceiling in a smoke house that has since collapsed. Frederick Collins sold the house to a man named Nance. His daughter recalled as a child seeing strange Negroes around the place and then seeing them no more. The house was then sold to a man named Norris. It is located at the beginning of a tributary to McKee Creek.

This is the hiding place up on the third floor under the eaves of the house.

When you come in the second floor bedroom, there's a fireplace and a closet that extends from the fireplace to the end of the wall of the house. When you walk into it, the ceiling of this closet is almost even with the top of the door. They built what looked like a brick coffin upstairs on the third floor near the chimney of the fireplace. The runaway slaves had to lie flat and then were covered by planks of wood. To get to this, you had to go under the eaves on the third floor. The chimney would keep them warm. The ceiling of this closet is solid brick and then plastered over. This is an unusual building feat to have lasted so long.

The following poem, given to me by Charles Brant, captures the lingering pressure of the people who passed through or lived in the stations of the Underground Railroad.

My Home

It's just an old house so some people say
It's just an old house slowly wasting away
Standing there so lonely, so silent and so grim
Like the echo of Amen at the close of a hymn.

The memories that linger as the melody dies
Bring a throb to my heart and tears to my eyes.
It is the home of my childhood, the place of my birth
More precious to me than any other place on this earth.

If this old house could talk, what stories it could tell
Of the guests entertained at this old country hotel
Some were men of distinction and of political fame
Some were great statesmen with world-wide acclaim.

I wish that I could tell you the stories I've been told
About the place I call home, it is so venerable and old
I have seen it sparkle with life, with love, laughter and joy
Oh, yes, I have seen this, my friend, when I was just a boy.

Father Time has taken its toll from the old house indeed
But it is still standing firm and I have a pleasant memory
To me it is the nearest thing to Eden under Heaven's vaulted dome
It may not look like much to you, to me it is home sweet home.

Charles Brant home used to be hotel.

Unfortunately, this house is not still standing firm but, like so many other stations, has since been torn down. After the passing of Charles Brant the house was demolished. It is sad to lose these homes with all the great stories they had to tell. I have written this book as a tribute to the brave men, women and children who lived in these storied homes.

Samuel McAnulty

This is the Samuel Holliday McAnulty house, and his son Samuel Ruby McAnulty's home.

The story, according to the McAnulty geneology is that Sam went out to the woodpile one day and behind the woodpile sat a Negro hunched up. Sam said "Never mind." This fugitive had been traveling for three days from the river without food. Sam had not had to act on his anti-slavery beliefs up to that time. Sam took him in, fed him and sent him on his way. He became very active in the Underground Railroad after that. This was told to me by Mrs. Ada Van Nosdall Mason of Golden, Illinois. "Some times they would show up in an old woodpile that was hollowed out to hide them. They were then moved after dark to Plymouth, Illinois, by wagon."

Samuel was born in Pennsylvania in 1806 and was of Scotch Irish decent. When he was twelve years old, his family moved to Greene Co, Ohio. In 1828 he married Lucinda McFarland. Four years later they moved to Camp Point Township, in Adams County, Ill. They had ten children. One child, Matilda, was born in the wagon bed on January 19, 1833, before the cabin was built. Matilda and her mother were kept warm with a bucket of coals on the inside of the wagon and a bonfire on the outside.

This picture was given to me by Mrs. Ada Van Nosdall Mason. On the back it reads: "This is a picture of The Old Stone Bridge where Runaway Slaves were hidden until dark, when they were taken in wagons to Plymouth. This bridge was in the Camp Point Twp., Section 3. My Great Grandfather, Samuel Holliday McAnulty, was one who helped in the Underground Railroad."

Griggsville Area Stations

One day, after giving my presentation at Pittsfield, Illinois, I received a letter from Mrs. Frankie Hatch Strahle. She was the great-niece of O.M. Hatch, who was a close friend of Abraham Lincoln and Secretary of State for Governor Yates from 1857 to 1865.
The letter follows:

Pittsfield, Illinois
April 15, 1971

Dear Mrs. Deters,

I am enclosing the McWilliams story – and am sorry I couldn't type it – My writing isn't very good anymore – arthritis in my hands.

I probably should tell you – the lumberyard he mentioned in the story I gave you Monday night was located south of Valley City, about where the old Griggsville landing was –

Now the home of Tom Coulson – The Mrs. Shaw lived on a farm two miles east of Griggsville – and we think was the great-grandmother of one of our friends, Miss Grace Shaw – She still owns part of the farm – It was her uncle and grandfather who helped the slave get across the river, and on his way to Jacksonville –

The O.M. Hatch mentioned was our grandfather's brother – who was politically minded, was Secretary of State under Gov. Yates from 1857 to 1863 – He was a close friend of President Lincoln.

Our grandfather came to Illinois overland from New Hampshire in the fall of 1835 with his parents, Dr. Durken Hatch & wife – seven brothers and two sisters. So we have been in Pike County quite a while. We lived in Griggsville till our parents died in 1954, then came to Pittsfield. My sister, Celia Hatch, is a retired school teacher.

We did enjoy your talk so much, especially since we knew very little about the "Underground Rail Road".

Most Sincerely yours,
Frankie Hatch Strahle

The following pages were enclosed:

Recollections of John McWilliams – p 105.

I was raised with a prejudice against Abolitionists, as it was that they were too radical – unnecessary agitators. There were two classes of anti-slavery men. One was rabid; the other had Lincoln with them, who would not interfere with slavery where it existed.

I was quite young, but I distinctly remember when a man came to Griggsville from Washington in 1837 with a petition asking that slavery be done away with in the District of Columbia. He was asking for signers.

The County was about equally divided; or, rather, there were more pro-slavery than anti-slavery. The pro-slavery men got hold of this man and took his petition away from him, and went around the neighborhood making people take their name off.

One night they came to the home of the Reverend Mr. Norton, a Congregational Minister, who, although small and delicate, was intellectual and unusually bright. They went into his bedroom and, showing him the petition, said he must take his name off. He replied: "Gentlemen, you can kill me, but I will never take my name off that petition!"

They did not succeed in intimidating him, and finally went away without using violence. Perhaps they were afraid of a minister of the Gospel.

O.M. Hatch, afterward our Secretary of State, and intimate with Lincoln, was a young man at that time, and he also signed the petition. The pro-slavery men got after him, and ran him into the Baptist church, which was being built, and had a high steeple. He went up in the steeple as far as he could and pulled the ladder after him so they could not get him.

We were living about nine miles from town (Griggsville) while these things were going on. Father got word one day that a mob had taken Griggsville, and he got about a dozen neighbors and they started with their guns; but when they got to the edge of town, everything was quiet – not a soul stirring. The mob had evidently gotten wind that men were coming who had no sympathy with their actions, and they got away.

It was about 1837 that Elijah Lovejoy started an anti-slavery free-soil paper in Alton, Illinois. The pro-slavery men came up from St. Louis, wrecked his office and threw his press in the river. He got another press, and they came the second time and not only threw this press in the river but broke up his office and killed him.

This Elijah Lovejoy was a brother of Owen Lovejoy, one of the greatest anti-slavery speakers we had in Illinois. Pike County was on the border and Republicans were in the minority. During the canvass of '58, Owen Lovejoy was billed to speak at Pittsfield, our County Seat, and the Republicans were afraid that such a noted abolitionist would lose more than he would make votes. Everyone wanted to hear him, Democrats as well as Republicans; and there was an immense crowd in the court house square which had trees all around and benches.

When Lovejoy got up to speak he said: "My Republican friends, I want you to vacate all these seats in front and I want my Democratic friends to come here. I want to talk to them."

So the Democrats gathered close in, and he made a great speech, and told them some incidents of the escape of slaves. Then he told the story of Liza, a Negro girl who was trying to get away from slavery, and whom he had helped. He told it sympathetically and well, and one old Democrat, Alex Taylor, was sitting right in front, with his mouth open, taking in every word. When Lovejoy concluded his story he looked down, pointed to Taylor, and asked; "would you not have done the same thing if you had been there?" and the old man nodded "Yes."

John McWilliams was born in Ohio, January 15, 1832 and came to Griggsville late in 1834 with his parents James and Margaret Latimer McWilliams. His book Recollections of John McWilliams describes his early days in the Griggsville area, his California "Gold Rush" days – and his Civil War experiences – After the Civil War he went to Dwight, Ill – and became wealthy as a lumber and building supply dealer. I do not know the date of the book's publication but it was somewhere between 1901 and 1920 – I think. It was a limited edition given by him to family & Friends – I received the book from a great aunt who was a neighbor of his sister Mrs. Elizabeth Farrand = two grand nieces = Mrs. Harry Kopps, and Mrs. Henry Seeds still live in Griggsville."

Another excerpt written by John McWilliams follows:

My own experience as a slave thief came about this way. Our lumberyard was four miles from town. After I got back from California, I was going home late one afternoon; and, in a lane about half way home there was a little thicket of hazel bushes in a fence corner. A Negro got out from there and said he wanted to give himself up. They had shot him in the back with fine shot which did not seriously wound him, and he had escaped and managed to get so far – nearly 40 miles from the Mississippi River. I told him to go into the bushes and I would have some help for him.

There was a family by the name of Shaw living opposite, and I knew they were anti-slavery. I went over to the house and found Mrs. Shaw alone. I told her about the Negro and she went immediately and assured him he was in safe Lands. She had to be very cautious because it was a public highway and people were constantly passing. Her son-in-law, Mr. Lyons, another son, that night hitched up their double carriage and took the Negro down to our lumber yard, then went up and crossed the river at the ferry, about a half mile above, coming down opposite the lumber yard to get him. That was the last I saw of him altho' I heard he got safely to Jacksonville.

It was strange respectable men would watch for run away slaves, trying to catch them for the reward which was $100.00 per person.

Agents 200 Miles Away

The tracks lead on to Lake Michigan in the Chicago area where the fugitive would get passage to Canada. A letter to Seibert written by Roderick B. Frary in August 3, 1896 tells of Underground railroad activity in LaMoille, Illinois about 200 miles north east of the Quincy area and about 100 miles west of Chicago. The station at LaMoille was kept by Deacon J. T. Holbrook and Benjamin Mather. A nearby station at Paw Paw was kept by Mr. Towne.

Frary tells that his uncle Parker, a Free Will Baptist Preacher lived next door to him. One morning he came to them very excited and asked if we knew who had taken his light one horse wagon. When we told him we did not take it "he was wrought up to about as high a pitch as was safe for a minister to get and said next time he would pull the linchpins out and then see if they would come in the night and steal his wagon". During the day he found out the Mr. Holbrook had an "urgent case to take a man to the next Station as the pursuer was close behind him. When Preacher Parker heard the reason the wagon was used he took the opposite extreme and offered his wagon for such use anytime it was needed.

I am often asked as to the time frame of the use of the Underground Railroad. Many people believe that it operated in the 1860s. Actually, after the passage of the Fugitive Slave Act in 1850 the climate was so intense regarding slavery in the United States that the Underground Railroad was getting more and more dangerous to operate. At the same time the political climate was evolving to the point where the abolitionists could begin to see that the tide was turning in their favor and they believed the Underground Railroad would not be necessary much longer. No one believed it would take a Civil War to make it happen. Mr. Frary's letter tells that the last "passenger" passed through LaMoille in the summer of 1854. Rev. Owen Lovejoy brought a man, his wife, two children and one or two other men and left them at the "Holbrook Station". They knew that the conductor on the Chicago Burlington & Quincy RR was friendly to this "competing line" (the Underground Railroad). Mr. Frary writes it this way: "So after sun down I took the passengers that were bound north on a summer vacation without the consent of their would be owners and landed them safely in Mendota – And with the assistance of J.J. Wante, the Agent at Mendota we took them all around the back side and hid them in the tall grass and just as the train was ready to pull out we landed them in the baggage car; and they were placed in good hands in Chicago.

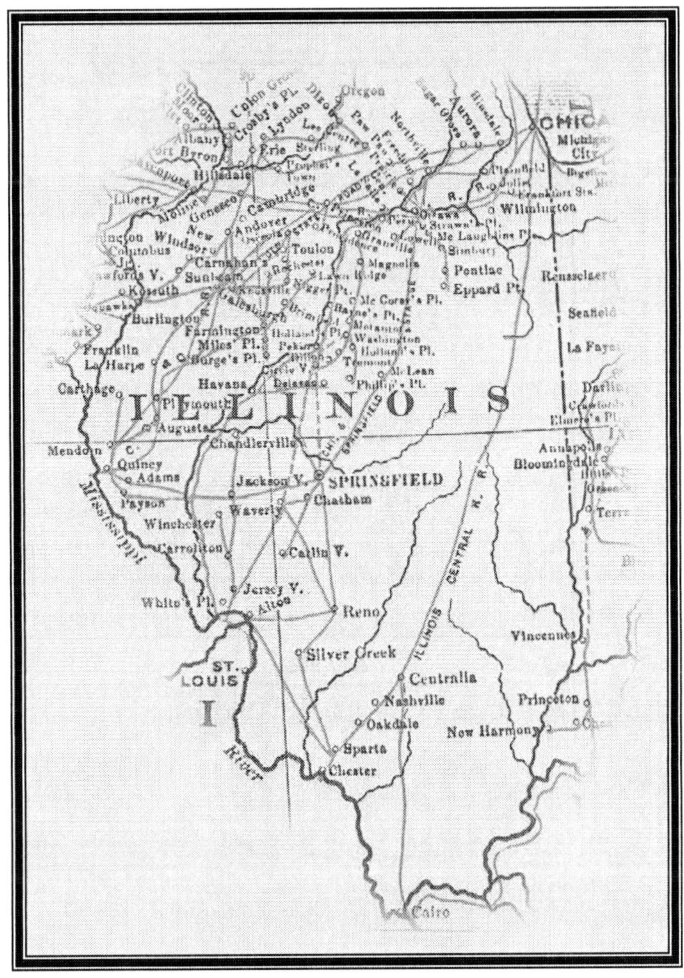

Map From: *The Underground Railroad from Slavery To Freedom*

By: Wilbur H. Siebert 1898

Chapter Eighteen

THE JOURNEY ENDS IN FRIENSHIP

So as we look back over Nelson's life as an abolitionist and a conductor on the Underground Railroad can we conclude that his efforts were successful? I doubt that Nelson died with certain knowledge of the answer to this question. There were many during Nelson's time that doubted whether the Underground Railroad was truly successful (they wondered what good it was to free one or two slaves at a time) or was it just further antagonizing those in the slaves states and perhaps hurting the chances of a potential political solution to the slavery issue. However in searching through many of Dr. Nelson's own handwritten materials, I found an interesting quote from Dr. Nelson which I believe gives us a clear insight into his philosophy regarding life but also perhaps his philosophy of the Underground Railroad. I think it undoubtedly demonstrates he was a determined yet patient person when it came to his expectations to end slavery.

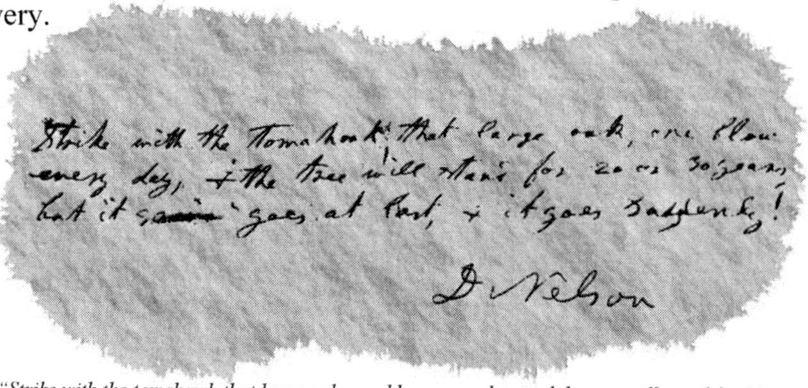
Strike with the Tomahawk that large oak, one blow every day, & the tree will stand for 20 or 30 years, but it goes at last, & it goes Suddenly!

D Nelson

"Strike with the tomahawk that large oak, one blow every day, and the tree will stand for 20 or 30 years, but it goes at last, and it goes Suddenly!"

D Nelson

Dr. David Nelson's last words, like so many he spoke have been remembered through the years and can today be found on a website noting famous deathbed quotes.

"My Master calls, I am going home; it is well."

The Quincy Daily Whig reported the following:

Died- October 17, 1844 at his residence near Quincy, Dr. David Nelson, aged 54. He died as he lived, tranquilly, and peacefully. All who ever were acquainted with him were impressed with the power and vigor of his mind, his excellent love of the souls of men, and the practical illustration of the truths and evidence of revealed religion.
Although always unmindful of his personal appearance, Dr. Nelson will always be remembered as a strong and original thinker.

(Actually Nelson was 51 at the time of his death.)

His friends felt his loss deeply and wrote many tributes about him. I have included several in the Appendix.

Originally buried on 24th & Maine on Mission Institute property, his body now rests in Woodland Cemetery overlooking the Mississippi River where a neat monument bears the following inscription:

Rev David Nelson, M.D. author of The Cause and Cure of Infidelity, born in East Tennessee, September 24, 1793 – a surgeon in the United States army – a distinguished physician in his native state – a devoted minister of Christ in Danville, Kentucky – a messenger of grace to multitudes – a founder of intstitutions of learning. Died October 17, 1844, aged 51. Erected by friends in New York.

(The friends in New York were believed to be the Tappans.)

Although I never knew him, I feel his presence daily in my home and I have had the privilege to meet his descendents pictured below.

Descendents of Dr. David Nelson visit their famous ancestor's grave November 8, 2003.

Front row from left: Forrest Irwin Bishop, Seth Michael Lanman

Middle row from left: Hazelle Lorene Nelson Lanman, MeKayla Elizabeth and Olivia Elatia Lanman,

Back row from left: Deborah Diane Lanman Bishop, Meredith Norman Bishop, Christie Lou Lanman Daugherty, Michael David Lanman.

Dorothy Ann Nelson-Watson & Hazelle Lorene Nelson-Lanman, descendents of David and Amanda Nelson.

Friendship

Throughout my journey on the mysterious Underground Railroad I have met many wonderful people and made friendships along the way. For them I share this poem given me by the late Charles Brant, owner of the Collins station in Columbus, Illinois.

Friendship

Friendship is like a golden chain
each link designed with care
Refined and drawn by the Master's hand
for mortal men to share
Infinite and ever increasing
in length, strength and in scope
Each depending on each other
for life, for love and for hope
Ninety and nine may be safe and sure
steadfast, strong and true
Depending each on each other
depending on me and on you
So may I be the hundredth one
that this chain strong may be
Having love in my heart for fellow man
may they also love me
Ironic but true we receive from life
in accordance to what we bestow
Proportionate to our friendliness
and the second mile we must go.

Charles Brant

Appendix A

Posthumous Tributes to Nelson

Nelson was so highly thought of that at one time Quincy had a street named Nelson. Tully Island in the Mississippi above Meyer was once called Nelson Island. There remains a village in Missouri named Nelsonville after its most famous resident. Nelson's legacy is best reported by the words of those who knew him.

The following tributes are reproduced in the writer's own words so that the reader can fully appreciate the impact of Dr. Nelson on those who knew him or read his writings. I believe it is important to appreciate Dr. Nelson's influence in order to understand the actions and convictions of those who believed in him.

In *Annals of the American Presbyterian Pulpit*, the history of the Presbyterian Church shares the following letters written by close friends and colleagues after his death. It begins with a synopsis of his life:

DAVID NELSON, M.D.

David Nelson, a son of Henry and Anna (Kelsey Nelson, was born near Jonesborough, in East Tennessee, on the 24th of September, 1793. His father was of English, his mother of Scotch, descent; and both were natives of Rockbridge County, Va. His father was an elder in the Presbyterian Church, and his mother was remarkable for strength of mind and ardent piety. The spot on which he was born was within two miles of the Nolachucky, a beautiful and brilliant stream that rises on the West of the Blue Ridge; and when he was taken there at the age of three years, he seemed almost entranced in looking at the cliffs and evergreens upon its banks; - the first development of that enthusiastic admiration for natural scenery for which he was remarkable in after life. As his father's residence was but two miles from Washington College, - an institution founded, and for many years presided over, by the Rev. Samuel Doak, D.D., it was here that he was sent for his education. Having completed his college courses at the early age of sixteen, he commenced the study of medicine under the direction of Dr. Ephraim McDowell, son-in-law of Governor Shelby, at Danville, Ky. Here he remained for some time, and then went to Philadelphia to avail himself of the superior advantages for medical education in that city. He returned to Kentucky at the age of nineteen, and had but just entered on the practice of medicine, when – the war with Great Britain having commenced – he joined a Kentucky regiment as a Surgeon, and proceeded to Canada.

During this expedition, (which was in 1812,) Dr. Nelson was subjected to deprivations and sufferings which had well-nigh cost him his life. He often made his bed in snow, and subsisted on frozen fat pork, and water, without bread. On his return through a wild Indian country, overcome by fatigue, cold, and hunger, he despaired of advancing any farther, and lay down in the snow, fully resolved to die there. But Providence kindly interposed for his deliverance. His friend and relative, the brave Colonel Allen, a distinguished lawyer as well as military man, who afterwards fell at the River Raisin, was instrumental in saving his life. Having missed young Nelson from the company, he returned in search of him, and found him just in time to save him from death; he lifted him upon his own powerful horse, and thus carried him on his way, encouraging his hopes, and administering to his wants, until he finally reached the end of his journey in safety.

On his return from this expedition, he settled as a medical practitioner in Jonesborough, with very promising prospects. But it was not long before he was again summoned by Generals Jackson and Coffe into the service, and he accordingly rejoined the army as a Surgeon, and went South to Alabama and Florida. In the wilderness of Alabama he was seized with a violent fever, to which he had well-nigh fallen a victim. In consequence of the great rains, the country was almost inundated; and the water was constantly rushing into his tent. For about three weeks, all who saw him supposed that his death was inevitable; though he himself, when at the lowest point, had the utmost confidence that he should recover; - and his expectation was not disappointed. The news of Peace reached him while he was at Mobile, - the very day before an expected battle; and in consequence of this, he returned to Jonesborough, and resumed his medical practice.

At the age of twenty-two, he formed a matrimonial connection with a daughter of David Deaderick, a highly respectable merchant of East Tennessee. They had twelve children, - six sons and six daughters; all of whom, with the exception of one son, survived him. The eleven children, with their mother, still (1857) survive.

Though Dr. Nelson had in very early life made a profession of religion, his serious impressions gradually wore away, and he became at length an open advocate of infidelity. This change occurred in consequence of some unfortunate associations which he formed while residing as a physician at Danville; and neither his creed nor his character was improved by his subsequent connection with the army. But, though he was avowedly infidel in his opinions, he had not been able to escape from all the influences of an early Christian education and profession. He at length became deeply impressed by the fact that the most distinguished infidel writers had greatly misquoted and perverted the Scriptures, as well as misrepresented history; and he became satisfied that justice to himself, as well as to Christianity, demanded that his reading should not be all on one side. He began now to read books illustrating the truth and power of the Gospel; and it was but a short time before his skepticism all gave way, and he was led to embrace Christianity, not only as bearing the stamp of Divine authority, but as the only foundation of his own personal hopes. Religion now became with him the all-engrossing subject; and it was manifest to all that his ruling passion was to do good, especially to the souls of his fellow-men. His profession, while he continued in it, he made auxiliary to the spiritual interests of those among whom he was thrown; not only administering Christian instruction and counsel, but distributing tracts and books on Practical and Experimental Religion, as occasion or opportunity offered. He found it exceedingly difficult at first, by reason of constitutional diffidence, to bend the devotions of even the smallest congregation; but he felt constrained to persevere in his efforts in this way, until, at no distant period, under the influence of a strong conviction of duty, and an unusual fervour of religious feeling, he could conduct such a service in the most composed and edifying manner.

Dr. Nelson's situation and prospects as a physician were in every respect what he could have desired. He was highly popular as a man, and had an extensive practice, which gave him an annual income of not less than three thousand dollars. But his heart glowed with the desire to preach that Gospel which had now become so dear to him; and this desire was not a little strengthened by a sermon on missions which he heard about this time, and which served to bring his spirit into the most intense sympathy with the missionary cause. He accordingly conceived and matured the purpose of the entering the ministry. In due time he placed himself under the care of the Abingdon Presbytery, Va., and was licensed to preach the Gospel in April, 1825.

He preached for nearly three years in different places in Tennessee, and at the same time, was associated with one of two other ministers in conducting a periodical work, published at Rogersville, entitled "The Calvinistic Magazine." In 1828, he removed to Kentucky, and became Pastor of the church in Danville, which had been rendered vacant by the death of his brother Samuel, the preceding year. He also, about this time, traveled somewhat extensively in Kentucky, as Agent of the American Education Society. In 1830, being deeply impressed with the importance of increasing the means of education in the far West, he removed to the State of Missouri, and was chiefly instrumental in establishing a College in Marion County, to which was given the name of Marion College, - twelve miles from Palmyra. Of this institution he became the first President. He visited New York, New England, and various other parts of the country, with a view to secure the requisite means for carrying forward this enterprise; and, wherever he went, left the impression that he was a man of extraordinary faith and power. The most distinctive feature of the institution was that the students were to support themselves by occupying part of their time in manual labour. But though it brought together a large number of young men, he seems to have been disappointed in the workings of it; and in 1836, owing to a difficulty which is more particularly referred to in one of the letters appended to this narrative, he removed to the State of Illinois, and in the neighbourhood of Quincy established an Institute for the education of young men, especially for missionary life. Here he exhausted his pecuniary means; and here, after a brief period, ended his days.

The latter part of Dr. Nelson's life was rendered sad from his becoming the victim of epilepsy. That fearful malady fastened itself upon him, and proved an overmatch for medical skill. His strong appetite for food he resisted continually from a conviction that indulgence would hasten the progress of his disease; but, however that may have been, abstinence did nothing to remove it. It advanced by slow but certain steps, gradually impairing his noble faculties, disappointing his hopes of continued usefulness, and finally terminating his earthly career. He was not, however, intellectually reduced to a wreck; nor was his mind at all embarrassed in its spiritual and devout exercises. Toward his family, and other near friends, it was remarked that be became constantly more tender and loving, as he approached the point at which he must leave them. When he became satisfied that his end was near, he called his wife and children around him, and said, "My Master calls- I am going home – kiss me, my children, and bid your last farewell, as I shall be in a state of insensibility and shall not know you." To the question, - why he felt sure that his end was near, - as he did not seem more ill than he had often done before, he laconically answered, - "Extreme debility." He then addressed most tenderly and impressively one of his children, who, he feared had not entered on the religious life, and, on the promise to serve the Lord being given, he turned over, and said, - "It is well;" and these were his last words. He died at Oakland, five miles East of Quincy, on the 17th of October, 1844, aged fifty-one years. His remains rest in the cemetery of Woodland, near Quincy, - a beautiful bluff overlooking the Mississippi, where there is a fine marble monument to his memory, erected by some of his friends in the city of New York.

Dr. Nelson's highest and most enduring fame no doubt is connected with his well known work entitled, "Cause and Cure of Infidelity." Most of this was written in a few weeks, in the summer of 1836, in his garden, and under clumps of tall oaks, at Oakland. It has already passed through many editions, and has taken a high place in the standard religious literature of the age. Dr. Nelson wrote another work entitled "Wealth and Honour," designed for publication, but the manuscript was unfortunately lost after it had passed from his hands, and has never been recovered. He also wrote many articles on Education, Baptism, Missions, and other subjects, which appeared in the New York Observer, and other papers of the day. A few of his poetical effusions also have appeared in print, showing that he had a talent which might, by due cultivation, have given him a place among the distinguished poets of his time.

FROM J.A. JACOBS, ESQ.

Danville, Ky.,
January 31, 1957

My dear Sir: I was much pleased to learn that you design to include a notice of my lamented friend, the late Rev. Dr. David Nelson, in your work commemorative of the distinguished clergymen of this country. The omission of it would, in my opinion, be the absence of one of the brightest stars in the constellation of ministerial piety, but of remarkable genius, distinguished by peculiarities and eccentricities of thought, manner, and conduct, which would have made him " the observed of all observers" in any profession or walk of life. His genius, sanctified and sublimated by religion, rendered him no unapt representative of an ancient prophet, rapt in Divine inspiration, and of whom the world was not worthy. His life, if correctly portrayed by the hand of a master, which it richly deserves to be, would be a valuable inheritance to the Church, to which, being dead, he would continue to speak with that strange and peculiar power with which, when alive and in the vigour of his strength, he captivated and entranced his hearers.

There was something strangely – almost preternaturally – unique in his manner. You listened as if to a being who lived in a world of thought and feeling, entirely different from the ordinary children of men – with a genius bold and perfectly original, ranging with burning zest through every field of imagination, and pouring forth thoughts that breathe and words that burn with the power of the true orator and inspired bard. His eloquence was not the cold argumentations of logic, but a succession of fervid, powerful and picturesque appeals, equally concise and vigorous in expression, and bold and original in sentiment.

I shall never forget the first sentence I heard the Doctor utter in the pulpit. It was in the month of September, 1827, in the Presbyterian Church, in this town, of which he shortly after became the pastor, and continued to be for several years. He had made a visit to the wife and family of his recently deceased brother, the Rev. Samuel K. Nelson.

It was a bright and beautiful Sabbath morning – the pulpit was shrouded in black, and the church was crowded to hear the brother of the late minister, the fame of whose eloquence and eccentricities had preceded him. He had lived in the neighbourhood when quite a young man, and some few of the congregation recollected him, when he was a wild and reckless youth, and actually professed that infidelity of which he has so ably written the "Cause and Cure."

His appearance was anything but clerical. He had on an old rusty black cloth coat, badly made and fitted, and his vest and pantaloons were not better – as he rose he hitched up the later, as if he wore no suspenders; and to make his garb as unministerial as possible, he had, for a cravat, a red bandana handkerchief. It is proper here to remark, that there was nothing in this garb intentionally eccentric. The Doctor was as far from affectation as a man could be. It was the result partly of a slovenly carelessness, and total inattention to, and forgetfulness of, external appearances, and partly of a conscientious and mistaken disregard for them. With his large and ungainly figure – with strong but harsh features, and totally destitute of all grace of manner, and thinking and caring nothing whatever about appearances, he made certainly a most odd looking occupant of a pulpit. His appearance and manner are now fully in my mind's eye and his first sentence still vibrates on my ear. It was abrupt and enigmatical – "Tether a horse to a stake in a rich meadow, and he is *perfectly* satisfied," – laying a strong emphasis on the word *perfectly*, in his peculiar intonation. What to make of this singular and startling exordium to a sermon, the congregation hardly knew; but they were not long in suspense. The Doctor proceeded in his concise, forcible and picturesque language, glowing with thoughts full of beauty and power, to illustrate the impossibility of satisfying the immortal soul of man with earthly things. The brute was entirely contented if its bodily wants were supplied; but not so the human sole. Restless, dissatisfied and unhappy, though possessed of every earthly good, it longed for immortality – a proof that it was made for the future, and of the duty of seeking our chief good in the present service and future enjoyment of God".

Dr. Nelson was then, and for several years after, in the prime and vigour of his intellect. The sermons that he preached in this place, which were written and delivered *memoriter*, and which he usually carried in the crown of his hat, if they could be recovered and published, would form a volume of eccentric, but singularly powerful, sacred eloquence. I anxiously applied to his widow, years ago, to know if the manuscripts were in existence. She informed me that they could not be found.

In after years, he probably lost, perhaps destroyed, them, under the conscientious feeling that the literary labour he had bestowed upon them sprung from vanity, and was sinful. Some years after he left Danville, his intellect became impaired from disease. He became extemporaneous, and rather tedious and rambling, in his discourses. It was painful to be witnessed by those that knew him in his prime.

Samson, shorn of his hair and strength, was hardly more changed. But his piety burned with a more intense and unearthly glow to the last. One of his daughters, who possessed a good deal of her father's wild and thoughtless character when young, half seriously and half jocularly said that, when traveling alone with her father, she sometimes feared he would ascend to Heaven, and leave her alone on the uninhabited prairie.

His soul seemed absorbed in spiritual realities – he was almost utterly careless of earthly affairs – made no provision for himself, and little for his family, leaving them as well as himself to Him who cares for the lilies of the field and the birds of the air. This did not spring from indolence; but partly from an almost total absorption of soul in religion, and partly from mistaken notions about the duty of devoting all our time and means to God's service, to the disregard of earthily interests, enjoyments, and appearances. In his latter years, he conscientiously wore a wool hat and the coarsest clothing. Had all men adopted his extreme notions, manufactures would have ceased, civilization would have retrograded, and pious people would have possessed but little to consecrate to their Master's service.

Yet Providence did not fail to provide for his faithful and trusting servant. Besides the attention to his wants given by his friends, his nephew, the son of his brother Samuel, died early, and left a large estate, a considerable portion of which fell to the Doctor, and administered to his and his family's wants for several years.

Not doubting that you will gather from other sources whatever may be necessary to illustrate the character of my friend, I will only add that

I am very sincerely yours,

J.A. Jacobs.

FROM THE REV. WILLIAM S. POTTS, D.D.

Mackinac, Mich.,
July 27, 1848.

My dear Sir: Yours of the 17th lt. was received in St. Louis, and I have deferred compliance with your request until I could obtain some relaxation from the press of cares and engagements incident to my calling. I came to this island with my family a few days since, and will now endeavour to call up my remembrances of Dr. Nelson.

My first acquaintance with him was in St. Louis, in the summer of 1828 or '29. He was then on a visit to the State, with a view to the purchase of land preparatory to the removal of his family from Kentucky. I found him, when introduced, a man of about middle age, prepossessing in his appearance, with a smile on his countenance, and very cheerful in his intercourse, but always directing the conversation to some subject of Theology or practical Christian duty, or to the condition and prospects of the Church. I had occasion to observe one of his peculiarities during his visit. I invited him to preach for me on Sabbath morning. A large congregation were in attendance. He took his text, stated his divisions, which were three, and proceeded in a plain, practical discussion of his subject for about twenty minutes, - when, having disposed of the first and second heads of his discourse, he abruptly concluded. Upon leaving the church, I inquired what had become of the third lead of his sermon. He was very thoughtful, and merely remarked, - "I would not preach to your congregation again for a thousand dollars. He gave no reason other than that everything was so orderly and precise about the whole appearance of the congregation that he could not preach. The difficulty I have no doubt was, that there was no emotion or visible indication of the Spirit's presence amongst the people; for, in my subsequent acquaintance and labours with him, I observed frequently the same thing, even during a revival of religion.

The following year, he removed to the State and settled in Marion County, about eighteen miles from the Mississippi River. His attention was directed immediately to the establishment of a school in his own neighborhood. A log school house was erected, and he invited the neighbors to send their sons and daughters, of all ages. His mode of teaching was unique. After prayer, and some brief exercises in reading, he sat down and talked to the pupils on subjects of history and science, producing endless illustrations, and giving much information in a most captivating form. But so frequent calls were made upon his time, to preach, to administer to the sick, and to attend to his own farm, it was not unusual, when he was tired of talking, to leave the school to take care of itself, and apply himself to some other work for hours. In this desultory way, no systematic instruction could be given, and there was danger of rearing his pupils with as little method as he had himself; yet a spirit of inquiry and desire for education was communicated to the families around him, which subsequently exhibited itself in the attempt to establish a permanent collegiate institution in his vicinity.

Marion College owed its origin to Dr. Nelson. Upon the same ground where his school house was built, other buildings for dormitories, recitation rooms, and boarding house, were from time to time erected. Pupils were called from a distance, teachers were obtained, and in 1832 a Charter was granted by the State, and Dr. Nelson became the President. The principal object of the founder was to raise up young men for the ministry in the West, and for heathen countries. Nine of these are now known to be laboring in the West, and one has been for many years in a foreign land. The wild, extravagant and speculating notions, which afterwards ruined this institution, were not, in any degree, attributable to him. Plain to an excess in his own notions of living, he had no idea of expending money on mere brick and mortar to accommodate the bodies of the students, without permanent provision for their intellectual wants.

Whilst these educational projects were in progress, Dr. Nelson was occupied mainly in preaching the Gospel in the Northern portions of the State. In this work he was greatly honored by the Head of the Church. Hundreds crowded to his ministry, and very many returned to bless their households, who had previously lived in ignorance and infidelity. The country was at the time without houses for worship, and this difficulty was obviated in a way of his own. He made known everywhere that he would hold a protracted meeting in any settlement where the people would erect a shed, consisting of a rude clap-boarded roof, supported by hewn pillars, and provided with seats. Around these sheds the people erected tents, or clap-board shanties, in which they slept, and thus two or three hundred people could be kept together for several days under the instructive and pungent ministry of this man of God. The converts were, at the close of the meeting, examined by such ministers and ruling elders as were upon the ground, and received by baptism into the Church of Christ. It was left to the particular churches within whose bounds they resided, subsequently to examine and deal with them as they pleased. Where it seemed expedient, a church was organized on the ground, and the converts, living in the neighborhood, received into it.

In 1836, a difficulty occurred in the county between Dr. Nelson and a portion of the inhabitants, which led to his removal to the State of Illinois. The revelations of the Doctor, aided by his frequent visits to, and preaching amongst, the more earnest opposers of slavery, led him, during the latter part of his stay in the State, to take higher and higher ground on that delicate and agitating subject. Before he came to Missouri, he had set his own slaves at liberty and in his social intercourse with his friends, pleasantly argued against the institution, and condemned it as an evil in the land. In 1835, he had so far adopted the abolition doctrine, that he accounted slaveholding a sin, and refused to sit at the Communion table with those who held slaves, although they had been brought into the Church under his own ministry. In the spring of the following year, whilst preaching his Farewell Sermon to the Greenfield Church, which he had organized, and served for several years, a member of the church requested him to read a paper to the congregation, which proposed opening a subscription to redeem slaves, by paying the price at which their owners held them, with a view to their being colonized. A great excitement occurred, and an influential citizen was stabbed by the person proposing the project. The Doctor was hurried from the ground by his friends. Mob law prevailed for several days, and he lay concealed in the brush in the vicinity of his own house, until opportunity occurred to retire to Illinois. It is said that, during the time of his concealment in this thicket, he projected and commenced his work – "The Causes and Cure of Infidelity".

Dr. Nelson was, when under the excitement of a revival, a most thrilling and powerful preacher. There was little apparent arrangement in his discourses. They were almost wholly made up of illustrations and historical facts, and the other matter was used only to tie his illustrations and facts together. He was a man of much prayer, and lived as nearly with a single eye to the glory of God as any one I ever knew. He looked upon this world as a field for working, and rejoiced in the marks of approaching age and of final dissolution.

On the whole, I have no hesitation in assigning to Dr. Nelson a place among the remarkable men of the age. With as much of native intellectual and moral nobility as is often seen in connection with our fallen humanity, and with a desire to serve God in promoting the spiritual welfare of men, that every body saw had all the strength of a ruling passion, he combined strongly marked eccentricities, which the essential grandeur of his character served only to render more conspicuous. But, however these eccentricities might blind some to his substantial excellence, and even interfere, to some extent, with his usefulness, it was impossible but that persons of intelligence and discernment should very quickly discover his remarkable piety and power; and it was equally impossible for anyone to be long in contact with him, and be insensible to his influence. Hence his career as a Christian minister was signalized in an unusual degree by the triumphs of Divine grace; and wherever he went, he seemed to be constantly gathering jewels to his immortal crown. He moved about in the most unostentatious manner; and though he did not literally have "his raiment of camel's hair, and a leathern girdle about his loins," yet he never appeared – at least in his latter years – but in the coarsest attire; and those who did not penetrate beneath the exterior, took knowledge of him only as a person of the most negligent and slovenly habits. But sadly were they deceived, who reached such a conclusion. Beneath that veil which false conceptions of Christian duty had drawn around him, there were the workings of a mind, which always moved in a path of light, and which was capable of some of the grandest achievements to which the human intellect ever attains. He was, in the most humble, yet efficient manner, performing a mission of benevolence among his fellow men, the importance of which, I doubt not, will be attested by the praises of multitudes whom he was instrumental of turning to righteousness. But it was the ordinance of God that his great mind should suffer an eclipse, before going to mingle in higher and brighter scenes; - thus completing the discipline by which he was prepared for the glorious change, and illustrating, in one of its aspects, the humiliating truth, that "man, at his best estate, is altogether vanity."

Very truly yours,
W.S. POTTS.

FROM THE REV. FREDERICK A. ROSS, D.D.

Huntsville, Ala.,
Feb. 4 1857

My dear Sir: My intimacy with Dr. David Nelson was, in some regards, greater than with Mr. Gallaher. For a time, indeed, we three were one – as Editors of the Calvinistic Magazine, and in other influences. No three men could have been much more affectionately united. We were about the same age. Gallaher was the oldest, Nelson next, I was the youngest. Gallaher was, as I have said, my spiritual father. Nelson led me into the ministry – after this wise: -

My religious change occurred, at one of our old-fashioned four days' Sacramental occasions, then, and now, so common in East Tennessee, - beginning on Friday, and terminating, usually with a sermon, Monday morning. It was Gallaher's Monday sermon which brought me to decision. It so happened that there was to be another similar series of days of preaching, connected with the Supper, at Jonesborough, about twenty-five miles from Kingsport, near which I resided. Gallaher, and another friend, Robert Glenn, to whom I owe eternal gratitude for his religious influence at that time, and before, - were solicitous that I should go over to Jonesborough, and with some others, (who, like myself, felt satisfied, that Monday morning,) add thereby to the good impressions hoped for.

I went, - and found there Dr. David Nelson. He had recently renewed, after years of relapse even into infidelity, his very early profession of Christ. He had been a physician, in the army of General Jackson, - for that was his Dr. and not D.D. He fell into many army habits – returned to Jonesborough, - a great over six feet, burley, drinking, card-playing leader of fun, in them one after next dissipated villages in the West, - now most remarkable for its piety. He ran away with the smallest girl you ever saw. She looked more like a fairy than a woman. Her family was one of the most respectable in the State, and, they thought all was ruin to their daughter. For, although Nelson's social position was equally good, his habits, as said, were, of course, such as to forbid all parental encouragement. His wife, however, often told me, she knew the genius, and the goodness, and greatness, there was in him. Well, he ran away with this little creature – beautiful in the extreme – and elegantly educated in Philadelphia. He soon returned to Jonesborough, and boarded, (ere the reconciliation,) in the house of my, after, father-in-law.

He was an admirable physician, and much beloved, as such dashing men often are, if full of genius, amiable, and whithal eccentric, as he was, to a high degree, till he died.

He one day took up Doddridge's Rise and Progress – some word arrested his mind. He read the work, - and like the look on Christ on Peter, that word led Nelson to go out and weep bitterly.

When, therefore, I went to Jonesborough, where I was an entire stranger, the latter part of September, 1823, Nelson had, a very short time before, re-entered the church with his wife.

During the Sacramental occasion, he, in the fullness of his renewed love, sought me. We were very kindred spirits, at least in our former habits, except the infidelity. I never doubted the Bible, and have defended it, even at the card-table, piled with money. Our intimacy began instantly. We were fascinated with each other, - both about twenty-seven years of age. He, a great lump of a man, - I, a little fellow, never weighing over one hundred and thirty-five; but we both were enthusiastic, and of very similar literary, among our other and formerly worse, tastes. I had no special eccentricities, but I was greatly *taken* with his. His wife was *sui generis* too.

It so happened that, at that meeting, I was called on, Sunday night, to lead in prayer – that prayer struck Nelson's fancy. He had it seems, been turning his mind to the ministry; for he was of an eminently holy family. His father was a ruling elder. His mother one of the very Scotch-Irish of the earth. His brother an esteemed preacher in Danville, Ky. That prayer had some important results.

In providence it so turned up, that, at this same Sacramental occasion, I saw the lady, whom I married a few months thereafter, - the intimate of Nelson's wife. So, I was often in Jonesborough, and with Nelson, a great deal.

A very short time after this last event, he wrote to me, giving his turn of conviction as to the work of the ministry, and inviting me to direct my thoughts to the same obligation. It resulted in our both putting ourselves under the care of Abingdon Presbytery, April, 1824, at Kingsport, near my home. We then studied theology, &c., at our own firesides, under some care of Rev. Robert Glenn. In April, 1825, he and I were licensed to preach the Gospel, in a log church, Glade Spring Congregation, Washington County, Va., and it so occurred that we were ordained on the same day, six months afterwards, (as Evangelists,) in Rogersville, East Tennessee, one of Mr. Gallaher's places of labor.

You perceive, then, there was more in my relations to Nelson, to make us know each other, than even in my connection with Gallaher. Indeed those years were the most attractive of my ministerial life – as they dwell in my thoughts. Nelson was one of most lovely of human characters, - with a charm about him, which, like all charms, can be understood only by those on whom the spell has fallen. Gallaher had much of that power; but it was different in type. Nelson was the most fascinating preacher I ever heard. His simple train of argument, - his combination of thought, so original, - his exquisite illustrations, inexhaustible, - his strange unearthly voice, - his noble face, - his sweet smile, which made you feel the light and love of Heaven, - made him the subject of undying affection in every heart which knew him. There were, you see, many things to make me love him living, and remember him as he was "very pleasant unto me." And I weep now, although sixty years of age, like a woman, as I see him and hear him, in his place, speaking for God, or in familiar talk by the way.

Poor fellow he died of the effects of epileptic fits, before his eye would have been dim or his natural force abated. His sun was going down when he was in Albany – clear and beautiful, but not in the greatest of strength.

He was very curious and ridiculous in his notions about dress, and he would have been worse but for me. What you say, however, evinces the correctness of somebody's remark, - that the minister, when he preaches in the country, must give his best sermon; when he enters the city pulpit, he must wear his best coat. Your Albany people, shrewd as they are, were caught napping that time. Nelson was a most refined and accomplished gentleman. His social position, aside from his ministerial, was equal to any, in the United States. And he was esteemed meet companion for the Clay, and the Crittenden, of Kentucky – where his brother was the son-in-law of the great Shelby of King's Mountain. I told him once, when I found him building a house – a cottage, unlike anybody's, with the stump of a tree left in the middle of the parlor, as a centre table – I told him I thought it might be well enough in *him* to dress as he did, - for it obtained for him all the more attention from refined people. "How is that," he said, sitting down upon the stump – "Why," I replied – "you preached lately in Washington, and the President invited you to dinner. You preached such a sermon as he never heard in his life; and then, I have no doubt, he paid you extra attentions, lest you might think he felt contempt for you, on account of your clothes." This hit did him some good. He tied his shoes afterwards, and wore a better hat.

After a few years in the ministry, he left East Tennessee, in obedience to the call of the Church of Danville, Ky., which had been his brother Kelsey's charge. But he remained no great while. Like Gallaher, he had no pastoral qualifications. He went to the extreme, then, of Missouri; in part, to have as many strawberries as he wanted, and the freedom of the prairie.

He was poor. But his faith was great, - and, strangely to the world, was it answered, in anecdotes of providence, curious and touching. Once he had no meal in his barrel, and said to his wife, he would go and see if the miller would trust him. On the way, a boy met him with a letter from a lady living at a distance, containing a piece of gold, &c., &c.

My dear Sir – I have just written on, intending, when I began, only to say I might some day give you a line about Nelson, and one word has followed another to the seventh page of this hasty reply to your kind favor of 26th January.

Yours very truly and affectionately,

F.A. ROSS

FROM THE REV. R. J. BRECKENRIDGE, D.D.

Danville, August 31, 1857

My dear Sir: Your request for my recollections of Dr. Nelson has found me in the midst of many pressing engagements; but I will endeavor to meet it as far as my limited time will allow.

He was a man of very large frame – not tall, nor fat, but powerfully built. He had a very full suit of rough, black hair, clear blue eyes, a Roman physiognomy, and swarthy complexion. His manners were grave, silent, but most gentle and sincere. He took no interest in general conversation, and ordinarily refused to hold protracted discourse except on some subject directly involving the salvation of souls. But nothing could be more tender, earnest and striking than his private conversation on all subjects of that kind. On one occasion of his crossing the mountains from one of the Eastern cities to Pittsburg, in a stage full of people, - after remaining profoundly silent for several days and nights, just before the journey closed, he said abruptly – “I have listened to all of you patiently during two days and nights, - now may I speak to you for half an hour?” This wholly unexpected remark, with his singular and striking appearance, secured the attention of the passengers: and he proceeded with the utmost tenderness and pathos to plead with them about their souls. One, who was present, told me, years afterward, that he dated his own conversion from that talk, and that no member of the party seemed unmoved. This is a specimen of hundreds of anecdotes told of him.

Two things were very noticeable about him, both of which struck every one at once. One was his remarkable appearance, augmented by the singularly mean, slovenly, coarse, and often dirty, apparel which he habitually wore, and steadily refused to amend. The other was the most touching and penetrating voice that was almost ever heard. Whoever saw him, paused to look at him – whoever heard him, felt his voice at his heart. I may add that he was most singularly careless about all temporal matters – utterly indifferent to his own wants and interests, and as profusely generous to all that he had the means of aiding. As a sample of both peculiarities – on one occasion, while he was Pastor of the Church at Danville, the late Judge John Green, an elder of that Church, met him going out of the town, on a trip that would occupy him several weeks, and knowing his habits, asked him if he had any money, - and forced about fifty dollars on him to bear expenses. It was afterwards ascertained that he had given the whole of it away before night.

There was perhaps nothing more wonderful about this man than his fervent and overpowering love for Christ. To say that he was a most engaged, earnest, devout Christian, does not convey the idea. It was, that he seemed to be consumed with a tender, ardent, solemn and unquenchable love for Christ Himself. Nothing was hard to him, if he could please or honor his Savior – nothing had any relish for him, if it was irrespective of his Divine Master. Nay, he never mentioned the name of Christ without visible emotion, manifest in a tremor of his voice, tears in his eyes, or a flush upon his noble and manly features!

As a preacher, I, who have heard most of the great preachers of America, Britain, and France, of this age, - can truly say his power in the pulpit exceeded all I ever witnessed. I have spoken of his voice and appearance – his manner was childlike in its perfect simplicity and naturalness. He spoke extempore always; but the pathos, the unction, the impression, of his preaching were amazing. His matter was compact; his words as few as could express what he meant; his tones low rather than high; and he could hardly be said to have any action. But such word-pictures were hardly ever surpassed by man – such insight into man and into Divine things – such love and pity for lost men – such conviction of eternal realities – such sublime exhibitions of a Gospel able to save sinners, and of a Saviour who had given Himself for them!

When Nelson entered the ministry, he has told me that all his friends derided him for thinking of preaching, - believing he had not a single qualification for the work. And that the Presbytery, which licensed him, viewed the matter as so singular, that all the examination they made of him was to ask him to read a chapter of the Greek Testament to them; after hearing which, and asking him a few questions, they licensed him on the spot; their notion seeming to be, that he would continue the practice of medicine, and merely preach once in a while. Yet he became one of the greatest preachers on earth!

His labours in the ministry covered an immense field, and were attended everywhere with the mighty power of God. Tennessee, Kentucky, Missouri, Ohio, Illinois, - nearly all the great Eastern cities – most especially, perhaps, Baltimore – witnessed as glorious and as repeated revivals of religion in connection with his labours as have been vouchsafed by God to any minister of his day.

I knew this man as well as I ever knew any one, out of my immediate family; and that for a period of nearly twenty years; and I can truly say I never knew a more godly man, a more noble gentleman, or a more illustrious example of a great pulpit orator. All this did not prevent him from having eccentricities, and from falling into errors and mistakes, and from being misled by persons far inferior to himself; and what is worst of all by far, from despising the Gospel, and deriding Christ, for the first half of his life. But, oh! he was a living monument of Divine grace!

In great haste,

Your brother in Christ,

R.J. BRECKENRIDGE

Dr. David Nelson--Beautiful Tribute from the Pen of Mr. Thomas Pope. 1886

The brief notice of the late Dr. David Nelson in The

Whig of the 14th, which was clipped from The Lewistown Democrat, prompts me to add some items and make a correction.

Dr. Nelson was born in Tennessee and became a skillful and noted physician. He was a free-thinker. Honest inquiry into the grounds of his disbelief in revelation brought him to acknowledge his error and to accept the scriptures as the word of God.

The processes through which his mind passed at this time eminently fitted him to write that wonderful book, "The Cause and Cure of Infidelity," which has greatly benefited many who were inclined to doubt.

Dr. Nelson gave up the practice of medicine and went into the ministry. Some time after he became connected with a movement to found a Christian college at Ely, Marion county, Mo., a few miles back of where Marion City was started with great preparation and great expectations; but the flood of the next year swept these away. It was from Ely he was obliged to fly from an angry mob on account of his anti-slavery sentiments, although he had been careful to avoid any overt act of opposition. From his hiding place at the bank of the Mississippi above Quincy he was rescued by two of our citizens. Capt. John Burns and, I think, either George W. Westgate or Peter McWorthy, and given refuge in our city.

It was while hiding that he wrote that beautiful hymn, "My Days Are Gliding Swiftly By," and not "On Jordan's Stormy Banks I Stand," as stated in The Lewistown Democrat's item, for that was in use in the churches long before.

Dr. Nelson, aided by friends, soon bestirred himself in the line of his cherished wishes, and Mission Institute No.1 was projected and put in operation near Burton, in this county. Its object was to enable poor young people of both sexes to secure an education and fit themselves for missionary work.

Here the good doctor located his family, Mrs. Rose Nelson Clapp, his accomplished daughter, still resides there, bringing at times the products of the garden and dairy to the tables of friends of long ago. From this school and another started at what is now East Quincy, quite a number of students went to missionary fields in Africa, the West Indies, Sandwich Islands, and the Dacota Indians. One winter a party of Missourians crossed the river on the ice, and burned the main building of the school at East Quincy.

Dr Nelson was always welcomed to the pulpits of our churches. He was a saintly man, revered by young and old. He was intensely interested in the prophecies of the Old Testament, making large use of them in his work on infidelity and in his versions, notably those relating to the coming and triumph of the kingdom of Christ. Often he spoke of the prophecy foretelling the extinction of the temporal power of the papacy, and grew eloquent as he claimed that day was very near, as it proved to be. While the Mormons were at

Nauvoo a joint debate between Joseph Smith and Dr. Nelson was arranged for. It was held near Quincy, but Smith remained silent, letting his more fluent speakers of the apostles do the talking.

Dr. Nelson died at the age of 54 years. His body rests in beautiful Woodland cemetery. Friends in New York placed an appropriate monument over his remains.

So long as his book is read, and his hymn sung, so long will it be true that "He being dead, yet speaketh."

The Quincy Daily Herald on Feb 7, 1908 tells this story:

State Historical Society Asks Our Representative of Dr. Nelson

At a meeting of the State Historical society in Springfield last week Campbell S. Hearn was asked to furnish the body with some information relative to the life and works of Dr. David Nelson, who was one of the early authors of this section of the state. This poet-physician was born in Tennessee, 1793, died near Quincy, 1844.

In 1830, after having spent several years with Andrew Jackson in Florida and Alabama, during the Seminole war, he came to Palmyra, Mo. and established Marion College, some twelve miles from that city. His attitude toward slavery was such that he was uncongenial to his slaveholding neighbors, and six years later removed his school of learning to Quincy. Although an eminent Presbyterian divine, he later became imbued with the idea there is no future existence. After groping for years after what he believed to be truth, the doctor again became convinced that God was and is. His book, "The Cause and Cure of Infidelity," is one of the strongest attacks on unbelief, with a remedy therefore, which has ever been given to the public. Among his poetic writings none perhaps is better known than an old hymn, "The Shining Shore," which has been set to music, and is sung throughout the civilized world. This was written in an ancient tavern at West Quincy, while waiting to cross the river into Quincy. The lights of the little city, as seen through the fog and night, suggested the theme of the song. The doctor is buried in Woodland cemetery, and a simple monument marks his last resting place.

From an article in the Quincy Daily Whig on May 9, 1908:

Nelson of Quincy—Doctor and Author

The old river towns of Quincy and Alton, in Illinois, have interesting memories running back to the days when there were neither telegraphs nor railways in the west and when Chicago was but a village, with far less prospect of greatness than towns on the great river claimed. The two places were the scenes of the last two debates between Lincoln and Douglas, in 1858, and are not a little proud of their connection with those historic point discussions. In fact, preparations are now making for a suitable observance this year, of the semi-centennial of those events. But Alton and Quincy became known widely through the nation many years before the time of the famous senatorial campaign. Each town possessed a celebrity who caught the attention of the whole country—Alton, Elijah Lovejoy's and Quincy, David Nelson. Each of these celebrities resided but a brief period in the city which he made famous. Singularly, each was a Presbyterian and a writer on religious subjects. Here the parallel ends. Lovejoy's tragic death at Alton made him of hero of national fame. Nelson's serene and beautiful life had in it nothing of the spectacular. Lovejoy's resting place is marked by a monument of marvelous design, which stands upon a commanding bluff and is visible for miles. Yet it is but ten years since this memorial was erected. For sixty years after the tragedy at Alton but little attention was paid to his grave. Nelson's monument at Quincy was erected shortly after his death by friends in New York and through six and a half decades has marked his tomb. The generation of today knows little about him. His name is but rarely spoken. His influence upon his time was deep and lasting but so silent, and in a great measure so indirect, that its source is not recognized except where the student of sociology traces it historically.

David Nelson, like Elijah Lovejoy, was occupied chiefly with secular work. He was a physician. He wrote a religious work on singular in its plan and so popular in its interests, that to this day it stands alone, and there is nothing on the same plane with it. Had there not been with Dr. Nelson, something peculiarly responsive to the needs of his time, it is not at all likely that its readers would ever have been numerous or its repute at all considerable. The river towns of the west were not producing authors in those days, and nobody looked to them for books of any kind. As a theme in sociology it is a matter if interest now to take up his old book for a little study in personal influence.

In Dr. Nelson's day, even the novels and romances were likely to prove very tedious for the first fifty pages when the reader "got into" them by wading through characters of dry description which had little or no connection with the plot of the story. The newspaper repartee had not yet been born. Dr. Nelson's book was alive with interest in every part. He caught the reader whose eye happened to fall upon any part of any page.

In Dr. Nelson's day there were no normal schools in the west, and the few established in the east were but initial experiments. We had developed almost nothing in the way of pedagogical literature. The true teacher must be "born," not made, nor even assisted. Had Dr. Nelson been trained by the Herbestians of today, he could not have been a better practical exponent of the "doctrine of interest."

Dr Nelson's book, "The Cause and Cure of Infidelity," has long been out of print, though for, some decades it was found in libraries everywhere, and was read with interest for all who read it. Perhaps there is now no need for it. Other books have taken its place. Other bright and joyous songs of religious character have replaced his hymn. Other teachers have learned to exemplify the "doctrine of interest." Yet Quincy can well afford to keep green the memory of the man who first caused this town to be known all the way to the Atlantic. It would mark the spot where, under the "four old trees" was written the book which was treasured by the people of the country, regardless of denomination. And if the student of literature in the school texts of today is required to know something of the old "religio medici" and its author. In a purely secular study, is it not equally in order to invite his attention also to Nelson's book, which probably had a much greater influence upon the minds of men?

HUBERT M. SKINNER

Bibliography

American Anti-Slavery Society. "Members Present." Fourth Annual Report of the American Anti-Slavery Society, with the Speeches. Proc. of American Anti-Slavery Society Anniversary Meeting. New York: William S. Dorr, 1837. 20. Samuel J. May Anti-Slavery Collection - Division of Rare & Manuscript Collections. 2006. Cornell Library. 13 Jan. 2008 <http://dlxs.library.cornell.edu>.

Biggers, Jeff. United States of Appalachia: How Southern Mountaineers Brought Independence, Culture, and Enlightenment to America, The . N.p.: Shoemaker & Hoard Publishing, 2007.

Blight, David W. "The Martyrdom of Elijah P. Lovejoy." American History Illustrated XII.7 (Nov. 1977): 20-27.

Boden, Linda. Personal interview. 15 Nov. 2007.

Burks, James A. "Quincy Diary of James A. Burks." Unpublished diary, 1889-1890.

Butler, Savina Cookie. Personal interview. 11 Jan. 2008.

Carriel, Mary Turner. Life of Jonthan Baldwin Turner. Jacksonville, Il: Mary Turner Carriel, 1911.

Carwile, Ruth "Kak". Personal interview. 31 Oct. 2007.

"Chapter Four Ephraim McDowell, Pioneer Surgeon." History of the Stanford University Medical School. 2006. Stanford University. 6 Feb. 2006 <http://elane. stanford.edu.wilson/>.

Class historian. "Class of Sixty-Three Williams College Fortieth Year Report." Thomas Todd Printer, Boston, 1903.

Collins, William H. "The Collins family." Unpublished essay, 1897.

Collins, William H., and Cicero F. Perry, eds. Past and Present of the City of Quincy and Adams County, Illinois. Chicago: S.J. Clarke Publishing Co., 1905.

Cory-Phillips, Diane. "Quincy, Illinois And The Underground Railroad." MA thesis. Quincy College, 1961.

Deaderick, David Anderson. "diary." Unpublished diary, 1825 - 1872. McClung Historical Room, public library, Knoxville, TN.

"Death Of A Pioneer ." The Quincy Daily Journal 5 May 1910: 3.

Deters, Greg J. E-mail to Ruth Deters. 13 Jan. 2008.

Dickey, Lyle Alexander. Portraits of American Protestant Missionaries to Hawaii. Honolulu: Hawaiian Gazette Co., 1901.

"Dr. Nelson's 'Mission Institute.'" Cincinnati Morning Herald 17 Apr. 1845: 2 column 4.

Duffield, Samuel Willoughby. English Hymns: Their Authors and History. NY, NY: Funk & Wagnalls Company, 1866.

Englert, Stuart. "Top Toys." American Profile 23 Dec. 2007: 11.

"Frisbie Pie Company." Wikipedia, the free encyclopedia. 18 Oct. 2007. 12 Jan. 2008 <http://en.wikipedia.org>.

Gallaher, James. The Western Sketch-Book. Boston: Crocker And Brewster, 1850.

Gallaher, James, Frederick A. Ross, and David Nelson. Editorial. The Calvinistic Magazine 1828: 1.

Genosky, Landry, ed. People's History of Quincy and Adams County, Illinois. Quincy, Illinois: Jost & Kiefer Printing Co., 1973.

"Henry Clay Work." Wikipedia, the free encyclopedia. 20 Jan. 2008 <http://en.wikipedia.org>.

Hill, Timothy, Rev. "The Early History of the Presbyterian Church in Missouri." American Presbyterian Quarterly Review X (1861): 94-117.

Holcombe, R. I., ed. History of Marion County, Missouri. St. Louis: E. F. Perkins, 1884.

Hubbard, Craig E. "Hubbard and Related Lines." RootsWeb.com. 18 June 2003. 12 Jan. 2008 <http://worldconnect.rootsweb.com>.

"In Memorium." Quincy Weekly Whig 18 May 1882: 3.

"Josiah Ells." History of the Reorganized Church of Jesus Christ of Latter Day Saints. 764-765. Rpt. in Centerplace.org. N.p.: n.p., n.d. 19 Apr. 2008 <http://www.centerplace.org/>.

"Kemper Military School." Wikipedia, the free encyclodedia. 3 Jan. 2008 <http://en.wikipedia.org>.

Ket White Hall Field Trip. 2008. 10 Feb. 2008 <http://www.ket.org///_1.htm>.

Kuhn, Kate Ray, ed. A History of Marion County. Hannibal, MO: Western Printing and Lithographing Co., 1963.

Landrum, Carl. "From Quincy's Past Civil War Composer Lived Here." Quincy Herald Whig 28 Mar. 1971: 5C.

- - -. “From Quincy’s Past ‘Underground Railway’ For Slaves.” The Herald Whig 11 Apr. 1971: 3C.

- - -. “In 1845, Private Schools Advertised.” Quincy Herald Whig 25 June 1995: 2A.

Magoun, George F. Asa Turner a Home Missionary Patriarch and His Times. Boston: Congregational Sunday School Publication Society, 1889.

- - -. Asa Turner and His Times, First President of Iowa College. Boston, MA: Congregational and Publishing Society, 1889.

Mendon Dispatch Mar. 1917: 58.

Mendon Dispatch Times 26 Nov. 1931: 113.

Muelder, Herman R. “Call For Convention.” Journal of the Illinois State Historical Society (Fall 1954): 321-323.

Narrative of Facts, Respecting Alanson Work, Jas. E. Burr ans Geo. Thompson, Prisoners in the Missouri Penitentiary, for the Alleged Crime if Negro Stealing. Quincy, IL: Quincy Whig Office, 1842.

Nelson, David. Appeal to the Church. New York: John S. Taylor, 1838.

- - -. The Cause and Cure of Infidelity. New York: John S. Tayor, 1838.

Nelson, Harry. "Autobiography of Harry Nelson." Unpublished diary, 1920.

Nelson, Seldon. "Cunningham Built E. T. & V. Railway." S. B. Cunningham Biography. 22 Feb. 1908. 20 Jan. 2008 <http://patsabin.com//.htm>.

Nelson, William. "Autobiography of William Nelson." Unpublished diary, 1898.

Nelson, William D. "Synopsis Of The Life Of Rev. David Nelson." Unpublished essay, 1900.

Oakley, Allen M. "Another Twist to Quincy's Underground Railroad Story." Letter. Quincy Herald Whig 25 Mar. 1990: 5A.

"Oregon Pioneer Biographies." RootsWeb.com. 15 Dec. 2002. 13 Jan. 2008 <http://weww.rootsweb.com>.

Orr, Christine L. Freedom's Highway, A Way Of Escape. Ms. Quincy College, Quincy, IL.

Payson Bicentennial Book Committee. History of Payson, Illinois 1835 - 1976. Payson, IL: Payson Bicentennial Book Committee, 1976.

Pope, Thomas. "Dr. David Nelson." Quincy Daily Whig June 1886: 6.

Quincy's Local Landmarks and Historic Districts. City of Quincy. 1 Feb. 2008 <http://www.ci.quincy.il.us///.htm>.

Rich, Ray. "Life of 'Buffalo Bill' Cody." Horse and Rider Magazine Sept. 1968: 39.

Rood, Emily. Letter to the author. 29 Mar. 1969.

- - -. Letter to the author. 13 Apr. 1969.

Schenk, Caroline. Personal interview. 25 June 2008.

Shaw, Benjamin, and Charles H. Spilman. Columbian Harmony,or, Pilgrim's Music Companion. Cincinnati, Ohio: Lodge, L'Hoomedieu and Hammond, Printers., 1829.

Shoemaker, Floyd C., ed. Missouri Historical Review. Vols. XLIV No3. Jefferson City, MO, 1950.

Siebert, Wilbur H. The Underground Railroad from Slavery to Freedom. New York: Macmillan, 1898.

Skinner, Hubert M. "Nelson of Quincy--Doctor and Author." Quincy Daily Whig 9 May 1908: 4.

Smith, Herman C. "History of the Reorganized Church of Jesus Christ of Latter Day Saints." Centerplace.org. 19 Apr. 2008 <http://www.centerplace.org///ch39.htm>.

Smith, Joseph. "Letter of the Prophet to John C. Bennett." Times and Seasons (Mar. 1842): 724. Rpt. in Centerplace.org. 19 Apr. 2008 <http://www.centerplace.org//>.

Sprague, William B. Annals of the American Presbyterian PulpitVolume Two. 1856. Birmingham, Alabama: Solid Ground Christian Books, 2005.

T., D. O. "Songs That Mother Used To Sing." The Prairie Farmer 11 Apr. 1931: 6.

Thompson, George. Prison Life and Reflections. New York: S. W. Benedict, 1848.

Thompson, Whitley. "Whitley Thompson's Diary." Unpublished diary, 1 Jan. 1837.

Tillson, John, Gen. History of the City Of Quincy, Illinois. Chicago: S. J. Clarke Publishing Co., 1992.

Tubb, Benjamin Robert. "Contemporary Commentary on Henry Clay Work." PD Music Site. 21 June 2003 <http://www.pdmusic.org>.

- - -. "The Music of Henry Clay Work." PD Music Site Index. 7 Feb. 2007. 20 Jan. 2008 <http://www.pdmusic.org>.

Turner, Steve. Amazing Grace. New York, NY: HarperCollins Publishers Inc, 2002.

Unknown. "The Abolitionists Of Illinois." Quincy Whig 25 July 1840: 2.

- - -. American Anti-slavery Society Twelve Tracts c 1840. CD-ROM. WWW.HISTORYBROKER.COM, 2000.

- - -. "Recalls Days of Abolitionists." Quincy Herald Whig 1 Mar. 1917: 9.

Wecter, Dixon. Sam Clemens of Hannibal. Cambridge, Massachusetts: The Riverside Press, 1952.

Wilcox, David F., Ed, ed. Quincy and Adams County, History and Representative Men. Chicago and New York: The Lewis Publishing Co., 1919.

Williams, George W. History Of The Negro Race In America From 1619 To 1880. New York: G.P. Putnam's Sons, 1883.

Index